Disaster Anarchy

'Commendable. Firth complicates the important concept of mutual aid, examining the danger of neoliberal recuperation while emphasising the subversive possibilities at its heart. She also brings to bear pithy critiques of both the liberal, mainstream practice around "natural disasters" and the ultimately demobilising, snarky-but-useless leftist takes that whether myopically or cynically conflate or confuse revolutionary practices of decentralisation and self-organisation with neoliberal practices of austerity and atomisation. The result is a book that prepares us to think about and react to the kinds of system failures, collapses, and other disasters that will become increasingly more common over the next decades.'
—Peter Gelderloos, activist and author of *The Solutions Are Already Here: Strategies for Ecological Revolution From Below*

'Supremely accomplished. *Disaster Anarchy* is a major step forward in the theory of anarchist practice and deserves our urgent attention as the collapse of capitalism unfolds.'
—Uri Gordon, author of *Anarchy Alive!*

'*Disaster Anarchy* is a clear, timely and rigorous account of anarchist responses to catastrophes. It avoids romanticisation, as Rhiannon Firth incisively unpicks state/corporate strategies of co-option. Nevertheless, Rhiannon's research also provides an inspiring record of achievement by mutual aid radicals.'
—Benjamin Franks, Senior Lecturer in Social and Political Philosophy, University of Glasgow

'This book disrupts disaster studies using an anarchist epistemology to question widely-held assumptions about the state, businesses and social capital in recovery. Drawing on a range of critical theories and empirical data, Firth finds anarchist practices underlie everyday actions in "fast" and "slow" disasters. Anarchism is often absent as a political and prefigurative theory in crisis and disaster. This ground-breaking book shows how imagination, radical pedagogy, and social movements are living components of disaster anarchy.'
—John Preston, Professor of Sociology, University of Essex

'Unpacking the beautiful possibilities of mutual aid, Firth reveals a glimmer of hope in this era of darkness and dismay. Anarchy is affirmed as the dawn light of our collective capacity to transform disaster into grace as we create a new day beyond the failings of capitalism and the state.'
—Simon Springer, Professor of Human Geography, University of Newcastle, Australia

'*Disaster Anarchy* makes an exceptional contribution to the existing literature. Highly original and beautifully written, it is a must read for any activist or scholar interested in exploring utopian alternatives to the status quo, and creating a new society in the shell of the old.'
—Richard J. White, Reader in Human Geography, Sheffield Hallam University

'Firth bridges the theories and methodologies in the continuing development of anarchist and liberatory frameworks of decentralised disaster responses, first articulated after Hurricane Katrina in 2005. They demonstrate through personal histories and analysis deeper paths forward in anarchist processes and practices that allow our liberatory imaginations to resist the collapse while creating viable alternatives without state coercion or interference.'
—scott crow, author of *Black Flags and Windmills: Hope, Anarchy and the Common Ground Collective*

Disaster Anarchy

Mutual Aid and Radical Action

Rhiannon Firth

PLUTO PRESS

First published 2022 by Pluto Press
New Wing, Somerset House, Strand, London WC2R 1LA

www.plutobooks.com

British Library Cataloguing in Publication Data

A catalogue record for this book is available from the British Library

ISBN 978 0 7453 4045 6   Hardback
ISBN 978 0 7453 4046 3   Paperback
ISBN 978 1 786807 92 2   PDF eBook
ISBN 978 1 786807 93 9   EPUB eBook

Typeset by Stanford DTP Services, Northampton, England

Contents

Acknowledgements

This book is dedicated to my mother, Moira Firth (1950–2016), who passed away during the early stages of this research. She was a mental health nurse who came into her own in a crisis.

The work in Chapter 5 was partly supported by the Economic and Social Research Council (grant number ES/K000233/1) through funds for data collection in New York. Particular thanks are due to the Principal Investigator of this project, and my long-term colleague, friend and collaborator Professor John Preston, whose encouragement, mentorship and good-humoured existential dread drew me to this interest in disasters.

The interviews with London activists during Covid-19 were undertaken independently and thanks are due to comrades in the Green Anti-capitalist Front, who invited me to present my research online as part of their lockdown series on 22 June 2020. This led to a fantastic discussion and feedback, which helped me develop my thoughts. Thanks also to my contacts at *Return Fire* magazine for our email conversations. I highly recommend their Volume 6, Chapter 2 issue, which contains several articles on the anarchist response to Covid-19.

My greatest thanks are due to my interviewees in New York and London. They wrote this book as much as I did, and that is the very least of their achievements. These pages can only scratch the surface of the meaning and value of their actions.

It has been a pleasure working with Pluto Press in bringing this book to publication. I would especially like to thank Jakob Horstmann, my commissioning editor, for inviting me to submit the proposal in the first place, and for ongoing support and encouragement. Thanks also to Sophie Richmond for meticulous and sensitive copy-editing.

For academic discussions, input, and feedback, I am grateful to anarchist studies comrades, especially Andrew Robinson, Erica Lagalisse, Uri Gordon, Lara Montesinos Coleman, Tim Waterman, Erica Cudworth, Stephen Hobden; and disaster studies scholars including Paola Di Giuseppantonio Di Franco, Sara Bondesson, and Emma O'Dwyer; and the cybernetics reading group at Essex University, especially Tara Mahfoud, James Fox, and Thomas Swann. I have presented various versions of this work at several conferences, most recently at a conference which I also co-organised: *Living in the End Times: Utopian and Dystopian Representations of Pandemics in Fiction, Film and Culture* hosted by Cappadocia University, 2021. Particular thanks to my co-organisers, Nora Castle, Emrah Atasoy, Heather Alberro, Conrad Scott, Martin Greenwood, Bridget Vincent and Burcu Kayışcı Akkoyun. Earlier versions of the work and draft chapters were presented at the 20th International Conference of the Utopian Studies Society 2019; the Millennium Conference 2018; the Anarchist Studies Network 5th International Conference 2018; the Political Studies Association 68th Annual International Conference 2018; and the International Conference on Critical Education 2018.

For friendship and emotional support during the pandemic, and the writing of this book, thanks to Elaine Sivyer, Richard Watson, Jim Diamond, Fiona McKenzie, Jacqueline McNee, Gus Rigon, Louise Abela, Simon Parker, The Lockdown Massive, Dad and Alison.

Abbreviations

ASMs	autonomous social movements
CMAGs	Covid-19 Mutual Aid Groups
COBRA	Cabinet Office Briefing Room A (UK Civil Contingencies Committee)
COIN	counterinsurgency
Covid-19	Coronavirus disease 2019
CSS	critical security studies
DHS	Department of Homeland Security (US)
DIY	do-it-yourself
DRR	disaster risk reduction
FALC	Fully Automated Luxury Communism
FBO	faith-based organisation
FEMA	Federal Emergency Management Agency (US)
FLOSS	free/libre/open-source software
GRASS	Green Radical Anti-capitalist Social Space
IDNDR	International Decade for Natural Disaster Reduction
IMF	International Monetary Fund
MADR	Mutual Aid Disaster Relief
NGO	non-governmental organisation
NHS	National Health Service (UK)
NYC	New York City
OS	Occupy Sandy
OWS	Occupy Wall Street
PPE	Personal Protective Equipment
PWC	Post-Washington Consensus
SAGE	Scientific Advisory Group for Emergencies (UK)
SAPs	Structural Adjustment Programs
XR	Extinction Rebellion

Interviewees

Pseudonyms have been used to protect anonymity. These have been substituted for numbers in the text to aid readability.

Occupy Sandy interviews, New York, USA, 2015
Q1   Daniel, Monday 26 October 2015
Q2   Blake, Tuesday 27 October 2015
Q3   Fiona, Tuesday 27 October 2015
Q4   Kieran, Wednesday 28 October 2015
Q5   David, Thursday 29 October 2015
Q6   Emily, Friday 30 October 2015
Q7   George, Friday 30 October 2015

Covid-19 Mutual Aid UK interviews, London, UK, 2020 (via Skype, Zoom and Jitsi)
S1   Bobbie, Thursday 14 May 2020
S2   Matt, Monday 18 May 2020
S3   Michelle, Tuesday 19 May 2020
S4   Ronny, 21 May 2020
S5   Nicole, 28 June 2020
S6   Amy, 6 August 2020
S7   Rich, 19 August 2020

1

Introduction

BACKGROUND AND CONTEXT: TWO VERY DIFFERENT DISASTERS

In late October 2012, almost a year after the eviction of the Occupy Wall Street (OWS) encampment at Zuccotti Park, Hurricane Sandy hit New York, with first landfall near Brigantine, New Jersey, with winds of 80 mph. At the time, Sandy was the second costliest storm in US history, costing around US $73.5 billion, second only to Hurricane Katrina. The human cost was significant: more than 600,000 homes were lost or damaged across New York City and New Jersey, and the storm was directly or indirectly responsible for at least 159 deaths.[1] In the context of this disaster, a new social movement emerged called Occupy Sandy (OS), which mobilised the latent skills, networks and activists of OWS into an effective relief effort, with volunteers distributing food and blankets, repairing communications, removing and remediating mould, and restoring properties. The movement was widely recognised as providing more effective relief than the official effort.[2] Even within mainstream paradigms, OS has been interpreted as 'outperforming' established relief organisations including the USA Federal Emergency Management Agency (FEMA) and non-governmental organisations (NGOs) such as the Red Cross.[3] There was widespread public anger with these two agencies in particular for their failures.[4] Indeed, official estimates are that OS recruited around 60,000 volunteers, at least four times more than those deployed by the American Red Cross.[5] The group also mobilised supporters to donate funds, raising more than US $1.36 million in cash,[6] and rallied people from all around the world to donate goods such as blankets, torches, hygiene products and tools using the gift registry system on Amazon.com, a facility usually used for wedding lists. This innovative use of the platform allowed sympathetic members of the public all over the world to order goods to be

1

dispatched to one of OS's distribution hubs using the third-party website's one-click system.[7]

OS was neither the first nor last movement organised on anarchist-inspired principles to mobilise disaster relief. After Hurricane Katrina, which affected New Orleans and surrounding areas in 2005, a decentralised network of volunteers and non-profit organisations emerged to organise relief for the residents, with key organisers including local community organiser Malik Rahim, a former Black Panther, and scott crow, an anarchist organiser.[8] The state response to Hurricane Katrina actively discouraged social movement and unofficial relief efforts and criminalised local responses, at times reacting with extreme violence. Just one year before Hurricane Sandy, Occupy activists had experienced the state response to OWS as similarly hostile and repressive, relying on militaristic social control, yet the response to OS appeared far more accommodating. Indeed, the Department of Homeland Security (DHS) published a document commending activists for their work. In my previous work, I have always been interested in thinking through the conditions for creating anarchist utopias and maintaining radical subjectivity, so my primary interest was charting the process by which an anti-capitalist movement geared towards occupying public space became a movement lauded by the state for their relief work with poor communities.[9] However, the DHS document led me to consider more complex issues, particularly the relationship between anarchist visions of mutual aid as anti-capitalist, and liberal/conservative visions of 'resilience' and 'social capital' as supplementary elements in the statist/capitalist order.

As I was nearing the completion of this book, a very different kind of disaster struck. Coronavirus disease 2019 (Covid-19) is a contagious disease first identified in Wuhan, which caused a global pandemic, spreading rapidly to almost every country in the globe by early 2020. Covid-19 is a very different kind of disaster from a hurricane, although its effects in accentuating crises of capitalism and exacerbating government authoritarianism have been similar. The virus is believed to be transmitted through airborne particles, and affects primarily the lungs, and sometimes the heart, kidneys and other organs. Much is still unknown about the range of symptoms and longer-term effects of the disease. As of April 2021, Covid-19 is implicated in 3.2 million deaths, though the real figure could be higher or lower due to differences in recording practices.[10] Worldwide, government responses have included a range of 'public health' measures intended to stop healthcare systems from being overwhelmed, including enforcement of 'social distancing', face masks, curfews, and lockdown measures such as closing businesses and telling people to stay at home, emerging only for 'essential' activity – which tends to mean 'essential' to capitalism: work, schooling, and shopping are prioritised over socialising, protest and attending funerals. The meaning of 'lockdown' varied by country and region: in some countries all going out was banned, enforced by the army; in others all measures were voluntary or only business closures were used. Although earlier advice counter-indicated lockdowns, the analyses rapidly shifted following the apparent (though questionable) success of similar measures in Wuhan, China. Initially intended to contain Covid-19 to particular areas (in the manner of traditional quarantines), lockdowns were later re-legitimised as attempts to slow the spread of the disease to prevent health systems (which have been decimated by neoliberalism) from being overwhelmed. There have also been campaigns to encourage personal hygiene such as hand-washing, workplace controls, and the promotion of use of Personal Protective Equipment (PPE), emphasising personal responsibility over the provision of social goods. An enormous mutual aid effort arose in the United Kingdom (UK) with the aim of providing aid to vulnerable people and those whose lives were affected by the virus – which includes everyone, but unequally. Where the government response to Occupy Sandy had been retrospectively accommodating, the UK government appeared to encourage and indeed expect mutual aid in advance, as part of its own contingency measures – with media signalling beseeching people to seek support within their communities. The pandemic brought to the fore a middle-class enthusiasm for surveillance and behaviour-shaming, and the irony of 'mutual aid' – an anarchist concept – being mobilised in support of the neoliberal state.

This book constitutes an attempt to document the achievements of Occupy Sandy and Covid-19 Mutual Aid, to think through the conditions that led to the state responses, and to offer a knowledge base and recommendations for anarchist praxis in terms of staying radical and avoiding recuperation. The concept of recuperation, used synonymously with co-optation, is very important to this book. Whereas repression (another important concept) refers to the action of subduing someone or something by force, recuperation means subsuming outsiders into the elite/mainstream in order to manage opposition and maintain stability.

Co-optation can either be by capitalism (in which case it is *commodification*) or by one of capitalism's states.[11] The concept of recuperation has its roots in Situationism, where it is the reverse process to *détournement* (subversion, redirection, turning-aside). While Situationists sought to *détourne* or turn-aside social processes from their functions/ utility within the dominant system, dominant actors sought to recapture these flows, turning their direction back towards some kind of systemic functionality and utility. The transformation of social movements into NGOs or political parties, of subcultures and countercultures into sources of commodified value, or of subversive discourses into legitimations of capitalism are examples of recuperation. The tension to *détourne* or recuperate is constantly present in the case studies, with recuperation taking various forms such as NGO-isation, subordination within state-led responses, and commodification as a 'brand'. Crucially, recuperation is neither an inevitable process nor proof a campaign or a concept is always-already non-radical. Rather, there is a dialectical or antagonistic process of contestation between people seeking to recuperate and those seeking to keep something radical (or conversely, between those seeking to *détourne* and those seeking to keep something systemic).

In a broader context, disasters are becoming more frequent due to the crisis of social and ecological reproduction in capitalism. Climate change, due to systemically promoted fossil fuel consumption and mass production, means the frequency and intensity of extreme weather events is increasing. Neoliberalism has also increased international travel and the interconnectedness of regions, meaning localised disasters reverberate globally, and also that infectious diseases spread rapidly. At the same time, earlier protective measures such as well-prepared health services, have been corroded. Neoliberal austerity and the decline of the oil economy, industrial civilisation and associated structures of governance mean we can no longer rely on our governments to save us from catastrophe (if we ever could anyway). Although a big enough disaster (in disaster studies terms, a 'catastrophe') might be enough to wipe out capitalism, modernity, or even human life, capitalism has found ways to normalise and profit from smaller-scale disasters. There is profit to be made from all aspects of disaster, from private security and construction firms to big data and technology companies. Disaster capitalism alongside the upheavals wrought by disaster and displacement of those who cannot afford to insure their livelihoods means that crises vastly accentuate inequality.

Billionaires, increasingly scared of the conditions they have helped to create, hide away in bunkers.[12] They also set up charities, making political choices as to who constitutes the 'deserving poor', turning aid into a competitive and consumerist enterprise. People who are already marginalised and barely surviving the 'everyday disasters' of normal capitalism (such as precarity, austerity and criminalisation) are usually the worst affected when disaster strikes.

Decentralised, anarchist-inspired mutual aid disaster relief efforts have arisen after nearly every major natural disaster in the United States since Katrina. These have included the Direct Action Bike Squad, which organised a bike team to Puerto Rico to deliver supplies to the mountainous regions after Hurricane Maria in 2017.[13] Several anarchist and autonomous groups arose in response to Hurricanes Florence and Michael in 2018,[14] and in the same year several self-organised neighbourhood groups emerged and organised relief alongside leftist groups including Food Not Bombs and the Houston Anarchist Black Cross after Hurricane Harvey.[15] In late 2017, activists involved in some of these groups set up the grassroots direct-action network Mutual Aid Disaster Relief (MADR), with a stable online presence, which provides training materials and workshops for activists and communities throughout the US on organising disaster relief based on anarchist ethics and organising principles.[16] Anarchist-inspired, autonomous and non-hierarchical movements have also mobilised disaster relief efforts in other countries, for example the self-managed autonomous brigades in Mexico after the 2017 earthquakes,[17] a grassroots village solidarity network in Indonesia after the 2004 tsunamis,[18] anarchist responses to Typhoon Yolanda in the Philippines in 2013,[19] and self-management and direct action against the militarisation of disaster zones after earthquakes in Italy in 2012 and 2009.[20] Mutual aid as a mass movement is new to the UK, but its nationwide visibility in the wake of Covid-19 was unparalleled.

The focus in the current book is on movements in the United States (US), and the UK, since they are two highly developed industrialised nations which also have well-established anarchist movements which draw on similar discourse, so the similarities and historical developments, particularly in terms of the recuperation of mutual aid into a neoliberal framework, are starkly visible. However, the argument in the book claims wider relevance, and it is important to acknowledge that anarchism is an international movement that does not recognise the authority of the nation state and places emphasis on local action tied to global critique. Therefore, it does not always make sense to bound 'case studies' by national borders, as one might in comparative political analysis, so the book also occasionally draws on examples from further afield. The national policy contexts in which the movements operate play an important role in shaping the possibilities and limits of action, but it is not a focus, since the book starts from a social movement perspective. The case studies are distinctly place-based around New York and London. A qualification is needed regarding generalisability: the global South is both disproportionately affected by disasters and has its own non- and anti-state movements which are significantly different from those of the North. This is a blind spot in the present book.

Since Sandy we have seen a growing trend for the state to rely on spontaneous community responses to compensate for its own incapacity and indifference; to covertly surveil and use policies to de-politicise movements rather than outwardly repress them; and to manipulate media to produce social effects that encourage citizens to surveil and police one another. In the UK, this is associated with the behavioural psychology of the 'nudge unit' set up by David Cameron's coalition government in 2010.[21] Rather than overt oppression, states increasingly move towards reliance on covert incentives, surveillance, mobilising fear and suspicion, moral panics, emphasis on individual responsibility, ideological co-optation and de-radicalisation, and other forms of social control. This often follows a counterinsurgency model, in which attempts are made to isolate the radical elements of a movement or community, which are then exposed to repression, by recuperating or demobilising participants. There is a depressing story in these pages of the increasingly cynical use of policy and rhetoric by government agencies that valorise the grassroots, only to turn them into a form of 'social capital' that is unthreatening and indeed helpful to capitalism and its states.

This book argues that anarchist relief efforts offer more than simply an effective practical form of relief that can be recuperated back into neoliberal policy. Rather, they operate as an ontological break, prefigurative utopias, autonomous expressions of agency and solidarity, and as mechanisms of consciousness-raising and pedagogy against the inequalities that lie at the heart of the ongoing disaster of capitalism. Mutual aid is a highly politicised, prefigurative phenomenon which links non-hierarchical organisation to structural critiques of disaster capitalism, climate change and disease, which tend to impact unequally on the most oppressed groups in society. The main aim of this book is to theorise the specificity of anarchist approaches to understanding and mobilising around disasters.

CONCEPTUALISING DISASTERS:
FROM ECOLOGICAL CATASTROPHE TO PANDEMIC

Definitions of disaster vary, and this will be explored in more detail in Chapter 2. In mainstream consciousness, disasters constitute a serious and devastating rupture in the normal running of a society. They are associated with human and economic losses and with the need to repair the damage and reinstitute order. Traditionally, disaster relief was seen as apolitical, and a humanitarian matter. In the 1970s, disaster literature began to divide into two camps: behaviourist and structuralist. The behavioural approach views disasters as events caused by 'physical hazard agents such as hurricanes or tornadoes',[22] and the purpose of disaster research is to understand how society does, and should, respond to these. In contrast, structural perspectives seek to understand disasters not as isolated, episodic events but as part of enduring social patterns.[23] The former approach views disasters as largely apolitical and best dealt with through technical measures, whereas the latter views disasters as intensely political and necessitating analysis of social factors that render some people more vulnerable to the effects of disasters than others.

These different epistemic approaches to defining disasters inflect the contemporary mainstream politics and practice of disaster management, which is usually considered to be divided into a series of phases: prevention, preparedness, response and recovery. Prevention refers to measures taken to reduce the likeliness of disasters occurring and the severity of their effects when they do occur, including measures to reduce the structural *vulnerability* of certain groups as well as increase the *resilience* of communities. Preparedness refers to the understanding and awareness of possible disasters within a community, and educative and other measures undertaken to ensure coordinated action. Response refers to actions taken in immediate anticipation, during, and directly after a disaster. Recovery refers to the process of restoration, redevelopment and improvement of services and infrastructure after an event. The shared assumptions in the mainstream paradigm lead to a politics that does not question the need for a state to provide a degree of redistribution of wealth and risk to reduce vulnerability, at the same time as individuals and communities are encouraged to absorb shocks and assume responsibility for losses as private citizens. While the approach gives some attention to structural causes of disaster, it remains a liberal approach that assumes the ongoing existence of unequal capitalism and a state whose primary function is to reinstate its normal functioning in times of crisis.

Some more critical contemporary approaches to disasters and resilience, including left-liberal, feminist and some Marxist-inspired approaches, place a heavier emphasis on the need to understand disasters not as episodic events but constitutive of the *longue durée* of capitalism, colonialism and ecological destruction. While these approaches, which we'll look at in more detail in Chapter 3, are useful for critique, and while they valorise resistance over resilience, they broadly concentrate on how the system reproduces itself even through those who resist it. They often conflate decentralising tendencies with capitalist deterritorialisation, and concepts such as self-organisation, complexity, autonomy and horizontality are seen as always-already complicit in capitalism, or at least the concepts themselves are seen to embody authoritarian tendencies as well as liberating ones. The problem with these approaches is that they leave no space for agency, expressions of autonomous desire and solidarity, or the prefiguring of non-capitalist lifeworlds. They are ultimately structuralist theories, in which every person or action is complicit in the reproduction of oppression, which the anarchist perspectives portrayed in Chapter 4 onwards dispute. It is argued that it is one thing to say that capitalism and its states seek to capitalise on all social relations, and even that it is possible and likely that decentralising tendencies can/will be recuperated in capitalism (which by definition refers to a system with a tendency to mobilise all social forces it can capture in the interests of creating profit for capitalists). It is another thing to conflate decentralising tendencies with capitalist exploitation per se – which ignores the fact that anti-authoritarian theories and resistance existed before neoliberal capitalism, and indeed before capitalism itself.

Previously, disaster studies scholars have tended not to include epidemics within their definition of disasters, because like other 'chronic, diffuse and long-term situations' such as famines and droughts, they tend to be associated with the 'Third World' and so are often lumped together with development studies and humanitarian work. They are seen to 'lack the suddenness' of traditional disaster work, and the agents involved are 'complex and diffuse'.[24] Covid-19 is therefore a very different kind of disaster from those usually considered within disaster studies, let alone within the much smaller field where academic anarchism and disasters intersect. Nevertheless, it felt important to include it in this book, which takes a radical perspective on disasters as events which accentuate, rather than cause, the crises of capitalism. The response to Covid-19, and to Ebola previously, seems to borrow from the disaster playbook, suggesting the securitisation of pandemics moves them closer to the 'disaster' category. Furthermore, from an anti-capitalist social movement perspective, climate-related disasters like hurricanes should also be seen as 'complex and diffuse', as the wholesale systemic change required to tackle each is similar. Anarchists understand disasters very differently from the mainstream approach, and this difference in understanding is simultaneously philosophical and practical. While statists, capitalists and neoliberals understand disasters as moments of exception and as episodic events that represent a rupture, anarchists understand disasters to be constitutive of the contemporary world system. Disasters are not merely a break in the normal running of things; rather, capitalism is an ongoing disaster. Anarchists promote degrowth and systemic change through creating small-scale, situated, prefigurative alternatives.

WHY WE NEED DISASTER ANARCHISM

Anarchism is many things. It is a diverse social and political theory and practice of anti-authoritarianism with a long and global history – sometimes traced back to ancient China and Greece[25] or to indigenous societies.[26] It is an ongoing social movement of decentralised networks and collectives around the world organising direct actions and longer-term projects, such as protests, camps, occupations, blockades, squats, social centres, intentional communities, zines, and cooperatives. Anarchism often encompasses a belief that humans are, by nature, able to cooperate without the need for external authority,[27] although some anarchists argue that anarchism as an ethical practice does not require such faith in human nature.[28] Whether anarchism entails a 'positive' view of human nature is controversial within the movement; some anarchists are constructivists, who see social arrangements or ecological conditions as central to possibilities, some are materialists in the Marxist mode, some are pessimists who distrust anyone holding too much power, and some are transpersonalists, questioning the importance of inherent individual traits. Uri Gordon argues for a definition of anarchism as a 'political culture' that infuses social movements and theory. He argues this culture involves a repertoire of direct action based on building grassroots alternatives, community outreach, and confrontation (as opposed to appealing to external authorities through the ballot box or other means). It also engages in particular forms of organising: decentralised, horizontal and consensus-seeking; and cultural expression in areas including art, music, dress and diet; and a shared political language around resistance to capitalism, the state, patriarchy, hierarchy and domination.[29] It is often possible to recognise anarchist movements from their distinct symbolism and culture, which involves a strong preference for 'horizontal', do-it-yourself (DIY) ways of engaging in social activities (including politics), often on a small-group basis. In many countries, anarchism is synonymous with insurrectionary and/or anarcho-communist currents, but there is also a wide range of variants including mutualist/cooperative, evolutionary, pacifist/non-violent, ecological/ anti-civilisation, feminist, hacker, etc. In the UK and US, these variants would be included under the anarchist label, and there is also no clear distinction between anarchists, autonomists and libertarian Marxists, although there are recurring antagonisms with Marxist organisations. Anarcho-capitalist and national anarchist tendencies are not usually treated as part of the anarchist scene as they are pro-capitalist and pro-state/nation respectively.

There is a need to distinguish between *anarchy* and *anarchism*. The former is a descriptive term that refers to a non-hierarchical condition of life and organisation of practices without intrusions from hierarchical governance. The latter refers to a conscious political and ethical theory that has the cultivation and expansion of anarchy as its goal. The distinction is important in the context of the book, because many communities organise for disasters in ways which might be considered congruent with anarchy, without being motivated by anarchist philosophy. Furthermore, while many movement activists are inspired by anarchism, and some self-define as anarchists, many do not. Mark Bray found 72 per cent of Occupy Wall Street organisers were either anarchist or anarchist-inspired,[30] but the figures are not available for Occupy Sandy.[31] Horizontalist movements that do not take a left-unity or Marxist approach, such as those covered in this book, tend not to self-define or follow a single ideology as they value diversity and hybridity and eschew identity – so to require that all movement participants 'identify' as an anarchist or 'call themselves' an anarchist would be unnecessarily restrictive. It would be impossible to talk about such movements if one aimed to represent them as a coherent ideological entity, and their anarchism resides in their practices and culture (non-hierarchy, prefiguration, etc.) rather than a monolithic theoretical vision. Movements will very commonly involve people identifying with a number of different varieties of anarchism, others loosely oriented to anarchism and still others attracted to DIY politics without specifically anarchist commitments. The book argues for the importance of building on anarchist political consciousness within disaster relief efforts, yet without colonising others' beliefs or imposing external values. This is a task that is already being undertaken by many social movements: an incomplete and not unproblematic task, and a discussion to which this book aims to contribute. Anarchism takes an holistic approach to mutual aid and seeks dis-alienation and commoning. Anarchist theory and its approach to understanding disasters is covered in more detail in Chapter 4.

POWER, CAPITALISM AND THE STATE

The key antagonists of anarchists are capitalism and the state, but this oppositional approach is supplemented by a critique of the ways in which people have a tendency to re-enact and internalise these structures of domination: authoritarianism can also operate through internal/psychological repression, or in-group repression, or social repression. Some anarchists (particularly anarcho-communists) adopt models of capitalism similar to Marxism, others are influenced by poststructuralist, decolonial, queer and feminist analyses of everyday oppressions, and still others adopt distinct views specific to the anarchist space, such as Stirnernian egoism[32] (all categories/identities can become forms of internalised oppression) and anti-civilisation (in which the role of capitalism in Marxist theory is replaced by the concept of civilisation, considered to have existed for thousands of years, and to correspond to domination over nature). Many will pick-and-mix aspects of different accounts, and there are often disagreements about issues at the intersection of different anarchisms (for example, pro- and anti-technology). In practice, these function similarly to other individual differences in the anarchist space: cooperative work requires mutual consent which may not entail ideological agreement, and people either opt in/out of projects based on their affinities or adopt particular roles congruent with their personal commitments.

Capitalism refers to an economic and political system based on the private ownership of the means of production, which are controlled by capitalists for their own profit. This means that people who do not own the means of production are usually forced to sell their labour in order to survive, which anarchists and Marxists alike view as exploitative. Anarchists tend to be less fatalistic than Marxists about the possibility of escaping this structure 'before the revolution'; a great many anarchist projects are designed around the seizure or DIY production of resources with a view to liberating time and space from the market in the here-and-now. Capitalism is also the basis of extractivism – the process of extracting natural resources to sell on the global market. Capitalism is arguably the basis of complex hierarchies like colonialism, patriarchy, racism, ableism, and ecocide, since the profit motive encourages people to objectify one another and nature. Anarchist alternatives to capitalist ownership often focus on ideas of *the commons*. Communal ownership is closely linked to strong community ties and collective decision making. This means that people who are affected by a particular decision are more likely to have intimate knowledge of their local ecosystem and also to be more personally invested in the decisions that are made. Commoning processes tend to involve localisation of both power and resources, and are associated with degrowth and smaller-scale socio-technical projects and frameworks.

The state refers to a collection of institutions, with sometimes seemingly different and contradictory interests, that combine to create and enforce laws on a given territory. In order to enforce laws, the state holds a monopoly on the legitimate use of violence. Anarchists reject the state on a number of grounds, often because it is coercive, violent, elitist, harmfully abstract and simplifying, and/or is associated with forces contrary to life. Most radicals agree that the state uses the law to protect the private property of capitalists and to justify and ensure the smooth running of the capitalist economy. Beyond this, anarchists and Marxists tend to disagree on the nature of the state: Marxists believe that revolution can occur by means of the state, or at least that the state can be mobilised as a terrain of struggle and a subordinate effect of class relations. Anarchists argue that there is something fundamental about the nature of the state that means it always tends towards alienation and objectification. They argue that when you concentrate power in the hands of people who are disconnected from the communities who will be affected by their decisions, the result will be larger-scale socio-technical projects which produce a more fragile system prone to crises. This is associated with the need to increase controls on movement of people and goods, which ultimately leads to inequality, exclusion, authoritarianism, and indeed capitalism, no matter who is in charge. For Kropotkin, for example, the state embodies the 'political principle' of top-down dyadic vertical control, and thus tends to decompose social relations; for Stirner, it attempts to reduce people's complexity to a single dominant identity or spook (the citizen) which overrides other identities and desires; for Bakunin, the bureaucracy and verticalism of the state ensures it will be the property of an elite.[33]

Anarchists are therefore happier with forms of action associated with small-group actions, self-management, and subcultural isolation than Marxists, who exhibit a stronger tendency towards human mass collectivism. In practice there is some overlap, particularly evident in Chapter 6, where we see Covid-19 Mutual Aid Groups becoming a terrain of struggle with the state. This overlap happens partly due to common anti-capitalism and partly because Marxists are also often reluctant to work with the *existing* state. Anarchists believe that any kind of state, even when composed of conflicting interests or captured by ostensibly progressive forces, will express a particular logic, which seeks to subsume autonomous action into a framework that is legible to the state, in order that the state can mediate and control that action (which deprives it of its autonomy). One of the original contributions of this book is to show how the nature of the state has shifted from a massified Fordist structure to a more decentralised post-Fordist model with cybernetic components, and that anarchists and other radicals need to find new ways to resist this. The anarchist critique of centralised power does not mean that decentralised power is benign if it is unequal. In this book, I argue that states no longer rely only on outright repression and social control, they also rely on new forms of biopower and surveillance.

In the context of Covid-19, this has been accompanied by a disappointing tendency on the left towards authoritarianism, such as calls for even tighter lockdowns backed up by more severe penalties, or for universally enforced mask-wearing and vaccinations. Public health has been almost completely conflated with morality with calls for greater 'controls', behaviour-shaming and little acknowledgement of the fact that not everyone has access to the goods being moralised (e.g. a safe home to stay in, educated understanding of vaccinations). This moralising discourse perpetuates classed and other oppression under the guise of virtue.[34] It also sidelines both the Marxist-inspired 'health as human right' approach and the eco-anarchist DIY approach. There has been a tendency on social media and the public sphere to deride attempts to imagine a stateless society as 'wrong' and 'dangerous', which shuts down many important conversations and thoughtful contributions about community-based decision making around health. Similarly, public discourse on the left around solutions to climate change have centred on large-scale techno-social interventions like carbon offsetting, carbon capture, electric cars and solar farming in a continuous growth paradigm under discourses such as a Green New Deal and Fully Automated Luxury Communism. This ignores potential rebound effects like over-exploitation of other resources, and the continued subordination of people and nature to the profit motive. This is accompanied by an abject refusal to countenance solutions that counter or reverse capitalist growth, such as local food growing, permaculture and forming local cooperatives, which are often derided as hopelessly utopian.[35]

There is a real danger of radical movements being co-opted into neoliberal discourses of resilience, and into NGO-ised funding structures, and even into authoritarian and exclusionary moralistic discourses of the middle classes. I tend to use the words 'anarchism' and 'anti-authoritarianism' interchangeably. Anarchism is not only against external authority, but also against vanguardist forms of knowledge. The purpose of this book is to contribute to a rigorous discourse of resistance while considering the possibility for tactical gains to be made by selectively and consciously adopting particular discourses or accepting resources. Anarchism offers a reversal of perspective, starting from the importance of bottom-up flows of life and activity, not from the standpoint of power. Where other political philosophies begin from the assumption of the necessity of the state, anarchism begins by assuming the possibility of a stateless society, and attempting to imagine and enact what that might look like.

METHODS

Anarchism is not only a political theory, culture and practice, it is also a methodology and a method that turns traditional political thought on its head, opening new possibilities for critique and political practice. Whereas the bulk of the tradition of political thought has sought to justify the legitimacy and limits of the political state, anarchists ask: What if the state is not necessary at all, in fact, what if it is harmful? How might this change the way we understand and act in the world? It offers a reversal of perspective whereby people are not simply cogs in a capitalist machine, with neoliberalism or cybernetic control as the 'end of history' or the least-worst option for people who are naturally rational resource-optimisers or nodes in a computer-like network. Rather, structures of domination are undesirable outgrowths that alienate humans from each other and from nature, and which perpetuate crises. The bottom-up force of life is pitted against top-down forces which seek either to repress or recuperate it. It is a core argument of the book that anarchist beliefs and ideals are actually (if partially) realised in social movements. This is a controversial claim, and not only the mainstream perspective, but also many forms of radicalism would deny the possibility of autonomous forms of cooperation without external authority. For example, many forms of Marxism would argue that all social relations are always-already co-opted in 'capitalist realism'.[36]

While the framework is broadly theoretical, it also draws on fieldwork and interviews. The first set of interviews was undertaken in New York from 26 October 2015 to 1 November 2015. My visit coincided with the third anniversary of Hurricane Sandy, a time when activists were involved in commemorative gatherings and events. I undertook in-depth interviews with seven activists, five of whom were involved in Occupy Sandy New York, one of whom was active in Occupy Sandy New Jersey, and one of whom was very active in Occupy Wall Street, and was affected by the disaster, but did not mobilise during Sandy. Interviewees were accessed by sending an initial email to the press department of the OS website,[37] and a contact kindly offered to send my email to the OS mailing list. Participants self-selected and approached me after reading the email, which explained the purpose of my research. Informed consent was sought from all interviewees, whose names have been anonymised using pseudonyms in the text. I also engaged in informal discussions, email correspondence and telephone conversations with activists prior to, and subsequent to my trip. The material on OS forms the basis of Chapter 5, where I attempt to show how the anarchist theory of disaster drawn out in the previous four chapters might be reflected in, and contribute to, existing anarchist practices.

The second set of interviews was undertaken in London, via video conferencing technology, after the first wave of Covid-19 infections, between May and August 2020. I undertook in-depth interviews with seven activists involved in mobilising mutual aid in London. I accessed the interviewees through my existing networks and purposefully spoke to people who either identified as anarchists or who had some sympathy for anarchism. Some interviewees I approached, and others self-selected after a call-out following a presentation I offered as a gift and contribution in return for interviewees' time.

Interviewees' views should not be taken as representative of the movement as a whole. Unlike an NGO, a political party or other organisation, grassroots movements do not share a single 'official' outlook, and activists tend to speak as individuals, yet their views are formed in conversation and in practice with other activists. I write this book as an academic researcher who has also been involved in social movements, including the Occupy! movement in the UK, and in mutual aid. My involvement with radical movements similar to those I research has (I believe) made me better able to understand some of the issues that movements face, to talk in a similar language, and to access spaces and interview participants who are sometimes hard to access because activists are often untrusting of academics. However, as with my previous work, I do not speak as an 'insider' or participant in the particular movement, nor as a highly engaged ethnographer, but as a theorist who takes the worldviews of activists seriously as sources of theoretical knowledge. The interviews were used to gain insight into individuals' experiences of participating, their motivations for participation, perspectives on the nature of disasters, strategies for social change in the context of disaster and ideals for alternative ('utopian') disaster communities. They are also used to compare personal assessments of how events unfolded and processes worked to the media and government portrayals of the movements' aims and purposes. In addition to the interviews, I draw on government reports, mainstream media accounts of the disaster and on independent media and activists' reports found online and in archives.

An important perspective that is missing in this book is that of affected communities. While mutual aid supposes an equal relationship between 'helpers' and 'helped', this is not always possible in a vastly unequal society. There are various practical and ethical reasons it would have been difficult to interview members of affected communities who were not consciously organised activists: for example, forced mobility and dispersal, lack of a platform or network for contact, ethical difficulties in requiring vulnerable groups to re-live traumatic events, and sheer diversity of social locations. This is not to say that interviewing affected populations is not an important task: it has been approached by Sara Bondesson through engaged ethnographic work in her excellent thesis.[38] My own work offers a very different contribution: it is an effort to build and contribute to an anarchist framework for understanding disaster by focusing on specifically anti-authoritarian movements, and also to situate their actions in a much longer history of anarchist and anti-authoritarian organising, and to try to contribute to dealing with some problems raised by movement activists – in particular issues of state co-optation and movement de-radicalisation. These issues were raised by both Occupy Sandy and Covid-19 Mutual Aid UK activists in interviews and online articles, and have also recurred periodically throughout the anarchist theoretical canon and history of organising. In this sense, anarchist theory and history have something to offer movements, and movements have something to offer anarchist thought, reflecting a recursive relationship between theory and practice that has often characterised the tradition of anarchism.[39] My book is thus also an attempt to produce 'movement relevant theory': Rather than seeking to use detached observations of movement activity to build structural accounts or reject earlier hypotheses, such research presents a dynamic engagement with theorising already being done by movement participants.[40]

OUTLINE OF THE BOOK

The book as a whole should be considered a work of political theory, although it is empirically informed and produces recommendations for pedagogy and practice within social movements. Chapters 2–4 are theoretical. Chapter 2 outlines the history and critiques the mainstream paradigm of disaster politics, considering how it has evolved under neoliberalism. It covers how the concept of 'disaster' is usually understood by academics, policymakers, and in mainstream media discourse. It reveals assumptions about roles played by NGOs and voluntary organisations in response to disasters, and how grassroots and anarchic views of disaster are understood as forms of 'social capital' to be mobilised alongside state and formal charity response in a rapid return to 'normal'. Chapter 3 covers a range of critical theories from left-liberal, neo-Marxist and poststructuralist paradigms that deal with disasters; showing there is a substantial body of thought that critiques the mainstream but is not anarchist. While I have many affinities with some of these perspectives, and they help me formulate my critique, I argue that they are not sufficient and merely displace the exclusions and oppressions of the mainstream elsewhere and replicate traps of statism: they either remain confined to critique, or they rely on modes of response that are vulnerable to co-optation. It is argued that disasters are constitutive of capitalism and embedded in the socio-technical frameworks of the state rather than merely episodic or symptomatic. I suggest that these wider aspects are more clearly visible from the standpoint of autonomous movements. This argument is developed in Chapter 4, where I formulate an anarchist theory of disasters. The chapter draws on various strands in the diverse history of anarchist thought to argue that much of everyday life is already anarchy and develops anarchists' theories of social organisation and mutual aid for the context of disasters. It is argued that the state seeks to recuperate mutual aid relationships and peripheral economies into political allegiances that can be subordinated and exploited by the worldwide capitalist axiomatic via the mediation of the NGO sector. It is argued that creating the conditions to expand autonomous activity may sometimes entail tactical engagement with the state in disasters but requires political consciousness and autonomous desires in order to resist co-optation. Chapters 5 and 6 seek to develop this anarchist theory of disaster by applying it in dialogue with two empirical case studies in anarchist-inspired mutual aid movements. Chapter 5 draws on the case of Occupy Sandy, with attention to the movement's organisational form, their values and ethics, their experiments in creating alternative economies and their use of technology. I also consider the ways in which the state attempted to re-order and recuperate their activities, and the extent to which the movement was able to resist this. I continue the argument that these movements should not be understood independently of their political content, nor as a form of 'social capital' compatible with the state. Chapter

6 explores the case study of Covid-19 Mutual Aid UK. It is argued that despite the seeming success of the movement, its de-radicalised nature shows that neoliberal techniques of covert population-nudging and the co-optation of radical mobilisations have become even more well-honed. Much of the movement was already recuperated from the start. In order to maintain the focus of the book on autonomous action and radical subjectivity, the chapter draws on interviews with a small subset of the movement that was explicitly and intentionally anarchist, with a focus on the ways in which they maintained their radicalism and sought to resist attempts by the broader movement to silence anarchist politics, co-opt their infrastructure into NGOs and block more radical actions, such as eviction resistance. The conclusion, Chapter 7, draws together key themes of the argument, considers the limits and possibilities for further application of the theory, and argues for the importance of political imagination, radical pedagogy and consciousness-raising in social movements.

CONCLUSION

My hope is to fill a gap in the media and literature around disaster anarchist social movements, which at present fail to systematically consider how these movements' impressive efforts in mutual aid might contribute to a radical and revolutionary reconceptualisation of disasters and the processes of relief and recovery efforts. While much has already been written about Occupy Sandy, the existing literature rests mainly within three camps: (1) personal accounts in independent media, written by activists who were involved in the movement, which tend to be factual, experiential, descriptive or polemical; (2) government-commissioned and mainstream media reports, and non-radical academic accounts, which tend to focus on what the state and/or wider society can 'learn' from the movement in order to integrate its practice into a conventional disaster management framework; and (3) Marxist-inspired structural accounts which understand social movements as social symptoms and/or reproducing capitalism, rather than in their own terms as autonomous forms of solidarity. Covid-19 Mutual Aid, as a very recent movement, has yet to attract a substantial academic body of thought, although it is likely that accounts will fall into similar camps. What is lacking in this literature is a theoretically rigorous attempt to understand these movements as engaging in radical critique while creating utopian alternatives to existing arrangements, at the same time offering a critical analysis of some of the movement's contradictions, tensions and obstacles, in particular the co-optation of anarchist approaches into the neoliberal rhetoric of community resilience. The hope is that the book will be of use to academics and activists interested in exploring utopian alternatives to the status quo. Disaster anarchy is one of the most important radical political phenomena to emerge in the early twenty-first century and deserves serious study and theoretical attention. The book aims to contribute to academic and social movement discourses and debates on social change, responding to crises, natural disasters and climate change, resisting the state and capitalism, and creating a new society in the shell of the old.

2

Backdrop:
Mainstream Disaster Studies

INTRODUCTION: NEOLIBERALISM, STATE AND CAPITAL

The dominant neoliberal paradigm of disaster politics is constituted by overlapping discursive and policy clusters which contribute to the overarching field of Disaster Risk Reduction (DRR), which has dominated global policy and disaster studies since the 1970s. These clusters are: (i) technocratic and behaviourist, focused on risk management and reduction; (ii) structural and development-oriented, focused on increasing resilience, reducing vulnerability and adaptation to longer-term threats such as climate change; (iii) associationalist, focused on moral humanitarianism and the role of civil society; (iv) a nation state-centred 'realist' approach, focused on exerting social control over conflicting forces within the domestic territory, and strategic positioning in international politics.[1] Mainstream neoliberal approaches tend to construct these approaches as partially in conflict – for example the political game-playing of the realist approach is seen to conflict with the altruistic globalism of the humanitarian sector, while top-down approaches to risk management appear to conflict with the networked organisation of institutionalised civil society and decentralising technocratic approaches. It is also commonplace to divide the field of disaster literature into two broad factions: behaviourist and structural. However, the purpose of this chapter is to argue that all are complicit in an authoritarian organisationalist view and in cybernetic forms of control, which either adversely incorporate social movement and community responses to disasters as *complementary* to top-down responses or degrade them as *illegitimate* or *illegible*. In so doing, dominant responses assume the legitimacy of the state and capital *a priori*.

The emergence and transformation of disaster studies is located in the context of the wider transformation of the relationship between the state and capital. The early twentieth century saw the rise of Fordism as a centralised and organised form of capitalism, based on mass production and consumption, where the state acts as an organiser and stabiliser for capital. In the late twentieth century and early twenty-first, the development of post-Fordist neoliberal capitalism has led the state to significantly relinquish this role, while at the same time, in developed countries, manufacturing gave way to the service economy and more precarious forms of work.[2] With the rise of New Public Management from the 1980s onwards, the autonomy of the professional/included stratum in both public and private institutions was largely lost to managerialists, who embodied a statist and capitalist logic with decentralised cybernetic components. Rather than acting as rigid Fordist bureaucrats and taking a top-down universalising approach to managing risks, the 'cadres' of 'the new spirit of capitalism' were trained to build scenario responses to risk in terms of behavioural nudges, proactive measures and gamification, quantification and 'flexibility'.[3] This approach simultaneously fuels uncertainty, insecurity and panic – as well as authoritarianism and top-down control, despite outwardly appearing to resemble decentralised organisation and endowing social actors with a sense of autonomy.

I hope to uncover some of the implicit theoretical assumptions underlying dominant policy and practice concerning the nature of disasters and the ways in which they should be managed. The chapter covers how the concept of natural disasters is usually understood by academics and policymakers, and in mainstream media discourse. It covers common understandings of the roles played by NGOs and voluntary organisations in response to disasters. It considers the way in which voluntary and anarchic views of disaster are understood, and the conditions under which post-disaster community responses might be constructed as 'good', for example as 'social capital', vs bad, for example as a Hobbesian 'state of nature'; as 'chaos', 'disorder', or 'looting', and the ways in which human subjects are constructed as competitive opportunity-seeking agents vulnerable to control via incentives or coercion.

DISASTER MANAGEMENT: A TECHNOCRATIC AND BEHAVIOURIST PARADIGM

The perspective on community response to disasters that dominates mainstream consciousness today dates back to the late 1950s and early

1960s. The behaviourist approach to disasters is situated in the scientific paradigm of *cybernetics*. Cybernetics is widely traced back to the mathematical and engineering work of Norbert Wiener during the Second World War, used to predict the trajectory of enemy aircraft.[4] During the post-war period and the Cold War, cybernetics was broadened, initially through dialogue with psychiatrists and neuroscientists interested in the human brain,[5] and then throughout the social sciences, especially within the nascent behaviourist movement, partially funded by the US military and the Ford Foundation.[6] Although cybernetics is incredibly diverse and less unified than is often thought,[7] it has been interpreted as the foundation of the interdisciplinary systems-thinking paradigm that came to dominate the social sciences in the post-war period, which attempted to model and control a full range of physiological phenomena, from human and animal behaviour to machine learning, by focusing on behaviour in terms of input, output, feedback and communication, rather than theorising about internal desires and motivations, or human meaning (as opposed to, for example, psychoanalytic models).[8] The behaviourist cybernetic paradigm views disasters as sudden ruptures in the normal running of events, and emphasises a rapid return to 'normal'. Such approaches may rely on rational-choice modelling or observed behavioural patterns. In either case, the view of social life tends to be 'flat', in the sense that the same motivations and structures are in play in every possible scenario, and these factors are equally observable and knowable in every case. Human actors are treated primarily as externally oriented nodes located in relational or opportunity structures which constitute what they are, or at least, how they 'behave'. Social control can thus be exercised indirectly, through technocratic design of the social environment, usually without a need for direct command or for dialogue. The influence of this paradigm on the development of disaster studies can be seen in many of the policies we see in force today, particularly in attempts to recuperate the energies of social movements into state-friendly disaster relief efforts.

The cybernetic model is in some respects a break with the earlier Hobbesian view of disasters as social collapse. Early North American disaster researchers and media reporters would laud the community action that arose in the immediate aftermath of a 'natural disaster' such as a hurricane, tornado or flood. Psychoanalyst Martha Wolfenstein coined the term 'post-disaster utopia' to describe a period of camaraderie and euphoria, where people put aside differences to roll up their sleeves and work together selflessly during the recovery effort.[9] Charles Fritz, the first renowned sociologist of disaster, argued contrary to others of his era who feared widespread panic and chaos, that large-scale disasters paradoxically appear to produce 'mentally healthy' conditions. He drew on evidence that people living in heavily bombed cities in Britain during the Second World War had 'significantly higher morale' than people living in more lightly bombed cities.[10] Fritz pre-empted later structuralists, arguing that disasters bring into focus the impact of ongoing systemic crisis on everyday life by erasing the contrast between normal conditions and 'disaster'. In particular, he highlighted the failure of modern societies to meet 'human needs for community' and argued that disasters produce a societal shock that helps people to build bonds through shared experiences.[11] Drawing on Fritz, later researchers used the term 'therapeutic community'.[12] According to these accounts, the 'utopian' period of solidarity, consensus, and mutual aid unavoidably recedes after the initial relief efforts as the everyday divisions and differences settle in, at which point it is necessary for a specialised bureaucracy to step in to administer the longer-term tasks of recovery.[13] Some of this earlier literature seems almost communitarian, though there is an emergent tendency to individualise the sociology of disasters by emphasising human psychology, pre-empting neoliberal discourses of 'resilience'.

Risk management as currently configured is a technocratic and behaviourist paradigm that grew out of this literature. Its historical background follows the transformation of liberal capitalism from social democracy to globalised neoliberalism. Early research on hazards had occurred in scientific disciplines like meteorology, hydrology, computing and engineering, with a focus on the specific issues involved in specific types of disasters. In the early post-war period (1947–58) an interdisciplinary technocratic paradigm emerged, linking these scientific studies with political models. Disaster research and policy was also internationalised, encouraging intergovernmental cooperation, scientific collaboration and technical assistance across borders as well as the coordination of research agendas.[14] The focus of this early research was on management techniques for administering disasters through top-down, data-driven models.[15] Disasters tended to be viewed as exceptional, episodic events representing a rupture in the normal running of things, and the purpose of disaster relief was a return to the prior state, while regulating population responses through behavioural sciences. This thread was largely developed by Enrico Quarantelli, a leading name in disaster studies from the late 1970s until the present day, and co-founder of the University of Delaware Disaster Research Centre.

Quarantelli was a student of Fritz, and following Fritz he ostensibly critiqued the top-down 'command and control' approach to risk management. Similarly to his predecessors, he saw the potential for disaster planning and management to manipulate 'prosocial behaviour' in the interests of restoring 'normalcy'.[16] Unlike his more communitarian and psychoanalytic forerunners, he espoused a cybernetic model which valorises feedback systems, arguing that disasters impact differently on different segments of society and communities have their own pre-existing 'patterns of authority' and 'autonomous decision-making' that ought to be left in place. Disaster planning deals with aggregate data and ought to 'focus on general principles and not specific details' and should also 'be vertically and horizontally integrated'.[17]

Quarantelli 'confessed' in an interview with Rebecca Solnit in June 2007 that his work was largely funded by governments who expected that the largest problem of disaster management would be crowd behaviour and panic – but what he found in his research was that really the greatest problem arose from bureaucratic inflexibility.[18] He is representative of the DRR paradigm even though he initially gives the appearance of advocating equal treatment and a role for horizontalist organisations such as mutual aid groups. The integration of the horizontal with the vertical relies on the planning and management functions of state agencies to oversee and coordinate their actions in order to differentiate between 'helpful' and injurious emergent actions – and ultimately to use generic structural adjustments, 'education' and 'nudges' to manipulate the beliefs and behaviour of populations in order to encourage those actions that are seen as helpful to the state.[19] Quarantelli's work also contributed to the emergence of a generic disaster studies field, connected to centralised disaster management agencies, and the relative marginalisation of the contributions of technical sciences, which focus on specific types of disasters.

DRR: STRUCTURAL APPROACHES

The early risk management literature rests on the assumption that risk and disasters are 'natural' and ought to be managed within the current structural framework rather than asking more fundamental questions about the ways in which economic and political constructs might actually create risk or magnify its effects on certain populations. This generated the impetus for the emergence of a rival, 'structural' school. These thinkers argue that the terminology of 'natural disasters' and 'risk management' means that we are more likely to view the loss of life and destruction of infrastructure and property, which often disproportionately affect the poorest and most marginalised members of society, as both inevitable and requiring top-down management within a problem-solving framework. Even conventional critiques have argued that this response can be ineffi- cient for emergent and unexpected hazards, as well as for the intersection of disasters with 'longstanding, wicked problems' such as poverty, crime and inequality.[20] The structural approach is based in anthropology and sociology and attempts to broaden the time-frame of disasters, to view them as part of the long-running socio-cultural 'patterns and practices of societies,'[21] showing 'disasters do not just happen'[22] and are compounded not only by human infrastructures but also political structures and cultural values and norms. However, despite this somewhat relativist stance, these writers view 'post-disaster solidarity' as an almost universal human response that cannot be explained by rational choice, resource mobilisation or other social movement theories that dichotomise reason and emotion.[23]

Structuralism initially emerged as a challenge to the technocratic focus of behaviourism and as a potentially distinct paradigm, loosely linked to the New Left and the growth of neo-Marxist, feminist, ecological and other radical critiques in the social sciences.[24] However, since the 1970s, and particularly during the 1980s and 1990s, the field of disaster studies began to consolidate around what adherents believed to be a broader and more structurally aware consensus of definitions and conceptualisations of 'disasters', corresponding with a groundswell of academic interest in disaster studies. This new, arguably Third Way take on structure either resolved or swept under the carpet the important philosophical disagree- ments between the behaviourist and structuralist schools, creating a kind of lowest-common-denominator consensus. In this revised structural- ism, researchers increasingly differentiated between natural hazards and disasters, with the latter encompassing social aspects.[25] Various factors were cited as causing a proliferation in disasters, including increasing population and the rising concentration in large cities with burgeoning infrastructures that were ageing and vulnerable to failure triggered by even minor events.[26] Another reason for the shift was the increase in communications networks and informational architecture emerging from the Cold War, which moved disaster research from a framework of 'voluntarist internationalism' to 'quasi-obligatory globalism',[27] where institutional powers to regulate technical systems concealed a technocratic political agenda.[28] The idea that the role of the state is basically well-meaning and technical was developed in the Third Way sociological paradigm of 'risk society' associated with sociologists Ulrich Beck and Anthony Giddens, concerned with a perceived increase in the political salience of risk in modern societies. The modern epoch and associated phenomena of globalisation and interconnectedness were perceived to have generated a future-oriented societal consciousness preoccupied with notions of hazard and risk. While pre-modern hazards were associated with 'nature' and characterised by uncertainty, Beck argues that modern risk emerges as a consequence of human activity, leading to greater concern over prediction, limitation and prevention, with the modern nation state carving out its role to protect and insure citizens against an array of personal and societal risks.[29] Giddens and Beck see a role for the state in the distribution of risk similar to the way in which the state plays a role in the distribution of welfare. The role of civil society and transnational public spaces is to build communicative bridges on unbounded risks. The risk society approach is conservative in its acceptance of high levels of risk and its focus on state responses. This paradigm was institutionalised in the International Decade for Natural Disaster Reduction (IDNDR) beginning in 1990, which focused on seeking low-cost measures of disaster preparedness and hazard reduction.

In 1994 the World Conference on Natural Disaster Reduction met in Yokohama encompassing three main strands: political conferences, technical sessions, and 'open/non-political' sessions for the development community. The involvement of the development community in talks led to an emerging interest in links between sustainable development and poverty reduction in the mitigation of natural disasters, but member states were reluctant to make lasting financial commitments to disaster reduction.[30] Towards the end of the IDNDR, leading meteorologists, dismayed at the failure of the decade to attract the attention or resources of policymakers and funders, argued for a switch in emphasis from post-disaster relief to preparedness.[31] This presaged the 2000 United

Nations International Strategy for Disaster Reduction (ISDR), consisting of partnerships between governments, NGOs and civil society, scientific and technical associations, and private sector financial organisations. Key concepts developed within disaster studies throughout the 1990s and 2000s were vulnerability, resilience and 'emergent togetherness'.[32]

The vulnerability approach emphasises that, when disasters are understood as temporally isolated chance events, the human decisions, actions and processes that put people at risk are rendered invisible,[33] which effaces the responsibility of those people and organisations who hold power and make decisions.[34] It challenges the purely technocratic approach to disasters as disruptive events to be managed, as it also looks at structural factors and imagines some form of longer-term redistribution and infrastructure building to manage this. Vulnerability researchers challenge the common view of disasters as great equalisers, showing that they have a tendency to magnify vulnerability. Vulnerability studies extensively catalogued examples of ways in which social inequalities impact on vulnerability to disasters considering factors such as gender,[35] age,[36] race,[37] class, and their intersections.[38] Some studies seem apparently critical, for example exposing the ways in which exploitative capitalist political economy leads to increased vulnerability to disasters in the global South.[39] However, these studies have been criticised because they fail to fundamentally challenge the structures that they identify as problematic, or to even make recommendations that challenge inequalities.[40] While they tend to consider inequalities over the *longue durée* of mounting structural inequality, they differ from the more radical neo-Marxist and poststructuralist approaches in their focus on the ways in which particular disasters exacerbate inequalities. They do not consider ways in which disasters may be constitutive of or beneficial for capitalism and other dominant structures. As a result, their proposed solutions tend to rely on capitalist development and liberal democratic welfare redistributive processes which are still within a capitalist framework. They thus fit comfortably into the post-Washington Consensus field, in which standard neoliberal policies are combined with unthreatening supplemental measures in attempts to reconcile social and ecological goals with established neoliberal arrangements.

Another key concept in the structural approach in DRR is resilience.[41] This is the crucial bridge between neoliberal demand and social/personal coping capacity, which enables the Third Way approaches to offer economic conservatism and social progress at the same time. Resilience theory arose in the natural sciences in the 1970s and 1980s, and rapidly spread through ecology, psychology and the social sciences. In the early 2000s, the discourse of resilience became popular as an approach to understanding and advocating community responses to natural disasters in the context of global climate change, and it often views resilience as a property that connects local ecosystems with communities and individuals (or more often, it seems, treats them as interchangeable). In theory, resilient people/groups will suffer less disastrous effects from the same disruptive events or hazards, and developing resilience thus offers hope of mitigating disasters without redressing structural inequalities or engaging in costly technological prevention. It is both similar to and subtly different from earlier ideas of 'toughness', 'fitness' and 'character' as attributes of healthy rugged individuals or useful productive bodies. Resilience is a key concept in this book and, I will later argue, a key discourse whereby neoliberal institutions attempt to co-opt and de-radicalise grassroots practices. Resilience operates by placing the responsibility for recovering from higher-level shocks onto lower-level communities and individuals[42] (my colloquial definition of 'resilience' has often been 'you need to take whatever shit gets thrown at you'). Ostensibly this kind of discourse can seem empowering for local communities, endowing them with agency in their own recovery and offering hope to offset the panic induced by externally imposed vulnerability. However, it leads to a set of policies and practices that operate comfortably within a de-politicised and managerial framework of natural disasters. It is thus part of the quasi-illusory 'empowerment' of structurally constrained, hyper-responsibilised individuals which is widely studied by Foucauldians.[43] It is also a state-centred discourse that attempts to reify human assets and ecological networks, treating these as exploitable sources of value conceivable in rationalistic, behaviourist, or structuralist terms, and thus open to productive management within state-led assemblages. This book will later illustrate, through the use of case studies, that grassroots responses are actually more spontaneous and organic instances of community learning.[44]

Vulnerability and resilience are sometimes seen as conflicting discourses. 'Vulnerability' is cast as a social democratic discourse seeking the redistribution of risks and welfare to reduce structural inequalities which unfairly expose poorer, racialised and other marginalised communities to hazard, although more recent variants tend to be complicit in

the privatisation of risk and in disaster capitalism. 'Resilience' is associated with smaller government and the privatisation of risk alongside
the need for individuals and communities to take responsibility for their
own exposure to shocks and recovery. Really these discourses are two
sides of the same coin, promoting an associationalist ontology of vulnerable private citizens in need of the state to provide cohesion and help,
in return for which they form civil associations which support governance through 'social capital'. The ideas of political radicalism, solidarity
and resistance to the state by means of social movements or everyday
networks are illegible from these perspectives.

INCLUSION, SOCIAL CAPITAL AND ASSOCIATIONALISM

In my view, this associationalist position on the relationship between
grassroots and top-down organisation is common to most mainstream
approaches. However, there is also a specific strand of the literature
which advocates for the importance of 'emergent togetherness', 'emergent
groups' and 'inclusive DRR' that discusses the importance of citizen
groups,[45] non-profits, informal grassroots groups and other entities.[46]
This literature emphasises how inclusive local-level participation is vital
in building resilience.[47] These authors argue that top-down, centralised
processes often fail in emergencies because they are not responsive
enough, suggesting that more participatory local groups are more
flexible and able to deal with unforeseen events. Drawing influence from
complexity theory, systems theory and ecology, they suggest that points
of instability have emergent properties that are better able to organise for
change than rigid structures.[48] This is often framed explicitly in terms of
neoliberal New Public Management discourse,[49] with a focus on organisational theory, for example on how grassroots groups distribute and
coordinate tasks and resources, how they make decisions and how they
produce knowledge.[50]

This literature is analogous to a broader 'social capital' or 'associationalist' standpoint in the social sciences and humanities, which informs
the mainstream liberal consensus on the relationship between 'civil
society' and the state. Many thinkers construct these spheres as being
partially autonomous, potentially conflicting and/or acting as checks and
balances.[51] This model deploys the assumptions both that movements can
be co-opted/channelled (NGO-ised) to promote cohesion, development

and community, and that state control can effectively impose cohesion. Grassroots, participatory groups are thus desirable, but only if they operate as components in a larger totality which produces stability and efficiency, not as distinct social subjects which pursue meaningful alternatives. Civil society is etymologically derived from the Ancient Greek idea of civilised society, as distinct from uncivil, barbarian society.[52] The idea was revived and elaborated during the Enlightenment. Civil society in this liberal tradition is seen as an independent realm, separate from state and market, which supports and promotes democratic values while independent associations, community organisations and volunteering act as checks and balances against state abuses of authority by demanding accountability. The concept went out of fashion for a while in the mid-twentieth century but underwent a revival beginning in the 1970s and became established in the 1990s. Robert Putnam's concept of 'social capital' creates a bridge between behaviourist models and the associationalist view of civil society. This concept treats trust and cooperation within society as a kind of capital, which, if well-established, leads to well-functioning and stable democracies. Social capital is seen to be fostered within society through flourishing egalitarian participatory voluntary associations.[53] Like monetary capital, social capital is seen to be a kind of universal, transferable currency.[54] Examples of institutions which generate social capital include communities, neighbourhoods, voluntary associations and churches.[55] Social capital theory is very prominent in disaster research, the argument usually being that societies with greater social capital are better able to prepare for and mitigate the effects of disasters, and that states can mobilise social capital in their organisation of recovery efforts.[56] The explicit monetisation of social bonds inherent in the idea of 'social *capital*' coincided with transformations in ideas around the structure and purpose of governments in the UK and USA, embodied in initiatives like the Obama administration's 'Open Government Initiative' and David Cameron's 'Big Society', both of which encouraged more socially active citizenry and the dispersal of information through an ethos of 'transparency' and decentralisation of knowledge, and the 'co-production of government services and democracy'. Much of the process was formulated by Silicon Valley cyberneticians and computer programmers rather than democratically elected politicians. This new group of technocrats started to treat networks of people, objects and machines like the 'transparent and controllable' flow of information within computer networks. Social media networks like Facebook embodied the new form of government, whose essential function – despite the seemingly non-hierarchical nature of networks – is policing.[57] When society and the state are seen as complementary and mutually supporting, this means that only the sections of 'civil society' that are legible to the state and which it can capitalise upon and control are seen as 'social capital'. Other social forces are a threat to be controlled – through recuperation or repression.

'NETWORK SOCIETY' AND THE STATE

As we shall see, anarchist approaches typically juxtapose state logics to those of 'society', mutual aid groups, or networks. The mainstream approaches discussed here, in contrast, treat the two as compatible and mutually supportive. This fits into wider discussions of the 'network society'. One of the distinctive features of the contemporary age and neo-liberalism has been the calling into question of the nation state as the primary political organising unit. Theorists of neoliberalism, globalisation and network society including Appadurai,[58] Hardt and Negri,[59] Held[60] and Van Dijk[61] have for more than 20 years been drawing attention to the ways in which place-based politics and culture are being replaced by international and transnational administrative bodies, corporations, investment and communication. The term 'network society' was originally coined by Jan Van Dijck and was elaborated by Manuel Castells[62] and Arquilla and Ronfeldt.[63] The idea of networks forms a recurring theme in this book and has both neoliberal and radical variants. In the neoliberal variant considered here, networks are sources of social capital and can be managed through cybernetic soft power.

Neoliberalism is often understood to be a less hierarchical, more networked alternative to Fordist capitalism and command economies – despite the persistent governmentality and limited subjectivities it requires. Castells argues that the information technology revolution played a large part in the collapse of the Soviet Union and the weakening of the nation state, which paved the way for a more effective and flexible version of capitalism – something like what we might now call neoliberalism. A defining feature of this new form of capitalism and the network society that underpins it is that 'dominant functions and processes in the information age are increasingly organised around networks. Networks constitute the new social morphology of our societies and the diffusion of networking logic substantially modifies the operation and outcomes in the processes of production, experience, power and culture'.[64] For Castells, the rise of new social movements is a response to the crisis of the nation state and democracy and traditional institutions of civil society and patriarchy. Social movements, for Castells, revolve around identities: religious fundamentalism, nationalism, sexual identities, feminism; yet there is a fundamental conflict between networks and identities, and new social movements are resisting in a manner that conflicts with the dominant logic of the network society. Network society is considered to be disruptive of such identities. Castells argues that the network society 'disembodies social relationships, introducing the culture of real virtuality'.[65] The diffusion of this network logic in modern society substantially alters production, politics, culture, relationships and even human experience.

Castells is an erstwhile neo-Marxist who moved towards a Third Way neoliberal position which seeks to learn from networked responses (e.g. social media, new social movements) in a way which integrates them with top-down functioning.[66] He is a structuralist and a technological determinist who leaves 'few political choices' for his readers.[67] The network society he conceives is primarily a society of loosely networked consumerist individuals. While Castells does not adequately theorise political resistance to and through the network society, Arquilla and Ronfeld argue that digital media put more power in the hands of non-state actors, allowing them to influence developments at a global level. Arquilla and Ronfeld binarise 'netwar' into the good guys and the bad guys; or, in their terminology, the 'enlightening' versus the 'dark side' of networks, to refer to conflicts waged 'on the one hand, by terrorists, criminals and ethnonationalist extremists', and by 'civil-society activists on the other'.[68] What these different groups have in common under the aegis of netwar is the networked organisational structure, leaderlessness and the ability to come together quickly in 'swarming attacks'.[69] From a more radical perspective, Karatzogianni and Robinson argue that distinctions need to be made between autonomous networks and similar structures which are nonetheless hierarchical. Networks only subvert the world system to the extent that they compose alternative social logics.[70]

NGOS AND CIVIL SOCIETY

The various strands of DRR research outlined earlier are embedded within and inform a broader policy field that defines the roles to be played by the state, social networks and civil society in disaster response. These discourses encourage the neoliberal rollback of state welfare and public service provision and offer an ideological justification for governments and funding donors to encourage NGOs to absorb former state functions, with an expectation of cooperation with state policies and regulations.[71] Humanitarian agencies are usually only allowed to deliver aid if they promise political neutrality, although arguably this is not possible as disasters are always-already political events with political causes and consequences.[72] Groups competing for outsourced state projects are often even more constrained, while governments increasingly regulate whether and how NGOs can legally operate in contentious fields (such as refugee support). There is therefore some question over the extent to which NGOs are an autonomous, associational realm of society which supports democracy through trust, egalitarianism and social solidarity rather than simply being absorbed into the interests of the government without having to undergo democratic election.

In the US, there is a long tradition of participation of volunteers in disasters.[73] In the policy field, there is emphasis on the participation of defined civil society groups rather than broader and more informal notions of community.[74] The participation of volunteers is usually formalised through affiliation with government-recognised NGOs or faith-based organisations (FBOs). This provides volunteers with particular rights and privileges that authorise them to serve in a close connection, particularly in the field, with FEMA. Other authors have commented that the DHS sees its legitimacy as 'a powerful bargaining chip to bring grassroots groups to the table'.[75] These NGOs often include quasi-autonomous NGOs (QUANGOs) and donor-organised NGOs (DONGOs). Some categories more than others represent a continuation of state functions,[76] and it has been argued that while their funding can mean they are almost entirely state controlled, they often operate with less transparency and without democratic accountability.[77] Most NGOs depend on funding from either states, private donors such as corporations, or international development agencies. This reliance on centralised funding undermines their status as autonomous organisations and their role in criticising governments and holding them to account. In the case of conflicts between funders and those groups and communities that the NGOs seek to serve, it is likely that the NGO will seek to appease the funder, without whose money they would not be able to continue. This leads to a top-down, donor-controlled model that can sometimes be to the detriment of the communities served.[78] NGOs have also been criticised as being co-opted into capitalism and as complicit in justifying the neoliberal state withdrawal of resources from the public sphere while supporting the provision of oppressive governmentality regimes.[79] Social capital theory in general and the NGO model of service provision have also been criticised because they fail to address pre-existent structural inequalities which mean that specific historical, economic and political contexts may be more or less fertile environments for the kinds of voluntarism and participation that underpins this model.[80] Furthermore, models of social capital seem to treat all forms of participation as interchangeable; there is seemingly no distinction between for example a bowling club, an interest group and a workers' party.

Many general criticisms of the NGO model also apply more specifically in disaster situations. For example, the Red Cross has been criticised for inefficiency and lack of responsiveness due to the top-down nature of its large bureaucratic organisation,[81] as well as for complicity in oppressive social control and systemic racism during Hurricane Katrina.[82] There is evidence that where internationally funded NGOs are present, governments will under-invest in preparedness.[83] Nonetheless, even critics of NGOs suggest that they do play a role in contesting neoliberalism.[84] Hannigan argues that, unlike DRR, the humanitarianism of the NGO sector is a moral rather than technocratic discourse. In the international realm, this is based on ideas of the moral duty of those in the developed world to 'rescue' poor people in the overseas peripheries – usually implying short-term needs rather than longer-term exposure to chronic poverty and risk exposure. However, the humanitarian approach also sometimes echoes the technocratic paradigm by drawing on a cybernetic or systems approach, whereby the goal of relief efforts is a return to 'normalcy', drawing on whatever organisational techniques are deemed most effective,[85] often leading to a valorisation of networks and social capital, but only insofar as these are compatible with a strong securitised state.

This can render NGOs unable to work with informal community structures which violate state norms, making NGOs either irrelevant or recuperative. This is a recurring issue in sources dealing with network versus state conflicts and is also part of the corporate discussion regarding flattening hierarchies. As NGOs take over the provision of services that were formerly the domain of the state, they become a conduit into marginalised communities for neoliberal state policy. Dolhinow has argued that a disabling situation is created by the three-way relationship between the state, NGOs and grassroots leaders (themselves created through NGO processes requiring representatives). She draws on the example of house-building in the Mexican *colonias* (neighbourhood communities) in the US, where she argues a focus on individual needs prevented collective action and donor conditions led to burdensome bureaucratic procedures. The requirements for planning applications funded by individual loans impeded effective projects. Since the residents were used to just building their own houses, the project collapsed.[86]

Ideas of associationalism and NGO-isation play a dual role in this book. On the one hand it is argued that movements like Occupy are very different from traditional NGOs, and indeed contest their co-optation into state-funded service-delivery roles. On the other hand, I will argue that there is a very real danger of mutual aid groups being co-opted. In the next chapter, I will consider more critical theories of civil society, which view it not as continuous with the state and governance but as a realm of conflict, while in Chapters 4, 5 and 6 I will consider anarchist alternatives.

DRR IN POLICY

DRR is not simply an academic discourse. It informs policy, which impacts on social movements. For example, a government report published by the US Department for Homeland Security (DHS) titled *The Resilient Social Network* attempts to co-opt the energies of Occupy Sandy into a neoliberal discourse and policy field, stipulating the need for control.[87] This provides a good case study of how associationalism can be used to recuperate radical alternatives. Agencies of the state, and FEMA in particular, were widely criticised after the storm by a very wide array of actors, including other authorities such as the New York City (NYC) Housing Authority, governors and mayors.[88] The state both needed the creative energies of the grassroots for the practical recovery efforts, yet at the same time was threatened by them, since effective response from the grassroots acts to delegitimise the state by undermining its necessity.

While many activists were not surprised to find that the DHS had been monitoring Occupy Sandy's activities, many were shocked to see that the agency commissioned a report that actually commends Occupy Sandy's work. Furthermore, the report recommends changes to the DHS and wider government response strategy based on the success of OS in order to encourage collaborations between government and grassroots efforts.

The document exhibits a fundamental ambivalence regarding Occupy Sandy (OS), praising the group's innovation and vibrancy while distrusting its anarchic nature. The report praises the 'volunteer army of young, educated, tech-savvy individuals with time and a desire to help others' that emerged from 'seemingly out of nowhere'.[89] However, the primacy of FEMA[90] itself is never questioned. According to the DHS, 'It is a well-established lesson of history that human group activity is most effective when it is orchestrated by someone or some group that has an overarching understanding of certain information.'[91] The result is an attempt to tap into OS's energy while also controlling it. The recommendations include coordination of response activities between FEMA and grassroots entities (such as OS); increasing capability for information sharing between official and 'emergent' relief entities (such as OS); and issuing guidelines on social media usage, inspired by the practices of OS. The desire for control inflects the tone of the entire report which simultaneously vindicates the flexible, responsive and non-hierarchical organisation of OS while, at the same time, calling for a 'unity of effort' and offering recommendations for introducing bureaucratic procedures whereby such groups might be monitored, regulated and controlled as part of the official relief effort, for example by insisting that volunteers are vetted and trained not to engage in 'risky behavior'.[92] The report cites 'rising public distrust of hierarchical institutions', while musing on ways that grassroots entities and their 'personal relationships and deep local knowledge and caring for the community' might be incorporated and controlled.[93]

The document appears to have benign intentions, yet the desire to either co-opt or repress movements is not far below the surface. There has been speculation that the DHS – a security agency established in response to 9/11 whose remit includes defence against terrorists alongside disaster management – did not have entirely benign interests in Occupy Sandy, and some commentators have linked the report on OS to a wider campaign of counterinsurgency (COIN) surveillance, secret monitoring and social control, which was exposed by the Partnership for Civil Justice Fund after Occupy Wall Street.[94] The document also encourages the NGO-isation of the grassroots movement, saying that being affiliated with a known NGO or FBO 'affords volunteers special rights and privileges to enable them to serve'.[95] Nonetheless, the state response to movement and community responses after Hurricane Sandy was very different to that which occurred after Katrina, which exemplified outright repression. Accounts of the aftermath of Katrina include harrowing narratives of how the state response criminalised community responses, often reacting with extreme violence and actively repressing social movement efforts. John Clark lists 'de facto ethnic cleansing, mistreatment and exploitation of migrant workers, widespread police brutality, denial of prisoners' rights, collapse of the courts and legal system, unfair evictions, price gouging on rent, discriminatory housing policies, discriminatory reorganisation of the school system, and gutting of the health care system'.[96] It is my contention that stimulus/co-optation and violent repression are two sides of the same coin, and both are implied in the cybernetic rationality of DRR outlined above.

In the UK, during the Covid-19 crisis, there is evidence that the state used both co-optation and repression. The state appropriated the language of 'mutual aid' in its calls for 'NHS (National Health Service) volunteers', and also incorporated the expectation of people providing mutual aid in their communities into its official social care policy for 'extremely vulnerable' people told to undertake an extreme form of social isolation called 'shielding', who were informed that they could have their needs met by taking personal responsibility for reaching out to 'friends, family or volunteers' or 'other voluntary or community services in your area'.[97] Such community support was one of the few activities permitted under distancing regulations. The more repressive aspects of the lockdown policy also relied heavily on crowdsourced policing by communities, with heavy use of media signalling to encourage mutual enforcement and silence opposing voices. While community was deemed desirable during the height of the crisis, the advice became more individualistic after lockdown was eased and people encouraged to return to work, with individuals urged to 'stay alert' in order to 'control the virus'.[98] This was also the frame used prior to the introduction of the lockdown, when the government relied on responsible individuals to contain the outbreak. In this more individualised frame, health is treated as a 'game' which the sick are perceived to have lost, with social structures largely ignored. The advice to 'wash or sanitise hands frequently' assumes constant access to bathroom facilities, running water and soap which are not always readily available for homeless people for example, and the ability to purchase sanitiser during a panic-buying crisis when prices were exorbitantly inflated. Conditions in workplaces, schools, prisons, care homes and hospitals are also outside individual control, while lockdown itself imposes additional risks on vulnerable people. Neoliberal public health emphasises personal responsibility for health outcomes, mimicking a decentralised approach while behind the scenes state, military, industrial and pharmaceutical capitalist technocrats are rigging the game to achieve desired (profitable) outcomes.

ASSUMPTIONS OF THE DRR LITERATURE AND CRITIQUE

In the next chapter (Chapter 3) I will go into more detail on a range of critical responses to mainstream disaster studies and policy, including critiques of disaster capitalism and securitisation. Many of these shade over into the more inclusive end of the mainstream literature. They also offer extensive critiques of associationalism and responsibilisation. Here, however, I would like to move towards a preliminary critique of the field, focusing on the problems with mainstream DRR.

Disaster as rupture

Despite a rhetoric of harm reduction, DRR is focused primarily on systemic stability. While it does not entirely neglect human consequences of disaster, its main focus is elsewhere. DRR defines disasters as ruptures in the normal functioning of society, and posits the desirability of using cybernetic forms of organisation and states of emergency to avoid recurring disasters becoming catastrophic for the system, that is, to allow the system to persist in spite of recurrent breakdowns of 'normality'. In relation to systemic problems such as climate change, economic instability, increasingly frequent natural disasters or pandemics, the approach is to let it happen and then manage the consequences through targeted and recurring emergency responses. This is clearest in the behaviourist version, in which the focus on management squeezes out other concerns. But the structuralist emphasis on reducing vulnerability and increasing resilience also leaves the social factors causing disasters largely untouched. DRR thus functions as crisis management in the sense proposed by Spivak: it papers over the occurrence of rupture, crisis and antagonism by disavowing it and attempting to restore a sense of normality. This generally provides reassurance to the less-affected groups while either neglecting or worsening the conditions of the worse-off.[99]

Indeed, one may wonder how far disasters are ruptures at all for some DRR scholars. The basic assumptions of behaviourism, cybernetics, rational-choice theory, or social capital theory are applied to disasters as mechanically as to any other process or event. The literature seems cut off from the affects and human impacts of disasters, treating them purely as a management problem like any other. The same neoliberal values which underpin normal governance – such as efficiency and cost-effectiveness – are expected to prevail. Indeed, the creation of a disaster field tends to normalise disasters as a distinct but recurring area of governance, which cease to be an existential threat precisely because this generic response-pattern exists. Disasters are still, however, sources of immense loss, trauma and death for those affected, and this leads to a persistent gap between popular and state-level perceptions. Disasters are now only disasters for human beings; they are not disasters for the state so long as control remains intact. They are a threat to the state mainly because they are disorderly, not because of their human impact. This disorder is managed or prevented through DRR, but the human side of disaster remains the same. States may thus become increasingly indifferent to the risk of disaster, secure behind the buffers of a resilient population and an efficient management regimen.

Disasters as generic: the need for disaster-specific agencies

DRR, in line with 'social capital' theory, seeks to treat all sorts of people, groups and associations, as well as the conditions they find themselves in, as equivalent and interchangeable. The capacity for DRR to engage with grassroots initiatives is also impeded by a set of formal models which are organisationalist, rationalist and behaviourist in focus. It is designed mainly to understand and mobilise the activities of large, hierarchical, formally structured entities such as branches of the state, public services, corporations, and NGOs. These are treated as similar 'stakeholders' which can be integrated based on their common rational-choice, behaviourist, or associationalist functioning. The isomorphism of different formal organisations is a large part of what allows them to be generically known and managed. Other kinds of responders – for example, social movements, community groups, or affected communities – are either ignored or assumed to be equivalent bodies operating like states, corporations and NGOs. The core axioms of all the variants of mainstream DRR are too rigid to allow any deeper engagement with situations where groups or individuals operating on completely different logics are either affected by disasters or respond constructively to them. In effect, the state looks at itself in the mirror; it is able to see others only to the extent that they seem similar to its own reflection.

DRR also tends to be associated with bureaucratic empire-building by specialised agencies like DHS and FEMA and their academic accomplices, at the expense variously of ordinary non-disaster agencies, specialised scientific fields of disaster-related knowledge, and non-state actors. The creation of a field of disaster-specific social power is conditioned on a corresponding creation of a field of disaster knowledge, which is focused on the management of disaster as such, not on characteristics of particular hazards or the needs of particular communities. This is reflected in Quarantelli's call to be 'generic' and not 'agent specific' (with 'agent' here referring to the natural hazard or other cause of the disaster) and to focus on 'general principles and not specific details'.[100] This recasts disasters not as specific events, but as an abstract concept – there is a pre-formed idea of preparedness that is relevant to all disasters, and the main problem of disaster response is that different responders are not coordinated. This further implies that it is better to respond to disasters through generic disaster-specialist bodies rather than through bodies specialising in types of disaster or in related matters. The same holds true for preparedness and planning: 'there should be only one major organisation responsible for coordinating the overall planning for all kinds of disasters. There should not be separate preparedness planning by different groups for different agent specific disasters.'[101] DRR thus often reads as an exercise in bureaucratic empire-building. In order to build up the power/knowledge complex of the disaster agency, the disaster agency has to transfer fragments of power from all kinds of other agents: the ordinary bodies responsible for a class of ordinary accidents (health services, fire services, etc.), mundane accident and emergency bodies in organisations, specialised disaster bodies relating to one class of disasters, military agencies with emergency jurisdictions, local community bodies, NGOs, etc.

The main role of the disaster organiser – a new role which DRR as a discipline seeks to carve out – is coordination. In the US, FEMA takes on this role, taking a 'Whole Community' approach – the key principles of which are apparently '(a) to understand and meet the actual needs of the whole community; (b) to engage and empower all parts of the community; and (c) to strengthen what works well in communities on a daily basis'.[102] In the UK it was assumed it was better to respond to the Covid-19 pandemic through the COBRA committee (that is, the UK Civil Contingencies Committee, set up initially for counterterrorism) rather than primarily the health service. This type of strategic choice draws attention away from the specific impacts of a specific disaster towards standardised practices of social, informational and cybernetic control which can be repeated for any conceivable crisis. Integrated disaster management is primarily an exercise in social control of different organisations, not in responding to the disaster. The underlying claim is that it is better to respond through a disaster agency than rely on ad-hoc local responses, existing community systems, through the central ministry responsible for particular types of disaster, or through the military (to take a few examples). The claim that this leads to more effective responses is true (if at all) only if the focus on generic aspects is accepted. The resultant focus on control and coordination comes at the expense of human needs, autonomy, empowerment, and nuanced responses to specific situations.

Despite the frequent associationalist attempts to incorporate non-state actors, DRR still seeks a largely authoritarian structure of response. DRR tends to advocate against the kind of militarised response that arguably happened after Hurricane Katrina, a style of response which is closer to the older Hobbesian fear of chaos and panic. Rather, it seeks to create a precarious unity between grassroots and top-down approaches. It tends to seek, in Quarantelli's words, 'vertical and horizontal integration',[103] or, in the words of the DHS report: 'neither the hierarchical centralised approach, nor the horizontal is a replacement for the other', yet as horizontal organising becomes more prevalent, 'it is increasingly important for unity of effort to build in order to deepen bridges between hierarchical institutions and emergent response groups'.[104] The assumption that there should be a coordinated response 'managed' by a central body, with a unitary integrated message and an orderly set of responses, is rarely questioned. At best, therefore, this approach is a recuperative modification of the Hobbesian approach, which makes concessions to non-state actors so as to remain in control. At its most dystopian, it involves a viral reproduction of the generic disaster script and its underlying (behaviourist, individualising, social capital ...) doctrines through the education and co-optation of bodies outside the disaster agency itself. Where 'participation' requires acceptance of centrally decided objectives, subordination to a central agency, collaboration in homogenised signalling, self- and mutual policing, and reconstitution of oneself as the desired kind of rationalistic/cybernetic subject, it may be more, rather than less, authoritarian than a purely top-down approach.

As we shall see in Chapters 3 and 4, anarchist approaches posit an antagonism between the logic of mutual aid and social cooperation on the one hand, and the logic of centralised control on the other. Marxists similarly posit a radical antagonism between popular organisations and neoliberal states. In terms of these antagonisms, DRR wants to have its cake and eat it: to have all the creative power, passion and improvisation of grassroots responses, while also maintaining strong centralised power. Associationalists would, of course, criticise the assumptions of these rival approaches and suggest that the contradiction is not in fact so sharp. However, their reconciliation of top-down and bottom-up power is often achieved rhetorically or at the level of assumptions – for example, by treating grassroots groups as equivalent bureaucratic 'stakeholders', or by seeking to blend apparently juxtaposed approaches without specifying how this is done. This rhetorical resolution may well fail to produce workable cooperation; people cannot simply be commanded and directed to freely and passionately participate. DRR models generally depend on the existence of unified objectives and some degree of trust. Yet neoliberal states may seek outcomes from disaster management which are fundamentally opposed to those of social movements or grassroots communities. DRR is too ready to paper over such disagreements.

Securitisation

The emphasis on generic responses also encourages authoritarianism and securitisation. Securitisation theory will be discussed in more detail in Chapter 3. It refers to a general dynamic in which issues are divided between normal and exceptional, with exceptional securitised issues excluded from normal restrictions and subject to extraordinary powers. As breaks with normality, generic disasters are an exemplary exceptional situation and thus facilitate securitisation. As a frame, securitisation generally undermines human rights and human security, and it does not necessarily lead to more effective responses either. Indeed, it tends to produce the kinds of authoritarian response which DRR in principle critiques.

For example, in the Covid-19 crisis, the promotion of a risk-based 'public health' frame, with a heavy emphasis on non-medical prevention and containment, may reflect the treatment of the crisis as a generic disaster. On the one hand, this led to an inappropriate reliance on police instead of health services and replication of measures (such as lockdowns and 'stay at home' guidance) historically used in planning for social control in very different types of disaster such as bombings, floods, nuclear war and terrorist attacks.[105] On the other, it led to the fatal neglect of various medical aspects of the situation: testing and diagnosis, PPE, antivirals, etc. Many deaths may well have been caused by oversight or policy negligence around such nuanced issues as sending people with Covid-19 infections to care homes or failing to provide PPE for hospital staff – problems which a more medical focus would have averted.

Like securitisation in general, DRR tends to de-politicise disasters. The focus on good governance, efficiency, and technocratic goals in a context of emergency measures undermines democratic processes, responsiveness to social movements or popular concerns, and consideration of the differing needs and desires of distinct social groups. In delivering DRR as a (compulsory) service, governments or disaster agencies also monopolise the power to decide what counts as a disaster and how to respond to it. DRR thus functions in the disaster field in a similar manner to neoliberalism in the economic field. This is the case even when participation is emphasised, and even when structural inequalities are taken into account. What is typically missing from the field is a sense that people are multiple, different, and distinct, and that legitimate disagreements exist regarding both the ends and means of social life. A group like OS does not simply deliver the same service in a more decentralised manner; it prefigures a different way of life with different goals. When such groups are incorporated into state-led DRR, these distinct trajectories tend to be overridden.

De-politicisation may also amount to covert side-taking, especially when combined with capitalistic assumptions. Mainstream DRR generally takes capitalism for granted and assumes the standard liberal account in which it is a system of cooperation for mutual advantage. However, critical approaches generally suggest that capitalism is instead a dominatory and predatory system which benefits some and harms others. If this is true, then DRR initiatives aiming to restore business-as-usual will also reinforce inequalities and oppressions. In particular, Naomi Klein raises the problem that not only is the technocratic and managerial authority undemocratic, it also acts in the interests of capital. Klein coined the term 'disaster capitalism' to refer to the way in which, in all kinds of disasters, powerful people use proxy global recovery agencies at a local level to clear out deprived communities and profitably reconstruct them as neoliberal developments.[106] Where DRR provides the military/policing force and the extraordinary powers to enforce such processes, it comes to seem far more sinister than its rhetoric of 'effectiveness' suggests.

CONCLUSION

This chapter has examined the mainstream disaster studies field and has shown that there are similar assumptions beneath its apparently distinct schools. In principle, DRR focuses on effective responses to, and prevention of, disasters; it is participatory, non-authoritarian and empowering. In practice, however, it relies on the construction of a securitised disaster field as the territory of centralised disaster agencies specialising mainly in social control. Activities of non-state actors are often valorised, but only as subordinate cogs in the DRR machine, or on the assumption that these actors replicate neoliberal structures and motivations. The desire to vampirise the creative power, passion and fluidity of mobilisations like OS and Covid-19 Mutual Aid coexists precariously with an overarching fixation on maintaining control and order in disaster situations, so as to prevent them from threatening established power. DRR thus oscillates wildly between a repression it disavows and a recuperation it usually cannot achieve. Behind this failure lies the problem that, in a sense, for DRR scholars, disasters are not all that disastrous at all. They are, so to speak, disasters only for human beings; for the state, they are manageable challenges.

3

Critical Approaches: Precarity, Securitisation and Disaster Capitalism

INTRODUCTION: DISASTERS AND TRANSFORMATION IN THE WORLD SYSTEM

This chapter tackles critical theories and discourses around the role of disasters in the world system other than the anarchist approaches discussed in Chapter 4. It covers critical responses in disaster studies, contextualising the theoretical discourses outlined in the previous chapter by describing how they are viewed by critical perspectives, particularly in the context of transformation of capital and how it reconfigures social forces, and the role that disasters play in this. In Chapter 2, I argued that the mainstream approach is underpinned by a range of assumptions and myths about the irrational or rational nature of humans and the apolitical nature of disasters. These myths serve the function of making the specialised yet generic disaster agencies of the neoliberal state seem both legitimate and essential as the only entities able to oversee and control the chaos ensuing from disasters, while portraying community responses to disasters as at best inefficient and at worst violent and dangerous. In highlighting some of the assumptions underlying this narrative, I have already moved some way towards a critique of this approach. The purpose of the current chapter is to go into more detail on a range of alternative frameworks for understanding disasters and for theorising the roles played by the state, NGOs and the market in disaster preparedness, relief and recovery. Critical approaches have shown that the cybernetic rationalism of the dominant approach creates conditions for securitisation, politics of fear, 'shock doctrine' and disaster capitalism. Theorists covered in this chapter come variously from liberal, neo-Marxist and poststructuralist paradigms. They thus differ somewhat from the anarchist approach outlined later in the book. It is argued that while these theories often provide an excellent critique of current conditions, their proposed solutions are insufficient because they fail to radically reimagine the temporality and scale of necessary social change and thus fail to situate disaster relief in the much longer duration of climate change and the collapse of industrial civilisation.

SOCIAL CONTROL, SECURITISATION AND FEAR

A first cluster of critical approaches focuses on critique of securitisation or the 'politics of fear'. Securitisation is the discursive process of success-fully framing a particular issue or policy area as an exceptional security issue. The securitisation of an issue typically results in exceptional powers, increased resource allocation, and greater use of militarised or policing measures. Different interest groups inside and outside states compete to securitise and de-securitise particular issues, often as ways to prioritise their own issues, capture resources, or increase their own powers. Milita-risation and securitisation of humanitarianism and disaster management have increased in recent years, even from a mainstream perspective.[1] Securitisation policies rest on the idea that a given phenomenon is an exceptional existential threat, and are thus particularly compatible with Hobbesian approaches which treat human actors as irrational and vulnerable to one another, thus requiring top-down prevention and control by (presumably more rational) elite actors. Disasters have proven a relatively easy area to securitise. With the exception of structuralists, dominant paradigms portray disasters as natural, episodic and random events which also surpass politics-as-usual. This combination leads to a policy framework for dealing with disasters that is state-led, with a particular emphasis on security and control rather than other state functions, such as social policy, welfare, community-based education or the 'normal' legal process. Perceived existential threats to the state or 'society' also tend to sideline individual rights and needs and community processes.

In Chapter 2, I portrayed the mainstream approach to disaster as 'risk management' requiring top-down management and control. This creates a state-led response set based on typical securitising moves, including an emphasis on security and control rather than other possible state functions such as welfare or legal rights and responsibilities. Here I discuss a range of theorists in the field of critical security studies (CSS) who take a critical approach to the choice of a security frame in policy. Underpinning this field is a denunciation of the de-politicisation of security in both policy and academia.[2] CSS scholarship seeks to open to theoretical scrutiny the statist and militaristic assumptions of dominant conceptions of security, such as those which underpin policy-oriented risk management. Contrary to the assumptions of these approaches, securitisation is not an indispensable response to disorder, chaos and threat, but an absence of normal politics, or, following Agamben (who is widely cited in the field of CSS), a 'state of exception'[3] which transcends 'the established rules of the game and frames the issue as either a special kind of politics or above politics'.[4] CSS thus works with a binary of 'normal' politics versus extraordinary, securitised politics.

While security discourse presents itself as apolitical and transcending politics, it is in fact intensely political and has political effects, in particular around the unequal distribution of risk and the arbitrary securitisation of some risks rather than others. Didier Bigo and Anastassia Tsoukala argue that International Relations (IR) scholars, along with mainstream policy discourse, have decided as an epistemic community that 'security is about "serious" things, i.e. war, death, survival, and not about everyday practices concerning crime, or about the feeling of insecurity, fear of poverty and illness',[5] issues which are elsewhere described as 'human security' concerns. This emphasis on survival and existential threat follows discursively from the earlier practices of state security, focused on great-power rivals. It often serves the purpose of legitimating violence and coercion, which are mobilised in the interests of a particular class or political community at the expense of others, while at the same time adopting a universalist discourse of 'security' which serves to estrange the voice that is speaking from any particular perspective or standpoint in time and space.[6] Security discourse can thus serve to simultaneously justify and enact very illiberal practices on the part of ostensibly 'liberal' regimes.[7]

Securitisation typically relies on a claim that a particular issue (such as disasters) constitutes an extraordinary existential threat (to the state, nation or society), which is qualitatively different from everyday risks. Declaring the 'threat' is a power move that CSS scholars call a 'speech act', a declaration with real consequences that is performed within unequal power structures and therefore impacts on people in very different ways, depending where they are situated in those power structures. The speech act identifies enemies and declares war, or a state of emergency, which is not open to negotiation or political debate.[8] By 'identifying' enemies, the speech act constitutes them, that is, it actually *creates* a group of people that may not previously have been a cohesive 'group' in the first place. There is considerable overlap between securitisation theory in political/ International Relations scholarship and the study of moral panics in media studies and sociology. A moral panic is a media event, often artificially generated, in which a particular form of deviance/crime is portrayed (usually misleadingly) as novel, exceptionally threatening, and exceptionally 'other'. Such deviance is usually associated with a 'folk devil', such as a racialised minority, supposed underclass, or youth subculture. It is also taken to stand for a wider social breakdown which is framed as an effect of moral collapse. Moral panics generate a discursive spiral which usually leads to escalating public, media, political, policing and judicial concern, culminating in extraordinary legislation or campaigns of repression.[9] Moral panics have become a staple of the populist media and dovetail with wider politics of fear in coverage of disaster-related deviance, such as Covid-19 lockdown-breaking, or supposed looting (often survival-related or misidentified) in the aftermath of earthquakes or hurricanes. This enables moralistic in-groups to find human targets for the fear and anxiety associated with disasters.

Securitisation studies also overlap with critical race theory and intersectional research. Securitisation and other distributions of risk and concern are usually structured along familiar lines of race, gender, (post)coloniality, sexuality, disability and class. Such distributions of risk, death and 'grievability' are central to the definitions of privileged and marginalised groups in much of the intersectionalist literature.[10] Without minimising other social hierarchies, securitisation theory particularly overlaps with 'racialisation' – a process by which a racial interpretation is imposed on a particular group and/or social practice. This was particularly evident in media portrayals and policy responses to terrorism after the New York 9/11/2001 attacks in the US[11] and the London 7/7 bombings in the UK.[12] In both situations, 'Muslims' (an incredibly diverse group) were declared as the enemy through speech acts, for example declaring 9/11 as 'an attack on freedom' by Islam. The security culture and anti-terror measures put in place after this event arguably are some of the most oppressive in history, impacting on the whole population, but utterly disproportionately upon Muslims and other racialised (e.g. black) people.[13] Framings of particular populations as 'risk groups' and other populations as being 'at risk' leads to grossly inegalitarian practices impacting heavily on the lives and bodies of the groups framed as 'risky', often putting them at much greater risk – for example, of being killed by police[14] or, in the case of migrants, of dying in transit. On the other hand, threats impinging on marginalised groups (such as far-right violence and femicide) are less likely to be securitised, and racialisation and other positional framings impact areas such as disaster preparedness and reactions to disasters, as we saw above in relation to Katrina and Covid-19. Securitisation thus typically involves oppressive choices as to which lives 'matter'. There is also a particular propensity for securitised issues (disasters, pandemics, migration, terrorism, crime) to be perceived as emerging from chaotic, marginal sites to threaten orderly, core areas or groups, even when driving factors are endogenous to Western societies or result from global structures.

If securitised and disastrous effects are closely enmeshed with discursive hierarchies, it follows that their roots lie in widespread cultural/discursive processes operating on a poststructuralist model of decentralised everyday power/knowledge. A vast array of everyday beliefs, feelings and actions go into the process of making certain groups 'risky' and others 'vulnerable'. Scholars have applied this idea to show that securitisation occurs not only in national and international policy, it also penetrates all levels of society, for example schools and education,[15] and identity formation.[16] Racialised people, alongside dissidents and political activists,[17] and asylum seekers and migrants are constructed as a threat to civilised society and the enemy of liberal democracy.[18] They are construed as such by not only authority figures, such as the government, police and teachers, but also possibly their neighbours and friends, and they may even come to be suspicious of themselves. This can lead to a culture of fear and conformity, backed up by the violent repression of social justice and community organising movements, even when these may have their own legitimate and embodied claims to seek 'security'.[19]

Another line of critique relates to atomisation. Both mainstream disaster studies and securitisation in general rest on the assumption that humans are essentially selfish, competitive and potentially violent. These beliefs are treated as transcending politics – for example, as part of the generic security field which applies regardless of the context of a disaster. Scholars from a number of traditions argue that neoliberalism actually works to produce the expected kind of rational, acquisitive, subject since people are encouraged to compete and fear each other, and discouraged from developing whatever skills or relations are needed to relate.[20] Beliefs about human nature can turn into self-fulfilling prophecies. First, if we believe that others are essentially selfish, we are more likely to behave in such a way ourselves.[21] Furthermore, we are more likely to place our trust in alienated institutions that we hope might protect us from one another. Mistrust of others leads to an everyday politics of fear,[22] which legitimises a culture of social control, for example increasing CCTV surveillance, private security guards and gated communities, which actually makes people feel less, rather than more safe.[23]

This may also be counterproductive because the competitive pursuit of security exposes others to risk or reinforces the social problems at the root of security problems. Different social groups also tend to become polarised, with each group fearing the others as sources of potential risk. This corrodes both individual freedom and social solidarity.

The politics of securitisation and fear have implications for disaster situations. Rather than being understood as people experiencing their own insecurity and fear, community response in disasters is frequently labelled as looting, anarchy, or chaos.[24] Hence, state policy responses to disaster are often top-down and treat community responses as dangerously unpredictable or as Hobbesian anarchy. Humanitarian aid increasingly adopts a militarisation and securitisation framework as opposed to a discourse of human needs.[25] People attempting to meet their needs are constructed as rebels or barbarians requiring control, as barbarous 'others' from which the general population must be protected. Again, this is a self-fulfilling prophecy: 'often the worst behavior in the wake of a calamity is on the part of those who believe that others will behave savagely and that they themselves are taking defensive measures against barbarism'.[26] The politics of fear can also be used as part of strategies of counterinsurgency and population management, with ruling groups consciously manipulating fear for purposes such as winning elections and marginalising protest movements. Such responses attempt to manufacture public legitimacy by spreading fear and mistrust and by undermining empathic affective responses.

ACCUMULATION BY DISPOSSESSION THROUGH THE
PRIVATISATION OF RISK/DISASTER CAPITALISM

While the securitisation, atomisation and positionality angles arise in a wide range of critiques, Marxist-influenced approaches are particularly likely to focus on the implications of disasters in terms of capitalist social relations. Marxists generally attribute major social shifts to the tendencies of capitalism, the development of its productive forces or relations of production, capital–labour conflicts, or the needs of particular stages of capitalism. This sometimes leads to an argument that risk management, securitisation and the growing importance of disaster are aspects of neoliberal forms of accumulation, production, consumption, reproduction and/or legitimation. Capitalism in the neoliberal period is characterised by recurring crises, often systemically if not deliberately produced. These crises themselves become opportunities for profiteering, regressive wealth redistribution, lucrative redevelopment projects and so on. While economic crashes form the model for this theory, this same model is increasingly also applied to other disasters which stop short of system collapse. Neoliberal capitalism is characterised as 'disaster capitalism', a model designed around recurring disasters and crises. It is argued that disaster capitalism is not an accidental by-product of particular policies, rather it is definitive of the ideological foundations of neoliberalism.[27]

While not a Marxist, Naomi Klein is clearly influenced by this style of theorising. In her book *The Shock Doctrine*, Klein argues that all kinds of disasters, as varied as terrorist attacks, financial collapse and tsunamis, are used by powerful people as a context at a local scale to clear out deprived communities in order to reconstruct neighbourhoods as neoliberal developments for profit. Furthermore, the trauma caused by such events can be used as a smokescreen for drastic changes at the level of the wider economy, such as imposing severe austerity measures on populations. Such actions are backed up by neoliberal ideology with little democratic legitimacy. This is what Klein terms 'disaster capitalism', where the original disaster puts the population into a state of collective shock, whereby 'like the terrorised prisoner who gives up the names of comrades and renounces his faith shocked societies often give up the things they would otherwise fiercely protect'.[28] Yottam Marom, an activist and writer who was involved in Occupy Sandy, writes that in the initial scenes of a disaster, 'volunteers and community organisers are not the only ones on the scene'. Before the recovery effort has even started, he argues 'an army of disaster-capitalist developers are plotting to use this opportunity to finally knock down the housing projects and replace them with the condos they've been drooling about for decades'.[29] The exploitative practices of disaster capitalism can occur between states – often a rich industrialised nation and a developing nation – where relief agencies 'operate as marionettes' for the selfish economic interests of the more powerful nation.[30] It can also be a tool of governments at the domestic level to disguise austerity politics, the privatisation of public spaces and public institutions.[31] Natural or unplanned disasters absolve the system of the difficulties which otherwise stand in the way of designs for gentrification, securitisation of spaces, removal of 'unproductive' populations, capture of land and natural resources, and so on.

The historical process of primitive accumulation, according to Marx, is 'nothing else than the historical process of divorcing the producer from the means of production'.[32] Once the historical dispossession is complete, capital can rely on standard, ostensibly peaceful processes such as market competition and wage labour to maintain and expand its profits. Marx's prediction that capitalism would rapidly lead to socialist revolution through the socialisation, homogenisation and pauperisation of labour seems not to have been accurate, although in some respects socialisation and wealth inequality have increased. However, later capitalist development has also involved fragmentation of labour through precarity.[33] The fragmentation of the labour force has led contemporary theorists to adapt Marx's theory in order to more accurately reflect present circumstances. One adaptation is David Harvey's idea of 'accumulation by dispossession'. This concept describes neoliberal capitalist policies in Western nations beginning from around the 1970s which cause a deepening of inequality, an increasing chasm of alienation between the rich and the poor and the centralisation of wealth and power in the hands of a very small elite. This process is reflected in the slogan of the Occupy Wall Street movement: 'We are the 99%', referring to the fact that the world's wealth is disproportionately concentrated in the hands of the 'top 1%', whose wealth grew by 275 per cent between 1979 and 2007.[34] 'Accumulation by dispossession' refers to the process by which capitalism (or capitalists) dispossess the public of their wealth. This is done through four practices: privatisation (the transfer of property from public to private ownership), financialisation (deregulated credit and stock manipulation), management and manipulation of crises (such as disaster capitalism!), and state redistributions.[35] This includes post-disaster clearance and reconstruction efforts which capitalise on disaster and austerity by dispossessing poor people of their homes and property. Disaster capitalism is thus taken to be a means of regressive wealth redistribution from poor to rich, with capitalists and their political allies either leveraging unexpected crises or actually causing crises so as to dispossess poorer groups, redevelop geographical areas for profit, and so on.

The ideological force driving disaster capitalism – 'the shock doctrine' of Klein's title – is the policy trinity based on the thought of Milton Friedman and the Chicago School of 'the elimination of the public sphere, total liberation for corporations and skeletal social spending'.[36] Friedman argued that 'only a crisis – actual or perceived – produces real change. When that crisis occurs, the actions that are taken depend on the ideas that are lying around'.[37] Neoliberal shock doctrine assumes inexorable technological progress and unlimited natural resource and the disposability of underprivileged people and communities. This ideology is disguised behind ostensibly neutral, de-politicised discourse of 'natural' disaster, 'recovery', 'rebuilding' and 'redevelopment'.[38] Dissent is quelled and compliance is enforced through securitisation and militarisation. The paradigm relies on a panoply of quantification technology for insurance purposes and remote sensing data. These technologies contribute to a new military-industrial complex in which surveillance and control technologies are easily shifted between military, policing and disaster management projects, with profits accruing to major technology companies. For example, the National Geospatial Intelligence Agency, which is part of the US Defence Department, supported Hurricane Katrina relief efforts by providing geospatial information to FEMA and purchased a technology ominously named 'Enhanced View' to make high-quality satellite imagery available to licensed federal customers. This has been used in Japan for emergency response and has been interpreted as the colonisation of the global field by corporate titans amid concerns that insurance logic will overtake humanitarian concern.[39] The major players in the emerging institutionalisation of disasters are international financial institutions, insurance/reinsurance companies, catastrophe modellers, defence policy analysts and geospatial analysts.

Disaster capitalism operates to the detriment of poorer, marginalised communities. In the case of Hurricane Sandy, for example, the ostensible economic success of the US as a whole, and New York in particular, obscures the vast inequality, precarity and poverty of many inhabitants, and the uneven effects that the disaster had on underprivileged members of society, who were disproportionately black and from ethnic minorities.[40] Empirical studies have shown that the residents of New Orleans who were displaced by Hurricane Katrina tended to have different experiences that were clustered around lines of homeownership, class and race. 'Purification discourses' in media and policy were intended to 'remedy the chaos, filth and negativity of the disaster area'.[41] This involved tearing down public housing and regenerating poorer areas in a manner that effectively forced poorer people out of the area and enacted 'essentially racialised purging'.[42] Katrina is only one example of a broader dynamic of disasters being used as a premise to 'deconcentrate' black poverty through 'displacement and racial cleansing [that] actually just disperses and makes poor people of colour even more invisible, arguably so that the clean, blank slate can be capitalised on'.[43] Miriam Greenberg traces the market-oriented approach to urbanisation back to the 1970s, when she argues that elite responses to financial crises and urban unrest produced a range of policies such as privatisation of public space, austerity, attacks on organised labour, and business incentives intended to attract private investment, development and to increase consumption. This created a vision of cities themselves becoming profit-making enterprises. Thus in New Orleans and New York after hurricanes Katrina and Sandy authorities were able to 'steer billions of public dollars to powerful industries, real estate developers, corporations and already wealthy neighborhoods'.[44] Marxists have argued that the process does not only operate at the observable level of cities and neighbourhoods; since the essence of capital is self-valorising value, it also seeks to invest in technology and create new markets at every scale,[45] and commodify even microscopic entities such as the Covid-19 virus.[46]

This process of accumulation by dispossession has also been referred to as the 'new enclosures' or 'commons enclosure',[47] a terminology which refers back to the sixteenth-century practice of 'enclosures' (Marx's paradigm-case for primitive accumulation), a process in which public land was taken out of common use and fenced in for private use. Enclosures entailed removing tenant farmers and peasants from the land and turning it over to capital-intensive or labour-light practices such as ranching and (later) factory farming. The historical practice is widely understood to have been cruel and unjust, since it created a landless working class to be fed into the difficult and exploitative industrial work in the developing economy.

Mainstream history tends to portray the enclosures as an event that was definitively in the past. However, the Midnight Notes Collective argue that: 'The Enclosures ... are not a one time process exhausted at the dawn of capitalism. They are a regular return on the path of accumulation and a structural component of class struggle.'[48] Neoliberal enclosures have created 'the biggest diaspora of the century',[49] uprooting people from land, jobs, homes, families and relationships. The root cause of this mass dispossession, according to the Midnight Notes Collective, are neoliberal financialisation policies such as the International Monetary Fund (IMF)-dictated 'Structural Adjustment Programs' (SAPs), inflicted on indebted countries, forcing them to undertake practices including the commercialisation of agriculture, demonetarisation of economy and the devaluation of money – all of which lead to the dispossession of poor people on the ground.[50] SAPs are in many ways the archetype for disaster capitalism. They leverage crises to impose policies which redistribute resources to Western companies and governments. Indeed, since aggressive US borrowing in the Reagan years was a major driver of debt crises elsewhere, these crises were arguably manufactured. Implementing SAPs also tended to increase export dependency and openness to footloose capital flows, raising the risk of further crises and further SAPs. Harvey suggests that the US Treasury, Wall Street and the IMF deliberately manipulate such crises to enhance US global power.[51] For example, the East Asian financial crisis eliminated promising rivals to the US and allowed US investors to buy up local companies at fire-sale prices. Resultant SAPs imposed open-market policies which undermined the earlier developmental statist policies of targeted companies.

The policy agenda promoted by global institutions such as the IMF since the 1980s is often referred to as the Washington Consensus.[52] Since the 2008 financial crisis, there has been a widespread loss of confidence in the neoliberal model,[53] and arguably a new Post-Washington Consensus (PWC) has emerged from the mid-1990s onward, which is somewhat more supportive of state interventions. The PWC includes 'pro-poor' development policies and conditionalities in areas such as labour rights, gender equality, health access and environmental protection. However, this is arguably a continuation rather than rupture since it serves to protect the functioning of neoliberalism through merely minor adjustments.[54] Indeed, measures in older SAPs are often simply rebranded as pro-poor or socially progressive in the newer versions. The PWC model intersects with the globalisation of disaster preparedness and resilience in the 1990s and with the spread of securitised disaster responses. For example, PWC approaches encourage 'investment' in basic healthcare based on strict cost-effectiveness criteria, thus stepping back from the drastic health privatisation agenda of the 1980s, yet still contributing to cuts in non-'basic' services. The resultant shortage of medical workers contributes to a trend towards securitisation of pandemics, using the rationalised, expanded security apparatuses encouraged in neoliberalism. For example, Paul Farmer criticises responses to multidrug-resistant tuberculosis in the 1990s and 2000s. Use of second-line medications and surgery was stymied by artificially raised prices and cost-effectiveness policies, leading to preventable outbreaks which were then sometimes securitised.[55]

In the case of SAPs, crisis is exploited to impose emergency austerity packages which may otherwise be politically impossible. The general trend is for SAPs to produce unemployment or at least reduce formal-sector employment, to corrode labour rights, undermine food security, and increase preventable deaths and suffering among the poor.[56] Significantly, the process has also been regarded as undemocratic because SAP policies are imposed top-down by unelected intergovernmental organisations on Southern governments, giving foreign investors and institutions a veto over national policies.[57] Dominant elites, the '1%', are the main beneficiaries of these processes. Even in the North, poorer groups often suffer. For example, William Robinson finds that US and Mexican farmers did not benefit from the North American Free Trade Agreement (NAFTA), while transnational corporate agro-industry on both sides of the US/Mexico border did.[58] Even within the world's richest economies, life is becoming more and more precarious for the majority of the population. SAPs arguably provide a model for disaster capitalism, with recurring emergencies creating an environment to shift power to unaccountable agencies which then engage in regressive redistribution under the cover of shock and terror.

PRECARITY, VULNERABILITY AND DISASTER

Neoliberalisation and precarity have also altered the relationship between states and citizens, and citizens with each other, which has implications for the ways in which people act and the support systems and networks that they rely on during disasters. The transition from Fordism to neoliberalism means that states no longer take on many of the welfare and social security functions that they used to; precarity also means that traditional communities people might have relied on for help have fragmented. This experience of fragmentation is caused by the logic of commensurability, which has always been basic to capitalism but has been intensified with globalisation. If a unit of labour time from anybody anywhere is measurable in the same way as another somewhere else, and always subordinate to profit for capitalists, there is no systemic impetus to sustain or reproduce particular communities and ecosystems. This operates to fragment shared experiences of time and temporal possibilities for sociability, since people no longer work similar hours to those in their neighbourhoods. It also operates to fragment people spatially; since they no longer live in the same neighbourhoods for their entire lives; or even for extended times that are long enough to form a community with those who live around them. Housing is now a precarious commodity and people move for work more often. At the same time, people can no longer rely on the state to help them through personal or social crises (if they ever could) because the nation state as a cohering force of social welfare redistribution has largely disintegrated.

Social structures, inequality and unequal distribution of risk mean that disasters are more disastrous for certain people at certain times. Zygmunt Bauman suggests that the likelihood of marginalised people to increasingly become victims of disasters is one of the most salient dimensions of social inequality of our time.[59] The same natural force (such as a hurricane or earthquake) may kill hundreds and leave thousands homeless in poorly prepared Southern countries while causing only limited damage in better prepared Northern ones. The effects of disasters are therefore in no way natural in the sense of unavoidable, but rather a product of a cumulative history of racism, deprivation and inequality.[60] In the provocatively titled edited collection *There Is No Such Thing as Natural Disasters*, the editors document the ways in which a history of racist institutional arrangements combined with failure to maintain critical public services and infrastructure in New Orleans during Hurricane Katrina. This led to the hurricane affecting black and low-income households in massive disproportion to their white, better-off counterparts.[61] The media portrayals of the aftermath of Hurricane Katrina reflect this dynamic of securitisation based on a pessimistic and racialised view of human nature. Paul Taylor, in his philosophical exploration of the concept of race, argues that '[t]he early depictions of Hurricane Katrina's aftermath read like a collaborative project of Thomas Hobbes and Joseph Conrad: The disaster, we heard, had broken the tenuous grip on civilisation long unevenly maintained by places like New Orleans and unleashed a wave of savage black barbarism.'[62] This is in spite of evidence of community cooperation during the disaster and the damage done by securitised responses.

Mainstream approaches often portray the networked, high-speed, ephemeral structure of the neoliberal economy in a positive light, emphasising autonomy, self-management, creativity, flexibility, mobility, identity-fluidity and the opportunities available to certain groups of skilled workers and professionals, while ignoring the increasingly insecure and unstable nature of work and social connections. Critiques of this perspective, which often come from autonomous Marxism,[63] explain precarity in terms of a general sense of fear and insecurity in the populace, which governments attempt to mobilise and manipulate into fear of 'the other', which finds expression in securitisation and moral panics. Amorphous latent fear can be manipulated as a basis for 'shock doctrine'-style disaster capitalism, which in turn reproduces such fear.

The mainstream framing of precarious labour portrays flexible and autonomous workers as endowed with a large amount of agency to determine how their time is spent. And there is of course some truth in this – many successful creative workers opt to work on flexible, self-employed contracts and enjoy the freedom that this gives. However, this glorified image of the precariat ignores the diversity of precarious contracts and positions, and the ways in which the precariat is fragmented in a way which enables the dispossession of the most marginalised classes.[64] Precarity is a situation in which people are vulnerable both to small-scale everyday disasters, such as arbitrary firings and delisting by platform-capitalist sites such as Uber, and as a result are less 'resilient' in the face of social-scale disasters which disrupt the various precarious income flows. For example, Covid-19 lockdowns have proven unenforceable among the informal-sector poor, who are at risk of starvation if they 'stay at home' as demanded; this group are thus disproportionately exposed both to lockdown-related repression and the risk of contracting the virus.[65]

Jason Moore[66] links the process of precarisation, which he terms 'accumulation by appropriation', to the exploitation of women and colonies as parts of the 'world-ecology'. According to Moore, capital seeks cheapness. It seeks to appropriate nature through violence rather than through sustainable reproduction as well as 'cheapness' of labour and material at 'frontiers' rather than within its existing territories, using violent appropriation at the margins rather than nurturing existing social relations and social reproduction. This is ultimately suicidal, with capitalism relying on an ever-shrinking frontier while failing to secure its own reproduction. '[V]iolence is fundamental to Cheap Nature – revealing capitalism's greatest "inefficiency": its destruction and waste of life.'[67] A good disaster-related example of this is the short-termist extractivism associated with the oil industry in the Niger Delta. In addition to polluting and expropriating land, the oil industry was and is responsible for a series of spills and explosions which undermine the local ecology. While the initial dynamic is accumulation by dispossession – the displacement of subsistence farmers for corporate accumulation – the long-term dynamic is to sacrifice potential long-term profits from agriculture for short-term oil profits.[68] In a change of perspective, one might view capitalism and precarity itself as an ongoing disaster which concentrates the effects of insecurity among those who are already the most vulnerable, while at the same time blaming them for their lack of 'resilience' and channelling their sense of risk away from the economy through the security discourses of terrorism and 'natural' risk.

DELINKING FROM THE WORLD SYSTEM

World-systems theorists argue that conditions for resisting and superseding capitalism lie not in the most developed zones, as Marx had argued, but in peripheral zones that were delinked from the world economy. Delinking was initially formulated by Samir Amin as a state-level alternative to global capitalism, an expanded variant of import substitution.[69] However, the term takes on more complex meanings as groups like the Zapatistas adopt similar strategies and swathes of the world drop out of the formal economy. While most states seek inclusion in global production chains, in practice many cannot generate globalised jobs for more than a tiny fraction of the population or a handful of extractive hubs.[70] Not only are rural areas often relatively autonomous from the world system, but the rapidly increasing concentration of capital and extreme inequality means that the urban poor, even in the most developed nations, are suffering similar dynamics. This has implications for both survival and resistance. Historically, the oppressed have risen in rebellion against their oppressors, yet in current conditions, power has no identifiable centre. Labour precarity and migration mean people are fragmented from traditional communities, work-based organisations and social networks, making it increasingly hard for people to organise politically, leading to a crisis of the traditional left. People – more often racialised people and women – are forcibly delinked from the world economy and treated as disposable. Contemporary capitalism has a tendency to destroy more livelihoods than it creates, with a trend towards the growth of 'surplus population' relative to employed.[71] Amin describes a massive broadening of precarity and pauperisation to the point where 80 per cent of the global periphery's population are precariously situated, and also 40 per cent of those within the global centre/core.[72] Thus, the new class division no longer follows the Marxist lines of exploitation but rather that of social exclusion and inclusion, corresponding to a new wave of social repression directed at non-conformity and precarity.[73] These dynamics are magnified by disasters, which already more often affect poorer communities, while rich people are more easily able to leave disaster-prone areas. Forced delinking is closely tied to corporate risk calculations and the risk–profit balance; poorer areas are often considered too crisis-prone to invest in. Delinking seems likely to happen even more in the future, as disasters become more prevalent due to climate change, and states become more austere as neoliberalism concentrates capital in private hands. Nevertheless, those who have been excluded or expelled from the world economy need to survive, and their survival tactics offer a very important emerging site of resistance.

Immanuel Wallerstein suggests that capitalism has partly overcome the traditional Marxist contradiction between the proletariat and the bourgeoisie by relying on cheap imports of primary goods from peripheral regions. The main contradiction is now between global capital based in 'core' (rich, industrialised) regions, and the peripheral regions seeking to free themselves from core control. Wallerstein argues that core–periphery actually refers to processes rather than spatial zones,[74] and while these frequently map onto 'First' and 'Third' world countries geographically on a world scale, we also see periphery-like processes occurring in 'First-world' countries.

Combined with the fragmentation of traditional communities, we are left with a situation which makes it increasingly hard for people to organise politically.[75] The 'oppressor' is transforming into a complex system that combines persons, networks and machines with no obvious centre.[76] Young people are blocked from accessing the same opportunities of those a generation before, and experience simultaneous stagnation and precarity, treated as a 'surplus population'.[77] When the powerful no longer have a need for the compliance of the poor (for example during a contraction of the world economy) the process of exploitation of workers most famously theorised by Marx tends to be replaced by exclusion.[78] Delinking is not simply economic, but can also involve exclusion from political participation and political rights, as with Agamben's 'state of exception', and military retreat from areas that the state no longer views as strategically useful.[79] Neoliberal states' definitions of security and disaster focus on the protection of capital, the state, and productive subjects, and involve treating unproductive populations as disposable barriers to progress.[80] Disaster management thus becomes management of those disasters which affect the included groups, ignoring the everyday disasters affecting the excluded.

Yet those who have been excluded or expelled from the world economy need to survive, and their survival tactics offer an important emerging site of resistance. This idea of 'forced delinking' can also be constructed as a form of 'exodus'[81] or 'exile'[82] from the neoliberal economy and from institutionalised politics that is both enforced and elected. Struggles tend to orient not around inclusion but around access to resources and land for subsistence and reproduction of life and sociality 'beyond the wage'.[83] Examples include historic Cossack *stanistas* (self-governing village settlements) observed and theorised by Kropotkin; the Zapatistas who declared a defensive war against the US in order to build an autonomous community based on principles of mutual aid;[84] and many projects of solidarity and mutual aid in Athens during the extreme austerity imposed after the debt crisis of 2010.[85]

Disasters are associated with forced delinking in several ways. First of all, disasters are more likely to occur to/in communities that have already been marginalised or delinked in some sense, since as discussed previously, rich people and capital are likely to move away from areas most prone to disasters. Second, disasters as they happen may involve further delinking as states are increasingly unable or unwilling to provide the extent of relief that they may have done previously, or that may be required. Third, delinking is likely to be intensified by disasters, which decimate public infrastructure in affected areas and increase existing poverty and inequality. Fourth, disasters therefore create prime conditions for organised resistance based on exile or exodus from the dominant system, as people and communities struggle to survive and subsist. This kind of resistance has the potential to come up against securitisation and militarisation and end in conflict; or it may be in danger of being co-opted or recuperated back into the capitalist cultural and economic mainstream, thus being emptied of its radical potential – when social bonds are recomposed and infrastructure is developed autonomously, the exilic space is often reincorporated by the state as a semi-periphery.[86] A key purpose of this book, therefore, is to explore such dangers and dynamics, and how they might be resisted in the immediacy of disaster and crisis situations.

SOCIETY AGAINST THE STATE: BEYOND ASSOCIATIONALISM AND THE NGO MODEL

Key to theorising the relationship between delinked communities, social movements and the state is an understanding of the relationship between society and the state. In the previous chapter, I considered various strands of associationalism, such as social capital theory, resilience theory, and risk society as the mainstream approach to understanding the relationship between civil society and the state. Associationalists view society as a necessary complement to the state; associations within society build forms of trust and solidarity and democratic knowledge that are essential for a functioning democracy. Forms of sociality that do *not* fit with this instrumental view (for example anti-state groups, riots or groups that are trying to meet their subsistence needs and come up against security forces or bureaucratic barriers; or groups that are trying to exist outside the state and capitalist economy without working towards inclusion) are therefore not legible as political entities within this paradigm. Theorists as diverse as Antonio Gramsci,[87] James Scott[88] and Michel Foucault[89] all argue that non-state resistance is not only a legitimate response to crisis and disaster, but essential, highly effective and ethically desirable.

Debates around the nature of civil society and its relationship to the state have a strong epistemological element; that is, they have implications for the relationship between knowledge and power, political subjectivity, and the extent to which social/local actors can resist political/global forces from a position of critical awareness. This is important for understanding how people organise in disasters, and the political implications of their actions, because it can help us think through the connections and differences between spontaneous community responses that almost invariably occur during disasters and a more politicised movement. For theories such as associational and social capital theory outlined in the previous chapter, the ideological motivations underpinning community organising are of little interest. So long as the action does not overtly conflict or resist the democratic functioning of the state, then it is legible as a form of social capital and thus as a natural complement to the democratic functioning of the state and, as was argued in the previous chapter, of neoliberal capitalism.

Gramsci understood civil society to be an extension of the state and a site for the production of political legitimacy, that is, consent/complicity in hegemonic governance, through everyday beliefs and practices. Where other Marxist philosophers understood capitalist ideology as totalising and monolithic, Gramsci offers a more dynamic concept of ideology which creates space for agency and struggle. Gramsci's argument is that 'common sense', contrary to the colloquial understanding of it as being a kind of practical and useful form of knowledge, is an ideological worldview which seems so self-evident that its adherents are unable to identify the extent to which it has been conditioned by institutions such as the media, religious institutions, voluntary organisations, societies and so on, many of which reproduce the agendas of state and capital. 'Common sense' teaches people to be happy with their lot, or at least to accept it as inevitable, and therefore to work to improve their corner of the world rather than to change the system as a whole. Civil society here acts as a bulwark against state collapse or revolution; while it is the political state that holds the 'monopoly of force' over a population, its power is ultimately dependent on the more diffuse hegemony of social power exercised through the associations and institutions of civil society.

However, Gramsci also saw civil society as a site of plurality and contestation, and of 'good sense', which is an emergent form of knowledge that transgresses or undermines those worldviews supporting ruling-class interests.[90] An effective strategy for social change would therefore involve contesting widely held beliefs at the level of civil society and forming groups and institutions to mobilise these ideas as a counter-hegemony. Nonetheless, Gramsci retains aspects of the Marxist belief in the totalising nature of capitalism – for example he believes subaltern actors have internalised the oppressor's mentality. He would probably view the inclusion of NGOs in state-led disaster responses as a variety of *trasformismo* or 'passive revolution', the process of 'beheading' social movements by incorporating their leaders or intellectuals into the existing power structure, thus maintaining bourgeois civil society against emergent challenges.[91] Gramscians generally believe that radicals can struggle within civil society institutions to change their class or ideological character in a progressive direction.

This view can be differentiated somewhat from poststructural and postcolonial theorists who believe that subaltern actors are formed by the discourses that oppress them; that there is no pre-discursive subject. Practices which shape people's subjectivity are termed 'biopower' because they are forms of power which act upon and determine life (bios). Such power is exercised through everyday life, and includes practices such as bureaucratic procedures, form-filling, metrics and regulations, and normative discourses; which require one to fit into predetermined categories or play a particular role in order to be legible/recognised by state actors. One ends up internalising and performing such roles, which come to constitute subjectivity. Neoliberal governmentality operates by seeking to manage people and render them conformist by plugging their lifestyles and desires into the dominant regime of power.[92] Poststructuralists typically see resistance occurring within structures of power/knowledge, through the re-inflection or subversion of dominant discourses. They would expect subaltern actors to operate within dominant disaster responses, but to subvert, frustrate, redefine, interrogate, and differently perform these from within.

Another group of theorists, whom I will term 'conflict theorists', have a lot of affinity with the anarchist conception of the relationship between the state and society, which will be put forward in more detail in the next chapter. James Scott, for example, portrays society as being in conflict with the state and capital, and as a site of resistance. He explicitly rejects Gramsci's theory of hegemony as only relevant in a very small number of contexts, suggesting that, in most cases, people are very aware of their situation and do not become ideologically incorporated into the system that ensures their oppression. They may accept it as inevitable if they are not aware of any alternatives, but this is not incompatible with 'a degree of distaste for, or even hatred of, the domination experienced'.[93] Thus, social forces and groups, rather than forming in parallel and complementary to hierarchical governance, actually form in order to resist or buffer the effects of global forces on their local conditions and to resist further exploitation. Much resistance is small scale rather than revolutionary, and often does not involve mass protests or incursions in elite politics. It is rather 'a patient and effective nibbling away in a multitude of ways', which can in fact have a huge cumulative effect.[94] The subaltern site of resistance for Scott is what is called a 'hidden transcript', an unofficial discourse that oppressed members of society speak among themselves while parodying the official discourse or 'public transcript' (akin to Gramsci's hegemony) in their dealings with dominant groups and in public. So, while for Scott there are still two competing discourses (complicit and resistant), the oppressed are generally defiant in opposition, but they tactically conceal this depending on circumstances. In situations where oppressed people mobilise to improve their situation, it does not make sense to interpret this in terms of 'social capital' nor in terms of the function of sustaining neoliberal democracy: 'Why, in a larger sense, should one expect those who benefit least – or who are actually disadvantaged – by a particular "public order" to contribute to its daily maintenance?'[95]

The important difference between poststructuralists and James Scott is that the former see internal (psychological) subversion of dominant discourses as the primary form of resistance because they think that subjects are made/constituted by these discourses. Scott sees public performances as consciously strategic and as deviating from what actors take their real beliefs to be. Scott would expect community groups to engage with state-led disaster responses for instrumental or extractive reasons, probably to a minimum degree necessary to obtain benefits or avoid dangers, and possibly while quietly sabotaging these initiatives from the sidelines, or simply criticising them in discussions with their allies/ friends while speaking the expected language to the people in charge.

NGO-ISATION AND CO-OPTATION

The concept of civil society has gained a renewed importance, both in policy discourse and in practice, due to the ascendancy of neoliberalism and the resultant withdrawal of the nation state's welfare and social functions. Mainstream disaster studies theories put forward in Chapter 2 understand civil society as an important alternative means of service provision and collective action, although this is done with the expectation of collaboration with the state. Conversely, the authors discussed in the previous section of this chapter understand society as a vital source of resistance. This debate is played out in policy and practice. Many researchers in this area believe that the relationship between NGOs and the state is problematic because this association undermines NGOs' autonomy, alters their values in line with state objectives and reduces their accountability to the communities they serve.[96] Civil society therefore becomes split into a sector comprised of NGOs, the institutional left and other organisations dependent on state funding (which are wary of challenging the policies of the institutions they depend upon) and a more critical and radical realm of autonomous social movements (ASMs). This split has been theorised by Arundhati Roy and others as 'NGO-isation',[97] and this section examines some of the problems of this process, arguing that when faced with powerful non- or anti-state movements, states always have the choice whether to seek to repress or co-opt/recuperate the movement, and its choice depends on the degree to which the movement imminently threatens the state versus the degree to which it offers energies or resources that the state cannot otherwise access. Disasters produce conditions which weaken state power and increase social movement energies, tilting the balance towards co-optation through NGO-isation. It is also a situation where state and movement goals are somewhat compatible, as both are seeking to relieve suffering and help survivors.

The way that we conceive the relationship between civil society and the state has implications for our understanding of the practices of the range of organisations that are involved in disaster preparedness, relief and recovery. In practice, 'civil society' is incredibly varied and composed of a hugely diverse range of groups and organisations with different forms and functions, motivated by different ideologies and politics.[98] This can lead to a situation in which the institutions of civil society become complicit in the policing and repression of the popular movements and struggles they arose from.[99] For example, governments have largely succeeded in making disaster-related NGOs desist from rescuing refugees in the Mediterranean and working in enemy-controlled conflict zones. In the UK NGOs now generally respond to disasters as a coordinated body (the Disasters and Emergencies Committee) with an integrated agenda. During the Covid-19 crisis, NGOs almost universally acted as signal-boosters for official public health messages.

Perhaps linked to their reliance on state funding, NGOs are often alleged to promote a neoliberal agenda by reorienting community groups into apolitical and individualised education and self-help programmes which fragment community struggles and undermine collective political awareness.[100] In the case of the Covid-19 crisis, for example, the South African government put considerable effort into persuading the community group Abahlali base'Mjondolo to focus on Covid-related education and organising, and abandon its early position that service-delivery (water and sanitation) issues and endemic diseases and dangers in informal settlements are worse dangers than the coronavirus.[101] Some activists involved with Occupy Oakland have argued that 'the exponential growth of NGOs and nonprofits could be understood as the 21st century public face of counterinsurgency, except this time speaking the language of civil, women's, and gay rights, charged with preempting political conflict, and spiritually committed to promoting one-sided "dialogue" with armed state bureaucracies.'[102] This reflects a wider critique of NGO-isation, which refers to the propensity of NGOs to de-politicise discourses and practices of social movements. In a disaster context, this will often involve NGOs and social movements encouraging self-policing in line with securitised responses, aiding 'resilience' as an alternative to mitigation, and acting as cogs within the coordinated disaster response.

However, development theorists have argued that some NGOs ostensibly focus on welfarism and service provision in order to satisfy elite demands, whereas their inner core is dedicated to social transformation. The orientation to social change is 'camouflaged by whatever packaging and labelling is required to cloud their actual intent'.[103] This is somewhat reminiscent of James Scott's understanding of society insofar as it presumes a 'public transcript' which is spoken to power about supporting state welfare and service provision, concealing a more radical hidden transcript dedicated to community empowerment, political education and social change. Indeed, some scholars argue that too little attention is paid to the ways in which organisations do resist and transform governmental agendas through their practices.[104] Nonetheless, the power structure of state–NGO relations seems to militate against effective border work of this kind, particularly due to funding dependence. 'This funding structure ties liberal organisations charged with representing and serving communities of color to businesses interested primarily in tax exemptions and charity, and completely hostile to radical social transformation despite their rhetoric.'[105] Disasters are a particularly difficult case for NGOs playing a border game, as securitisation creates hard dividing lines between compliance and dissent, requiring border groups to either endorse the entire state agenda or openly oppose it.

DISASTER ONTOLOGY: TEMPORALITY AND SCALE

The potential complicity of NGOs and states does not neutralise the transformative potential of social movements. It is also possible for movements to remain radical, resist co-optation and NGO-isation, and offer alternatives to authoritarian disaster response models. In this section, to be elaborated in the next chapter, I argue that anarchist and autonomous social movements operate with a fundamentally different set of ontological assumptions which are better suited to dealing with climate catastrophe and disaster capitalism. They operate with a more flow-based and longer-term temporality of disaster awareness, situating their disaster responses within broader, ongoing responses to the structural problems inherent in capitalism. Beliefs about the time-frame within which an event occurs fundamentally shape our understandings of the boundaries of that event, and what we might consider as connected events or contributing factors. As we saw earlier, Hannigan and others argue that natural disasters have usually been treated in international politics as episodic, short-lived events that are best handled as humanitarian issues.[106] This approach means that important connections – such as the relationships between disasters and climate change, or disasters and longer-term national, international and development policies, or disasters and everyday life – are often ignored. Disasters are constitutive of capitalism rather than merely episodic or symptomatic, and I would suggest that these wider aspects are more clearly visible from the standpoint of autonomous movements. Dealing with impending climate catastrophe will require us to fundamentally rethink our relationship to each other, the planet, and non-human others, and our understandings of the time and space of politics.

The theorist Walter Benjamin suggests that capitalism is always-already a disaster, and that history is nothing but the accumulation of ruins caused by a 'storm blowing from Paradise'.[107] This is in sharp contrast with dominant conceptions of disasters as exceptions. Interpreting Benjamin, Andrew Robinson argues that: 'It is common for such disasters to be portrayed as a violent eruption of an "outside", which breaks into the otherwise peaceful development of (white, Northern) humanity. Benjamin reverses perspective, seeing such events as the Hell of the present.'[108] Paul Virilio also resituates disaster in a broader frame. He conceives the state primarily in terms of military and surveillance systems, which tend to colonise all of society through the ways of seeing and relating that they promote. Consumer society, television, the internet and robotics are among the many technologies Virilio sees as contaminated by a military way of seeing. Military strategy is today based on spatial or logistical control, in which territories are redesigned or occupied in ways which render them difficult for adversaries to use. Risk is controlled through blocking/controlling the flows of life so as to disempower and observe actors, rendering them predictable or powerless. Such deadened, controlled territories are also poisonous for civilians, but serve well the interests and needs of military agencies and their personnel, who are hardened to survive in such environments. Virilio thus concludes that ecological crises are only crises for civilians. They tend to shift power from civilians to the military, because the military is designed to operate in crisis conditions. Constant crisis thus goes hand in hand with endocolonialism, or the militarisation of everyday life.[109] One sees in mainstream disaster research how disasters which are managed in quasi-militarised ways do not pose an existential threat to states; in Quarantelli's terms, they are not 'catastrophes'.[110] Yet they remain disasters for the (mainly) civilians affected by death and devastation. And, as discussed above, disasters may even aid the state in expanding securitisation and capitalists in accumulation. If disasters are only disasters for civilians, then it is important to remain autonomous from the state-led disaster response and, in some cases, to confront it.

Furthermore, the discourse surrounding 'natural disasters' presumes a binary opposition between nature and culture so that an emphasis on the former disguises the interrelationships between the two, particularly evident in the twenty-first century in light of increasing knowledge about the association between human activity and climate change.[111] Disaster researchers have moved away from the term 'natural disaster', based on a conception of the world as a cybernetic system subject to continual management. Nonetheless, the nature/culture binary remains central to popular and media conceptions and lurks in the background of disaster studies' distinctions between the disaster agent or cause and the social/ political response. Yet, as discussed above, 'the same' natural force can have disastrous effects in one locality and not another. In addition, a sizeable proportion of disasters are anthropogenic, arising from dangerous industrial practices (Chernobyl, Bhopal, Aberfan, Fukushima …), as side-effects of environmental degradation (e.g. flooding due to deforestation), or as complications arising from massification and mass production (e.g. livestock-based pandemics).[112] On a broader scale, human/industrial impacts increase both the frequency and impact of disastrous events, with the impact of climate change on extreme weather events particularly prominent. Climate change has been implicated in a great many recent disasters, such as increasingly severe wildfires, floods and hurricanes. The state agencies which head disaster responses and the capitalists who profit from them, are often the same groups that manage the social processes causing climate change. It thus seems counterintuitive to work under the leadership of these groups to mitigate disasters which, in a sense, they have caused.

We shall see more examples of broader conceptions of disasters in the next chapter, dealing with explicitly anarchist approaches. For now, it is important to note that a broader, systemic awareness tends to generate autonomous forms of activism. If a given crisis (such as Katrina, Sandy, or Covid-19) is simply a local manifestation of the human-made disaster of capitalism, statism, patriarchy, civilisation, coloniality, or whatever longer-term structure activists focus on, then the long-term causes and impacts will also be more apparent. For example, Marxist-influenced activists quickly see the connections between capitalism, health service spending cuts, and the lack of pandemic preparedness, while ecological activists see the relationship between population concentration, unhealthy living environments, and disease vulnerability. Activists with longer-term awareness are sometimes less susceptible than others to episodic panics and less ready to sacrifice 'big picture' issues for the emergency of the moment. Often, they will have alternative, grassroots responses based on their own perspective of what the core problem is. Even if they broadly agree with the dominant disaster response, they will seek to keep a critical distance and avoid being co-opted in state-led responses. While this is not always the case – there are people who 'know better' and yet mistake recuperation for reform or are emotionally overwhelmed by immediate crises – it creates the beginnings of other ways of responding.

CONCLUSION

This chapter has surveyed a range of critical approaches to disasters and to trends identified in Chapter 2. Without going the whole way to an anarchist critique of the statist disaster management model, critical approaches have demonstrated a number of vital points which will be carried through to the following chapters. First, dominant disaster responses form part of a broader trend of securitisation, which is a political and contentious process of naming exceptions and escaping 'normal' political constraints. Second, disasters impact unevenly on differently situated people and groups, in a grossly oppressive distribution of threat-perceptions in which socially recognised 'vulnerable' groups are protected from marginalised 'risk' groups. Third, disasters are exploited (or arguably even generated) as part of the core dynamics of neoliberal capitalism, as a form of accumulation by dispossession, an exceptionalist basis for austerity, and a means of regressive redistribution. Fourth, the organisational models used in disaster studies rely on contentious theories of civil society which are challenged by critical approaches. These approaches show that NGO-isation is often a form of institutional capture which weakens social movements. Fifth, disasters have systemic dimensions and are in a sense only local manifestations of the greater disaster which is the dominant social system. The limits to these approaches are that they either remain confined to critique, or rely on modes of response which are vulnerable to co-optation. For example, traditional left politics seems to be undercut by disaster capitalism, as is shown by the failure of Syriza in the face of imposed crisis in Greece, while poststructuralist internal subversion of dominant texts seems to force people into embracing the unconditional emergency imperatives of disaster situations. These approaches are also insufficient to address the climate crisis, which requires envisioning and actualising entirely different forms of social life. In the following chapters, I will explore what I take to be the main viable alternative: autonomous organising along broadly anarchist lines. In pursuing mutual aid instead of resilience, autonomy instead of coordination, and empowerment instead of control, this approach offers a way of responding to disasters which does not fall into the statist trap.

4

Towards an Anarchist Approach to Disaster

INTRODUCTION: SPONTANEOUS ORDER VS STATE CONTROL

The previous chapters have examined the main existing approaches to disasters in the academic literature and shown major limitations to these approaches. In this chapter, I aim to construct an anarchist theory of disaster. The focus is on so-called 'natural disasters' (in which the 'disaster agent' is a natural, biological or physical event), although, as was argued in the previous chapter, there is no clear-cut line between natural and social disasters. It is argued that disasters have not been a significant theme for anarchism in the past, in part because classical anarchists were optimistic about human nature and the future of humanity and in part because anarchism creates a reversal of perspective where state and capitalism have been viewed as an ongoing disaster, contra the mainstream understanding of disasters as a rupture in the normal running of things. The chapter draws on various strands in the diverse history of anarchist thought to argue that much of everyday life is already anarchy and develops their theories of social organisation and mutual aid for the context of disasters. It also draws on contemporary anarchist texts, often written by and for activists, which deal more explicitly with disasters and theories of commoning and communisation theory, that are linked to but distinct from anarchism. The chapter considers the characteristics of anarchist and related theories of disaster and their understandings of the roles of NGOs, grassroots actors, and the state in disaster. It compares these to views outlined in previous chapters, arguing that the anarchist approach is both more effective and ethically desirable than associationalist models which view the state as necessary to arbitrate conflict and mobilise welfare. I argue that spontaneous order is incompatible with state control and co-optation, which undermines the mainstream approaches to disaster in which social cohesion both supports and requires conformity and governance. The central difference between anarchist and other approaches to disaster is thus the assertion of a difference in kind between spontaneous/horizontal and statist/vertical approaches.

THE SOCIAL PRINCIPLE AND THE POLITICAL PRINCIPLE

Anarchists have constructed the state/society boundary as antagonistic and exclusive, which differs from the associationalist view. The seminal articulation of this distinction is found in Kropotkin's treatise on the historical rise of the state.[1] In it he argues that revolutionaries who seek to achieve social change through state power are misguided because the state rests on a logic, the 'political principle', which is incompatible and incommensurable with direct social connection (the 'social principle').[2] The social principle is conceived as a type of life-energy, whereas the state is a deadening force. Kropotkin portrays communities as 'organisms bubbling with life', with mutual aid, communal ownership, concrete freedoms, and social associations all part of this picture. He depicts a historical process in which the social principle is periodically eclipsed by, or reasserts itself against, the political principle. While Kropotkin sometimes appears to base his theory on a somewhat idealised version of the history of the Middle Ages,[3] he does not theorise the social principle as conflict-free. Rather, conflict-resolution involves free debate and creative compromise rather than suppression by outside force.[4] The social principle is the 'complete negation of the unitarian, centralising Roman outlook', that is, the political principle.[5]

Kropotkin's definition of the state or political principle involves the 'extinction of local life',[6] which is suppressed and replaced by a primary dyadic relation between individual and state. This encompasses legal subordination, self-interested elite power, role-based conformity in institutions, and restrictions on, or elimination of, direct horizontal connections.[7] All relationships are mediated by the 'triple alliance' of state, Church and military which take on a monopoly in the task of 'watching over the industrial commercial, judicial, artistic, emotional interests'[8] for which individuals used to unite directly. Conflicts are not resolved directly between conflicting parties but are arbitrated by the state, and so one perspective is always repressed and silenced rather than incorporated when the state adds its 'immense weight to the battle in favour of one of the forces engaged in the struggle'.[9] The state demands from each subject 'a direct, personal submission without intermediaries'.[10] Land is pillaged or enclosed; vibrant local groups are bureaucratised and sustained by 'brainwashing education'.[11] Statism is thus associated with the shutting down of the direct connections which are the source of life itself. The political principle is 'the principle that destroys everything',[12] and in the end 'it is death'.[13]

This account of the rise of the state as a violent process of dispossession, enclosure and destruction of communal folk knowledge has been echoed and developed from feminist, ecological and decolonial standpoints. Barbara Ehrenreich and Deirdre English show how the witch hunts of the late Middle Ages were a well-orchestrated campaign financed and executed by the Church and state in order to deprive women of reproductive autonomy, targeting folk-healers in particular.[14] Sylvia Federici conceives the transition to capitalism as a process of accumulation by dispossession of women, who had previously had material and reproductive autonomy.[15] Maria Mies links this 'housewifisation' of women to processes of colonisation and the international division of labour which relied on the objectification and exploitation of the procreative capacities of slaves.[16] Carolyn Marchant connects the formation of the modern scientific worldview to the objectification of nature as a machine rather than an organism in a root metaphor that sanctioned the domination of women, workers and the environment.[17] Similar arguments that Western/ colonial global power involves an epistemic authoritarianism empowering a dominant 'subject' at the expense of nature, women, colonised peoples and everyday knowledges are made by post-development theorists such as Escobar and Shiva,[18] and decolonial theorists such as Mignolo and Lugones.[19] Though not necessarily anarchist, these theories repeat Kropotkin's focus on the interconnection of state and capital as agents of alienation which impose top-down, impoverished relationships to secure political domination/colonisation and economic exploitation.[20]

The political principle requires a dyadic vertical relation to the state, and, therefore, the decomposition of horizontal social associations. The state permits people to relate only through its own mediation, which organises the people through the division of labour to meet the needs of the market. There is also a subjective component to the anarchist critique of statism. A variety of anarchist and libertarian Marxist theorists, such as

Max Stirner,[21] Gustav Landauer,[22] Martin Buber[23] and Wilhelm Reich,[24] have theorised the state as not only the imposition of external control but, more insidiously, as an alienated psychological state. An authoritarian-statist psychology involves the dual elements of forming or intensifying desires to dominate and/or objectify others (to boost one's ego, reduce fear of disorder, etc.), and also repressing one's own authentic desires in order to embrace conformist social roles. People come to relate to each other through performance of a false self (based on an internalised oppressor, an image of how one wishes to appear, or an abstract view of what one 'is') and functional or manipulative 'I–it' relations to others. This destroys unmediated and intimate communal relations between authentic desiring subjects, theorised by Kropotkin as mutual aid,[25] Buber as I–Thou relations[26] and Stirner as a 'union of egoists',[27] because people can only relate and act through abstract categories related to external roles and status rankings, with the state as intermediary.

Kropotkin explicitly argued against the Hobbesian and social-Darwin-ist myths that humans are competitive, rational-choice monads. He drew on studies of human and animal behaviour to show that both animals and people often cooperate, even in conditions of scarcity and emergencies. Cooperation can be just as important as self-protection, and the struggle for survival is often against circumstances rather than between individu-als.[28] Drawing on these analyses, Colin Ward made the argument that a lot of everyday life is already anarchy. Similarly to Kropotkin, Landauer and Buber, Ward uses the social/political principle in such a way as to suggest they can be present in impure or hybrid combinations. For example, a group can operate on the social principle among its own members but politically or hierarchically towards non-members or subordinate members. Many everyday groups, such as neighbourhood associations and musical subcultures, are examples of anarchy in action, even if the groups' stated aims are apolitical, arise from people with mainstream jobs and lives, are legally registered as associations and have elected or unelected officers and official committees.[29] This echoes Kropotkin, who also based his studies not only on peasants and indigenous groups but also on mutual aid among the rich, in medieval guilds and in religious brotherhoods.[30] Ward argues that rather than *supporting* state power, as is assumed by mainstream views outlined in Chapter 1, associations actually play a role in *warding off* state power: 'if any community can't organise itself, it is going to find governmental bodies filling the vacuum'.[31] Ward's approach to anarchism is to expand the field of the social principle across as much of life as possible, until it gets to the point where it strains at the limits set by the state and bursts out into the whole of society.[32]

The idea of an authentic 'outside' to state mediation and control in the form of a different social logic has been alluded to in different terminology by many different anarchistic, anti-authoritarian, and non-statist Marxist theorists. In Marxist-inspired approaches, the idea of labour as a creative power alienated in capital can function similarly to the social principle. For instance, Negri argues that capital and the centralised control it engenders is vampiric and sucks away the creative energy it exploits, while 'constituent power' is a form of collective subjectivity which 'wrenches free from the conditions and contradictions' of this control.[33] Holloway makes a similar distinction between 'power to' and 'power over',[34] while Castoriadis theorises a 'socially instituting imaginary'.[35] Paolo Virno contrasts oppressive sovereignty with concepts of the multitude and exodus as the expression of a radical politics that does not want to construct a new state.[36] Poststructuralist thinkers have offered overlapping theories, for example Agamben's 'whatever-singularity'[37] and Deleuze's concept, drawing on Nietzsche, of 'active force'.[38] Eco-anarchists such as John Zerzan have extended the possibility of dis-alienated relationships beyond those between people to the natural environment, describing a place of 'enchantment, understanding and wholeness'.[39]

Ethnographic works offer empirical evidence for a social way of relating that exists in tension or contradiction to the state. Kropotkin himself supplemented his historical and ethological studies with ethnographic material from his contemporaneous society.[40] In the twentieth century, anthropologist Pierre Clastres, in his work *Society Against the State*,[41] argues that indigenous stateless societies contain complex, purposive mechanisms for warding off centralisation and coercive power. Nurit Bird-David, in her study of the Nayaka forest-dwelling group of south India, proposes what she calls 'oil-in-water sociology'[42] of the 'band society', where individuals are conceived to be already whole, yet they are able to join and coalesce with other individuals in the way that drops of oil in water amalgamate into a greater drop. She contrasts this to English society and sociology, where individuals are understood to be rational, unique and autonomous individuals, yet in a sense are incomplete; they are '"socialised" into their parts within society'[43] like cogs in a machinic totality.

There is also a literature on horizontalism in autonomous social movements (ASMs) of the late twentieth and early twenty-first centuries, which often contains an ethnographic element. Georgy Katsiaficas differentiates ASMs from 'old' and 'new' social movements because they do not seek reformist change through statist structures, nor to seize state power, but rather to 'create free spaces in which self-determined decisions can be made autonomously and implemented directly',[44] asserting freedom from conformist values and hierarchical structures. Richard Day differentiates 'counter-hegemonic' movements from 'anti-hegemonic' ASMs, where the latter eschew not only representative democracy but also identity politics and Laclau and Mouffe's hegemonic integration,[45] whereby the goal of politics is to liberate an assumed essentialist identity such as class, race or gender, which simply substitutes another social role for those expected by the state and capitalism. To this logic of identitarian counter-hegemony, ASMs counterpose a logic of 'affinity', which creates multiple connections across differences rather than relying on sameness of identity to create an in-group.[46] Marina Sitrin shows how ASMs prefigure the change they want to see in the world through their everyday practices such as non-hierarchical decision making and horizontal, non-hierarchical organisation.[47] David Graeber's ethnography of direct action shows how movements can make decisions and resolve conflicts without the mediation of an external authority, which involves amalgamating different perspectives rather than silencing certain perspectives through unequal power.[48] Raúl Zibechi finds anti-state forces in the everyday relations of Bolivian indigenous social movements.[49] All of these ethnographic accounts echo Kropotkin's distinction between two different logics, one social, vital and horizontal, the other political, hierarchical and dominatory.

In these anarchist and related literatures, the authentic, dis-alienated subject–subject relationship, akin to Kropotkin's social principle, is portrayed as more or less ontological. It is an ever-present, or always possible, aspect of human existence. Since this distinction is vital to the approach taken by this book, I would like to briefly cover some possible objections. We shall see later that an issue exists regarding whether activists arriving from outside communities can be said to engage in *mutual* aid.

The first objection relates to the account of human nature given by proponents of the social principle. I have already debunked essentialist views of competitive/selfish individuals in Chapters 2 and 3. There is a critique from other anarchists, post-anarchists and poststructuralists that Kropotkin's view is overly optimistic and/or essentialises human nature by assuming people are naturally drawn to community and mutual aid.[50] Classical anarchism is portrayed as a mirror image of Hobbesianism, creating an untenable, essentialist, moral opposition between 'good' humanity and 'bad' state power. This optimistic account cannot explain the rise of states, individuals' desires for power, or the power inherent in anarchist accounts. Some variants emphasise the importance of hierarchical yet dispersed or capillary power structures, in which 'subjects' are produced and enmeshed rather than dominated. Post-anarchists thus argue that radicals must recognise our own complicity in oppressive regimes rather than seeking external enemies.[51] I agree with the post-anarchists that relations of domination can arise within spaces structured mainly by the social principle, and also that there is an always-present danger of turning anarchism into another fixed, exclusionary moral or rational discourse. I will consider these problems in more detail throughout the chapter. However, it is not clear that Kropotkin and other classical anarchists deny these dangers. Hence, Ferretti argues the classical anarchists created a basis for non-essentialist geographies because they stressed the importance of individuality and variety as the basis of agency and social transformation.[52] Similarly, Morris points out that the classical anarchists anticipated the poststructural critique of productive power, for example in Kropotkin's analysis of the ways in which power produces institutions, propaganda, laws, ideologies and modes of resistance,[53] while Turcato adds that the anarchist tradition was never just an abstract ideal but a complex set of debates linked to real movement praxis.[54] Ferretti also questions the post-anarchist critique of anarchist humanism as essentialist and anthropocentric, arguing that Kropotkin's portrayal of humans and animals as agents of mutual aid assumes them to be 'protagonists with agency, feelings and freedom' rather than 'hostages of mechanical "laws of nature"'. Kropotkin sought to construct an 'antimetaphysical' method where 'the source of ethics is the concrete behaviour of beings'.[55]

This ongoing debate has practical implications for social movement strategy in disasters. There is both an empirical question here (Is there an outer enemy? Is power mainly 'inside' each of us requiring self-change?) and a political question (Are social movements still effective if they focus on self-change instead of outer-directed struggles?). Given the affective basis of social movements,[56] the loss of outer-directed struggles is arguably fatal; movements either dissolve into atomised individuals or become fratricidal.[57] If an external power exists, then a self-change focus is useful as deflection and divide-and-rule. Indeed, this is very much the basis of languages of responsibilisation and adaptation-focused therapies, such as 'resilience', critiqued in Chapter 2. In what follows, I would like to follow the understanding of mutual aid, not as an essentialist humanist concept but a highly political concept that links immediate relief to structural change, which rests on different views about human nature, the space and scale of political community, and the temporality of social change to the mainstream Hobbesian view outlined in Chapter 2.

A second question is: If the social principle is 'essential' or always present, why does it not triumph? Classical anarchists tended to emphasise the role of external repression and the oppressive role of the state, for example the pillaging of common land and the massacre of popular movements.[58] Today, such external repression is less blatant and often entails securitisation (see Chapter 3). Alternatively, control may involve 'recuperation', whereby the state attempts to insert itself as mediator to alienate social relationships, a process which will be examined in more detail later. In practice, state repression and recuperation/co-optation often coexist, although the state will frequently emphasise one or the other depending on conditions, a dynamic that will be examined in more detail in the next chapter. Repression may also operate as internalised repression, or in-group repression of out-groups. Later theorists have attempted to explain the inertia of consumerist subjects, and the popularity of conservative or fascist social forces as forms of false consciousness,[59] or effects of mystification,[60] or as effects of desiring subjects being inserted into social machines that are not of their making (the patriarchal family, the capitalist economy) which distort and pervert their desires, creating docile individuals.[61]

A third question focuses on the issue of exclusivity. In an extreme example, an anarchist group might be composed entirely of white, male, middle-class, socially conventional people who are completely unaware of and unconcerned about other people's oppression, or may even be outright prejudiced in some ways. One might imagine a 'Neighbourhood

Watch' group who band together with the purpose of excluding ethnic minorities from the neighbourhood by mutually agreeing to restrict house sales. Such a group might still be anarchy in the sense of operating on the social principle within the group of the included. It might not even be too much of a stretch of the imagination to think that private groups of billionaires might engage in mutual aid among themselves as part of their everyday capitalist operations. The question, therefore, is whether such groups count as expressions of the social principle. They appear at first glance to have little relevance to anarchy, yet the issue often arises in anarchist texts and in social movements. For example, Clastres' depiction of the warding-off of statism in Guarani (Aché) bands includes the objectification of women as means of exchange among bands. It seems unlikely that such relations would appear powerless or egalitarian from the women's perspective.[62] Erica Lagalisse argues that 'gender-blind constructions of anarchoindigenism fail not only indigenous women but any anticolonial, anticapitalist movement'.[63] Lagalisse also examines the history of exclusion in anarchism through anarchists' long history of involvement in secret groups; for example, the anarchists Mikhail Bakunin and Pierre-Joseph Proudhon were both freemasons.[64] She highlights the way in which the secularisation of religious tendencies in the anarchist movement has frequently operated to exclude feminised and indigenous knowledges. Furthermore, anarchist social movements are often accused of being overly homogeneous, creating a kind of 'activist ghetto' which is often isolated from the wider community,[65] while it has also been argued that it is harder to sustain non-hierarchical structures among diverse and heterogeneous groups.[66] Some of these arguments will be addressed in the following chapter and, while it is important to note that activist groups, particularly Occupy, are often much more diverse than is often assumed,[67] it is also true that they can sometimes be intentionally or unintentionally exclusive.

Does the fact that the social principle can operate in exclusionary ways invalidate the basic premises of the anarchist social/political split? There are a few ways of dealing with this issue. Ultimately, most anarchists would assume that the elimination of the political principle requires getting rid of coercively enforced hierarchies. Ward and Kropotkin take an evolutionary and gradualist approach of increasing the relative weight of the social compared to the political principle. This renders the destruction of exclusionary social groups, particularly by coercive/political means, undesirable. This can be qualified somewhat by additional qualifications from theorists including Buber, Landauer and Levinas, and, from a slightly different angle, Stirner. These theorists stipulate that not only must the social principle involve a lack of hierarchy and mediation, it also requires participants to relate to the other authentically in what Buber calls an I–thou relation[68] and Levinas calls humanism of the Other.[69] For these thinkers, a group that excluded on the basis of fixed identities would not be counted as anarchy because the social principle consists of an I–thou relation rather than an objectifying relation. The I–thou relation is extra-positional: one cannot enter into an I–thou relationship based on an observed characteristic, because one relates to the other as a singularity, so entering into I–thou relations seems to preclude racism, sexism, classism and requires a more extensive sense of proactive responsibility to others than Ward or Kropotkin require. Stirner adds the concomitant that individuals must have freed themselves from alienating ideas called 'spooks' before they can authentically relate to the other in a 'union of egoists'.[70] Several interviewees in Chapters 5 and 6 express similar views that mutual aid is not truly mutual unless one is able to accept the others' needs as different to one's own and forego moralising judgements.

Despite these complexities, the important point to note here is that, rather than offering much-needed direction and cohesion, state control is actually corrosive of spontaneous order, while capital is vampiric and sucks away the energy it exploits. Conversely, spontaneous order can be understood as an authentic site of resistance because it involves direct relationships that undermine state control. The point of creating this conceptual distinction is not about ideological purity. In practice, it means that resistance needs neither to be pure anarchy nor build a one-off event, but to build and expand the field of the social principle across as much of life as possible. Creating the conditions to expand autonomous activity may sometimes entail tactical engagement with the state in disasters but requires political consciousness in order to resist co-optation.

MUTUAL AID AND DISASTER UTOPIAS

The social/political distinction is useful in understanding the phenomenon of 'disaster utopia'. As described in Chapter 2, the idea of the 'disaster utopia' has conservative origins dating back to the 1950s and 1960s, when North American disaster researchers and media reporters would laud the community action that arose in the period immediately following a natural disaster. The terminology 'post-disaster utopia' would be used to describe a period where people would put aside prior differences in order to 'roll up their sleeves' and 'pull together' to selflessly help others during the recovery effort.[71]

According to such accounts, the 'utopian' period of solidarity, consensus, and mutual aid soon recedes as the everyday divisions and differences settle in, at which point it is necessary for a specialised bureaucracy to step in to administer the longer-term tasks of recovery.[72] In Chapter 3, I considered how this account has come under increasing criticism, for example in Klein's theory of disaster capitalism as dispossession. Rebecca Solnit expands this critique by turning the idea of disaster utopia on its head, positing that it is not a momentary suspension of division that leads communities to unite in mutual aid. Rather, mutual aid is the norm that is normally hindered by the minorities in power and by media hegemonies.[73] Disaster utopia is thus a reappearance of the social principle due to the weakening of political order. Solnit draws on records of the 1906 San Francisco earthquake, the 1917 Halifax explosion, and the 9/11 attacks. She illustrates how, time and again, 'without orders or centralised organisation, people had stepped up to meet the needs of the moment, suddenly in charge of their communities and streets'.[74]

For Solnit, disaster utopias are different from other types of social change because they are not chosen or intentional so are thus independent of political preference. Such situations 'require we act, and act altruistically, bravely, and with initiative in order to survive or save the neighbours'.[75] In disasters, the Hobbesian view of human nature is dangerous because '[w]hat you believe shapes how you act'.[76] The very belief in a brutish, violent and selfish human nature creates the conditions for its emergence. People who believe that others are likely to act ruthlessly will do so themselves, while a policy intervention that assumes self-interest is more likely to encourage it, even if the intention is the opposite.[77] Beliefs also have implications for the ways in which we interpret the actions of others. A Hobbesian ontology can lead to misrecognising cooperative action, such as a group learning to find food in a disaster, as a selfish act of 'looting'.[78]

Disaster utopias provide relief and reconstruct communities through mutual aid, but they also change lives, shared beliefs and perspectives. People in a 'culture of silence'[79] may go through life not thinking about

84

what they desire, because they do not think that radical change is possible or they are focused on surviving. Utopias indicate, stimulate, point to, ask questions about what people desire, which can be transformative. Affected communities can suddenly experience an 'outside' during the aftermath of a disaster, and this experience makes the present order seem both intolerable and changeable. Sometimes it is only with the experience of the constituent power of the social principle that the question of the desirability of the present is even asked.[80]

Mutual aid in the context of disaster utopias differs from neoliberal conceptions of resilience outlined in Chapter 2 and offers a counterpoint from the standpoint of the social principle. Mutual aid initiates a reversal of perspective by creating direct relationships outside of state mediation. These ultimately must become resistant to incursions of state and capital, rather than resilient. Disaster utopias do not begin as social movements, they begin from necessity. However, they have much in common with radical 'newest'[81] or autonomous[82] social movements insofar as they mobilise the social principle and mutual aid to solve problems through horizontal relationships rather than deferring to external authority. Mutual aid occurs between equals and involves people 'helping one another directly', unlike charity aid, which is mediated by federal institutions or NGOs.[83] It involves an ethic of mutual recognition that is not mediated by political institutions or identity politics.[84] Disaster utopias involve a process of 'world making' and knowledge production,[85] and arise from the bottom-up through spontaneous order and through horizontal relationships.[86] They cannot be designed from the top-down through technocratic means, as the neoliberal concept of resilience assumes. Disaster utopias have a different relationship to space and scale than territorial nation states. They are local but, like the disasters that create the conditions for their emergence, they are unbounded by national borders; they are not exclusive to particular groups or identities, and they may connect to global struggles. They open prefigurative space for new ways of practising politics.[87] Because they exist outside the state and are defined by unmediated relationships, they are 'demandless' and non-representational.[88] Disasters create alternative forms of sociality and ways of being that do not require state mediation and must ultimately resist externally imposed power if they are to survive.

The concept of prefiguration is an important one in anarchist theory and practice. It resonates, but is not identical with, the idea of

a disaster utopia. Gradin and Raekstad trace the concept of prefiguration as it is currently understood to Carl Boggs' analyses of tensions
between Marxism and the New Left in the 1970s, although they argue
the practices that the term refers to have a much longer history, for
example in anti- and de-colonial movements.[89] Prefigurative politics is
characterised by an antagonistic relationship with vanguard revolution
or approaches advocating seizure of state power. This is accompanied
by attention to informal as well as formal power relations, such as class
relations, patriarchy, white supremacy and ableism. Boggs' definition
focuses on prefigurative politics as the embodiment of the social
relations, decision making, culture, and experience that are the 'ultimate
goal' of a movement or organisation.[90] There may be some rigidity and
teleology implied in this idea of an 'ultimate goal' that belies some of the
more self-reflexive and recursive aspects of anarchist movements, which
face changing and unforeseen conditions as they attempt to transcend
domination and new values emerge.[91] I prefer definitions of prefiguration that emphasise experimentation and the experience of future-facing
desire in the present, rather than a deferred goal, for example that offered
by Raekstad and Gradin: 'the deliberate experimental implementation of
desired future social relations and practices in the here-and-now'.[92]

The relationship between prefiguration and disaster utopias is
complex. Even with a definition of prefiguration that emphasises uncertainty and experimentation, a degree of intentionality is assumed at the
level of desire. Disaster utopias problematise the orientation of utopia
towards intention and the future. Nobody wishes for a disaster, yet they
can produce affects such as desire and hope for change.[93] The idea of
the 'disaster utopia' does not require any political ideology or intent, nor
an orientation to the future (e.g. prefiguration). However, as we shall see
in the following chapter, social movements such as Occupy Sandy 'plug
in'[94] to these disaster utopias with various aims, including solidarity and
mutual aid, but also more political aims, such as raising awareness of
the dangers of disaster capitalism and climate change. This introduces
issues of hierarchy, vanguardism and separation that will be explored in
more detail in the next chapter. In the following sections I will consider
how an anarchist language of prefiguration may need to be adapted to
encompass tactical engagements and use of resources in the context of
disaster anarchism.

ALTERNATIVE ECONOMIES, INSURRECTION
AND THE COMMONS

In the last two decades, anarchists and allied anti-authoritarian theorists, particularly autonomous and insurrectionary communists, have begun to contemplate the collapse of civilisation through climate catastrophe and the need to compose immanent utopias as 'lifeboats'.[95] This line of thought arises in reaction to Marxist ideas of teleological progress, technological optimism, and millenarian tendencies within anarchism, with the earlier project of post-scarcity transformation seeming less viable today.[96] We live in a state of 'truly catastrophic dispossession', and a 'disastrous relationship to the world'. It is precisely separation and alienation from land, locality, place, production and environment that renders us utterly vulnerable to the 'slightest jolt in the system' and at the same time opens us up to control and authoritarianism: 'As long as there is Man and Environment, the police will be there between them.'[97]

Communisation theory unites insurrectionary anarchists, autonomists and ultra-left communists[98] and refers to a process of transfer of ownership of goods, land, resources and means of production from private, capitalist hands to the commons. There is an emphasis on local place-based politics, recomposing public space and social bonds in an era where 'we have been completely torn from any belonging'.[99] Communisation draws on the tradition of utopian social experiments and countercultural attempts to reconstitute social bonds and common ownership with a history that traces back through squats and traveller sites of the 1980s and 1990s, intentional communities of the 1960s and 1970s, all the way to the utopian socialists of the nineteenth century. However, while previous attempts at creating secessionist communes aimed at prefiguring a brighter future for all of humanity, contemporary efforts are as much about bracing for oncoming catastrophe, facing crisis with dignity and care, and developing community subsistence in the present in the context of pervasive repressive control and the withdrawal of state welfare functions.

The Out of the Woods collective link communisation theory directly to climate change and climate-induced disasters. They distinguish 'disaster communities', which are the 'collective, self-organised responses to disaster situations',[100] from 'disaster communisation'. The former are disaster utopias based on the social principle, discussed above, but are short-lived, apolitical, and vulnerable to co-optation. Revolution would require a process where 'self-organised social reproduction of disaster communities came into conflict with existing property relations, the state, and so on, and overcomes these limits'.[101] This requires disaster communisation: building links between different disaster communities, class struggles and social movements, recomposing public spaces and social bonds, and building temporal links between episodic disasters and the longer historical process of disaster capitalism.

There are voluntaristic and class-political variants of communisation. The first approach starts with intentional exodus from the system.[102] Neoliberal forces that subjugate us also socialise us to prize our adaptability and resilience as forms of intelligence, which are techniques of separation and individualisation. This renders radical such traits as inadaptability, fatigue,[103] passivity, refusal to work,[104] and 'direct self-abolition of the working class'.[105] For some, such as Berardi and the Endnotes collective, exodus is not a prefigurative revolutionary practice but an inevitable response to collapse, similar to delinking. It composes self-reliant communities but does not require prescriptions for particular sharing or commoning practices.[106] A key tactic of this approach is invisibility: 'The task of the general intellect is exactly this: fleeing from paranoia, creating zones of human resistance, experimenting with autonomous forms of production using high-tech-low-energy methods – while avoiding confrontation with the criminal class and the conformist population.'[107]

Another approach, associated with Tiqqun[108] and the Invisible Committee, is closer to insurrectionary anarchism. Recomposition is a first stage that presages insurrection, a form of action that advocates the creation of self-valorising autonomous affinity groups or communes. This involves the creation of new values: forming new complicities, attachments and forms of resistance. This recomposition begins with political aspects of personal authenticity and friendship.[109] People first form a 'commune' or affinity group of like-minded people, then engage in 'insurrection', encompassing subsistence practices, economic localisation, and networking among different communes, as well as militant resistance. Disaster appears in this approach as an opportunity for exodus. Alienation and separation produce constant crises and disasters, but the interruption in the flow of commodities and suspension of normalcy and control can be exploited to liberate potential for self-organisation.[110]

Although rooted in Marxism, communisation theory is similar to anarchism and influential in anarchist circles. Discourse associated with communisation theory has permeated the disaster relief and recovery groups that will later be studied. Anarchists have also theorised conditions for social change in an age of collapse in similar terms. For example, Uri Gordon echoes the themes of exodus, recomposition and insurrection in more recognisably anarchist terminology, calling for 'delegitimation, direct action (both destructive and creative), and networking'[111] with an emphasis on retrieving commons and on self-sufficiency.[112] Rejecting both pessimism and earlier revolutionary hopes, Gordon calls instead on concepts of 'anxious hope' that it is not too late to act, and 'catastrophic hope'[113] to describe 'the choice to sustain ethics and dignity even through the passage of a way of life'.[114] Anarchists have frequently articulated the idea of prefigurative economics in terms of the 'gift economy', often drawing on anthropological studies of indigenous societies and the work of Marcel Mauss.[115] The idea of the gift refers to a mode of exchange where goods are not sold or exchanged on a market, but given unconditionally, without the expectation of equal return, which has the potential to decommodify relationships, remove feelings of guilt and obligation, and create new commons.[116]

The anonymous author of the popular anarchist pamphlet *Desert*[117] echoes and develops many of the themes discussed above, but in a context where bottom-up action may be forced rather than chosen through the continued withdrawal of the state and its redistributive functions and the crisis and collapse of peripheral economies. The author suggests that as the libertarian extreme of the European Enlightenment, anarchists have tended to reject dominant social forms and values, yet retain vestiges of religious myths of salvation and the presumption that the entire world is moving towards a better future: 'the illusion of a singular world capitalist present is mirrored by the illusion of a singular world anarchist future'.[118] The pamphlet suggests that climate change will extend 'the unevenness of the present' between overdeveloped zones and those subject to depletion. Civilisation and central power will be challenged or vanquished in some areas of the globe, opening up possibilities for wildness, while in other areas civilisation will extend its reach.[119] Insurrectional possibilities are greatest in those areas that have been *deserted* by capital and civilisation, similar to theories of delinking in the previous chapter. The pamphlet plays on two meanings of the word 'desert', referring both to depleted, abandoned territories and acts of desertion.[120] The author also draws on urban slums and vagabond plants to illustrate forms of wild survival within and against civilisation's frontiers. Localised disaster becomes an opportunity for autonomy.

There are many similarities between communisation theory and post-left and anti-civilisation forms of anarchism. Anarchists tend to place more emphasis on wildness and dis-alienated relationships with nature while communisation theory favours the hacking, reappropriation or making-common of infrastructure and technology.[121] Some strands of communisation theory prefer forming new values in revolution and struggle, whereas anarchists veer towards mutual aid and DIY culture. Some of these differences play out further in debates on technology, infrastructure and resources, which I shall examine in more detail now.

TECHNOLOGY, INFRASTRUCTURE AND RESOURCES

Understandings and uses of technology have immense practical implications for social movements' tactics in disasters, which will be explored in the next chapter. Anarchist approaches to technology take positions ranging from pessimistic to optimistic. There has been a recent surge in non-anarchist techno-utopian thought in radical circles which infuse the context. These include Fully Automated Luxury Communism (FALC) – a moniker that began as a joke in London activist circles[122] and was taken up by Aaron Bastani, whose book of that title attempts to turn it into a serious political programme.[123] FALC seeks to head off or solve disasters by means of speculative advanced technologies, such as asteroid mining to thwart mineral scarcity. Such overtly utopian speculations are symptomatic of a broader trend of accelerationism, which seeks to capture and repurpose the material infrastructure of capital for emancipatory ends, including ideas such as abolishing work through automation, a Universal Basic Income (UBI) and the Green New Deal, a neo-Keynesian economic solution focused on techno-fixes like solar power and carbon capture.[124] Fantasies of intensifying economic growth and technological development tend to arise in times of crisis, and accelerationist fantasies can be read as a symptom of 'stagnation, deceleration and decline' of capitalism.[125]

Traditionally, anarchists have tended to be wary of modernity and progressivism and have focused on present action rather than future technologies. Nevertheless, there is a persistent thread of techno-utopianism in anarchism, ranging from the classical anarchists, in particular Proudhon's desire for 'domination over nature',[126] through to Murray Bookchin's commitment to utilising technological development to alleviate toil and scarcity.[127] This approach is still committed to humanism and progress and, similar to Marxist approaches, constructs a binary between the positive potential of technology and its dominating nature when inserted into capitalist relations. A techno-optimist view in social movements studies literature around the use of social media to enable protest is echoed in the interviews discussed in later chapters. Scholars variously argue that social media undermines governmental authoritarianism[128] and aids the logistics of protests by building networks and trust[129] and by distributing information that may contradict 'official' sources.[130] While the internet is a highly developed technology, it might be seen as amenable to anarchist organisation, in particular because of its decentralised, networked structure and ability to share a global information commons for use in local peer production.[131] While some optimistic positions value the internet mainly as an associationalist means to deepen participatory governance or active citizenship, or as part of anarcho-capitalism, others draw on the anarchic logics of hacker culture, peer-to-peer production, FLOSS (free/libre/open-source software) programming, meshnets and cryptocurrency as ways to connect in more horizontal ways and bypass statist and capitalist middlemen.

The frontier of the techno-pessimist stance is encapsulated in anarcho-primitivism, which critiques the totality of civilisation and its technologies from the standpoint of 'primitive' human nature.[132] In Zerzan's work, a positive vision of hunter-gatherer bands is the point of departure for resistance to a vast dystopian cybernetic machine that has grown out of all control and threatens humanity to its very core.[133] Perlman characterises civilisation as a giant machine-like 'Leviathan', with humans giving up their authentic and autonomous desires in order to become dead segments of this enslaving machine in which humans and machines become interchangeable units of labour.[134] Rather than being exposed to the vagaries of nature, hunter-gatherers and other uncolonised indigenous groups may be better able than modern societies to avert disaster by maintaining ecological (not capitalist) resilience and to read warning signs ahead of natural events. Primitivists also emphasise the idea that civilisation is an ongoing disaster, for modern 'domesticated' people as well as for ecosystems and the remaining hunter-gatherers. There is an overlap with eco-feminist critiques which show how technological accumulation is inseparable from a Western scientific epistemology and consciousness that was developed through violent dispossession and continues to sanction the domination of women and nature.[135] 'Rewilding' often includes developing low-tech DIY and survival skills which are useful in disasters. However, the emphasis on returning to a state of nature may offer little practical succour to communities and activists seeking to engage in mutual aid disaster relief and resisting disaster capitalism, where quick decisions using available resources are essential.

A techno-pessimist perspective might draw attention to the ways in which technological development in hierarchical societies is cumulative and has a path dependency that crystallises and magnifies existing social hierarchies.[136] Langdon Winner cites the example of a nuclear power station, which by its nature demands centralised power and a strictly hierarchical chain of command.[137] Similarly, one might note that a society predisposed towards hierarchy, competition and inequality creates a strong push towards the invention and implementation of technologies of control and surveillance. Ivan Illich argues that manipulative and habit-forming technology becomes de facto compulsory in hierarchical societies and creates artificial scarcity.[138] The techno-pessimist stance also offers a critique of the use of social media for protest. 'Slacktivism' or 'clicktivism' becomes a narcissistic form of virtue signalling which substitutes for real action.[139] The internet is portrayed as complicit in the social and temporal fragmentation of contemporary neoliberal precariousness, undermining political participation through anxious overstimulation and attentive stress[140] and the time-consuming obligation to be always available for communication, which is mediated, inauthentic and superficial.[141] The internet is also heavily, and increasingly, commercialised, with social media dominated by a small number of powerful corporations.[142] These corporations have a large amount of power over the architecture of social media platforms, and so they are able to structure and define the nature of interactions.[143] Thinkers including Ivan Illich and Ran Prieur attempt to distinguish between manipulative, centralising technology and 'convivial tools' which aid individual autonomy, communities and ecology, and can be used or dropped at will for multiple purposes by autonomous users, for example the telephone system or bicycles.[144] Technologies can be judged liberatory when they meet principles such as freedom of refusal, possibility of reversal (no forced path dependency), use autonomy, make-repair autonomy, ecology of manufacture and use, and the enhancement of consciousness and skills.[145]

Deep ecologists[146] and posthumanists[147] offer systemic accounts that emphasise connections between humans and non-human nature, arguing that the more we try to ontologically separate ourselves from our entanglements and exert control of nature, the more control eludes us through complex interactions, leading to unstable emergent system effects such as climate change and climate emergencies.[148] Techno-fixes for environmental issues have a tendency to displace problems to new areas, or to create new problems.[149] Disaster might even be valued as a way of checking the hubris of modern egos.[150] Resultant political proposals focus on transpersonal awareness and humility but also bottom-up reconstruction similar to the communisation approach.

What does all this imply for a practical anarchist politics of technology in disasters? One might wish to avoid technologies that are unnecessarily exploitative of humans or nature. At the same time, participants in mutual aid groups should also avoid an unnecessarily purist approach if particular technologies have the potential to provide effective aid to communities in crisis. Core/periphery relationships are replicated on a smaller scale within core cities, and one might wish to consider the intersection of varying access and skills for technology with vulnerability. Differential access, technological knowhow, and the impact of deskilling may lead to issues of unwanted hierarchy and lack of trust between (often techno-literate) activists and community members.[151] Paying attention to the situated nature of action may involve offering skill-shares or knowledge sharing around technology. One may also wish to acknowledge that technologies embed intrinsic political qualities and power relations that manipulate their users and lead to cumulative tendencies and path dependencies that are difficult to change. Uri Gordon calls for a multifaceted approach to technology. Some technologies, such as those of warfare and surveillance, can only be sabotaged, whereas others can be productively repurposed.[152] Although the techno-pessimist account that the internet has become more heavily surveilled, controlled and commercialised is partially valid, there are praxis-based movements and means to counter this. These include alternative media networks,[153] the hacker ethic,[154] and the FLOSS movement which encourages free circulation and open collaboration.[155] The hacker ethic extends beyond software and indeed electronics, and also includes a now global network of hackspaces and makerspaces which provide community access to tools as varied as 3D printers, robots, woodworking machines and sewing machines for building and repairing anything the users desire based on a DIY ethos.[156] As we shall see in the next chapter, open-source software and the hacker ethic were mobilised to remarkable effect during Occupy Sandy relief efforts. Anarchism also has a constructive or utopian aspect in its attitude to technology, which involves technological innovation for decentralised living in the spheres of energy, building, food production and sewage, and can often be observed at intentional communities, eco-villages and autonomous social centres.[157] I will examine how some of these varying tactics are used by disaster anarchist movements in the next chapter. Now I would like to turn to the problems of recuperation and repression, which have particular urgency in the crisis which often follows disasters.

REPRESSION, RECUPERATION, DECOMPOSITION

Earlier in this chapter I argued that the basis of anarchist theory is a distinction between the social principle (non-hierarchy) and the political principle (hierarchy). It was argued that the key function of the state is to decompose and mediate immanent networked social bonds, subordinating them to the political principle. It has also been argued that while it is conceptually vital to distinguish between these two forms, they can exist as proportions or hybrid combinations, and sometimes the infrastructure or techniques of the state can be strategically appropriated, repurposed or hacked to create conditions for social recomposition or communisation. This section explores the opposite dynamic: when the state appropriates the creative values, techniques and energies that properly belong to the social principle and either destroys them or mobilises them in its favour.

The most obvious and visible way in which social movements can be suppressed is through outright repression. Systemic repression is usually associated with totalitarian regimes and dictatorships. However, the tactics of these regimes have been linked to COIN tactics used by modern state agencies such as the CIA and FBI in the US and MI5 and MI6 in the UK.[158] A 'boomerang effect'[159] uses colonised lands as a testing ground for repressive techniques and technologies, then bounces counterinsurgency tactics used on colonial populations back to Western nations. This has been interpreted as a 'primitive or permanent war' against people and populations, involving the proliferation of counterinsurgency warfare in everyday life,[160] or in Virilio's terms 'pure war'.[161] This sets the stage for 'hard' COIN repressive measures undertaken by states to suppress political uprisings and insurrections; these rely on overt force, violence and social control, for example human rights violations, police brutality, imprisonment, state terror, army occupation, massacre, executions and extrajudicial punishment.[162] There are also various 'soft' COIN tactics that aim to prevent uprisings before they even happen through state conspiracy, which attempts to change the rules of engagement by changing laws almost overnight, making previously legal activity into a criminal offence; or, alternatively, instituting measures gradually, one by one, with a cumulative effect that would spark revolt if enacted all at once.[163] Softer COIN tactics also aim to win over populations through emotional and intellectual manipulation. In the contemporary political climate, the global 'war on terror' as well as securitisation responses to 'natural' disasters outlined in Chapter 3 create a backdrop of moral panics in order to 'create a sense of fear which is used as a pretext to close space'.[164] State repression certainly occurs during disasters, even violent repression, as the following chapter will illustrate drawing on the example of Hurricane Katrina.[165] Indeed, disasters can very much create the climate of fear that might legitimate state violence in the eyes of a wider population. Nonetheless, repression is not the only tool at the disposal of the state to quell uprisings and insurrections and de-radicalise radical movements. The concept of recuperation also plays an important role in understanding some of the empirical material in the following chapter, in particular the ways in which state agencies have tried to simultaneously cover their own ineptitude while politically neutralising radical movements' discourse and culture. Recuperation has been interpreted as a way of defeating insurrections that is 'quieter' and 'less obvious' than outright repression.

Andrew Robinson distinguishes between three related but different anti-authoritarian perspectives on 'recuperation'.[166] First, the term is usually traced back to the Situationist school of thought, in which it describes processes through which radical ideas and practices are co-opted into a mainstream, socially conventional perspective, and distorted to suit the needs of state and capital. The world that we experience is a 'spectacle',[167] an unreal and mediated collection of images, and in order to survive, it must have total social control: any threat must be recuperated through 'creating dazzling alternatives' or 'embracing the threat and then *selling* it back to us'.[168] Second, autonomous Marxism views the whole of capitalism as a kind of recuperation-machine. Workers' labour is a creative force, which capitalism objectifies and alienates from the commons or multitude.[169] The third theory includes anarchism, particularly post-left anarchism, and poststructuralist accounts such as that of Deleuze and Guattari, who portray the rebellious creative force that escapes recuperation as *desire* rather than labour.[170] Robinson argues that this account is the most useful because it opens up possibilities for theorising radical intentionality and a difference between hybrid and recuperated formations: it is intentionality at the level of desire (conscious or unconscious) rather than 'work' that defines exteriority or autonomy.[171] This creates the possibility for autonomous subjectivity and desire, a way out of the logjam of the more Marxist portrayals of 'Capitalist Realism'.[172] Where exteriority exists at the level of desire, it is possible for radicalism to exist in hybrid forms, as in James Scott's studies on slave and peasant communities whose 'hidden transcripts' sometimes force small changes in the official public discourse,[173] or Colin Ward's emphasis on partial everyday resistances.[174]

Recuperation can involve 'addressing real problems with the same responses which might occur in a liberated context',[175] and in a way which tolerates and recognises autonomous action. Nonetheless, there is a cost to recognition, as the forces of recuperation seek to 'alter the future strategic balance by decomposing the basis for resistance' by drawing marginal people inside.[176] Once insurrectionary actors have been drawn into the logic of the state, they become alienated from one another and their direct relationships, which are then regulated and controlled by agencies of power. This leads to the decomposition of 'networks sustained by resistance' and also the emotional and affective states which sustain resistance.[177] Recuperation can occur through community representation, identity politics, politics of recognition, and politics of demand.[178] As soon as a force or a group is provided with representation or recognition by the system, or defines itself in the system's terms by seeking recognition, it opens itself up for recuperation if radical intentionality at the level of desire is not maintained. Furthermore, the state often gives recognition to autonomous action when it has no other option but to do so, such as Kropotkin's example of a time the French state 'gave orders for the return of the communal lands to the peasants – which was in fact only done when *already achieved by revolutionary action*. He goes on to argue that it is the destiny of all revolutionary laws that they are only 'enacted after the *fait accompli*', yet in the process the law must 'add some of its bourgeois venom'.[179] This dynamic is described similarly nearly a hundred years later by Deleuze and Guattari in their theory of axiomatics. The state takes on the role of the model of realisation for the capitalist axiomatic by putting in place legal frameworks and by mobilising political alliances to co-opt peripheral economic systems and creative flows in the service of the axioms of the time.[180] In the next chapter we will see how this plays out in practice in the context of disaster capitalism, where the state attempts to recognise and capture the energy of mutual aid disaster relief movements to mobilise them in the service of profit.

In the context of social movement studies in general, and disaster relief movements in particular, the process of NGO-isation, covered in Chapter 2, can be seen as an example of recuperation. This is because the process refers to the capture of autonomous movement energies through professionalisation, institutionalisation and bureaucratisation. NGOs arise from and draw on the energies of social movements and civil society, claim to represent them and advance their interests, but at the same time become complicit in the policing, surveillance and repression of autonomous spheres of action.[181] They may be perceived by the public as a mechanism for social justice and a platform for participation and democracy, but anarchists have interpreted the third sector as a tool of mediation between government, corporations and the people, which operates to diffuse anger and therefore convert potential dissent and uprising into 'a calm, peaceful, legal, controlled, institutionalised and completely harmless discontent' by creating a mere illusion of struggle for change.[182]

Attempts to respond in empowering ways to disaster must thus be wary of being captured in the webs of recuperation. Nonetheless, there may be circumstances where radical desires for mutual aid can be realised through hybrid actions, and 'using the master's tools' can sometimes be tactically useful to create conditions for communisation. There is a division among theorists discussed here as to whether partial recuperation is always a bad thing (as in Situationism, autonomia, and post-left anarchy), leading to a wider-ranging refusal to collaborate with the system, or whether there are cases where collaboration can create conditions to expand the sphere of the social principle (as seems to be indicated in Ward, Scott, and Deleuze and Guattari). In the Chapter 5, I will go into more detail on how processes of recuperation and repression have operated in disaster situations, for example by redefining the concept of mutual aid. This has led to a position where state funding is offered for ostensibly radical groups to pursue longer-term mutual aid projects, with conditions attached.

CONCLUSION

In this chapter I attempted to sketch an anarchist theoretical approach to disaster: a distinction between the social and political principle; an exegesis of the concept of mutual aid; a theory of social and economic change appropriate to disasters and ecological collapse through communisation/commoning; a theory of technology, infrastructure and civilisation; and a theory of state repression and recuperation of movement energies. The core of my argument is that while the state needs the grassroots to survive, the opposite is *not* the case. It was argued that the state and capital are vampiric and corrosive of spontaneous order, sucking away the energy they exploit while re-coding and re-ordering mutual aid relationships and peripheral economies into new political allegiances that can be subordinated and exploited by the worldwide capitalist axiomatic. This is sometimes done via the mediation of the NGO sector, but more recently it has also been mobilised via the global discourse of 'public health' and associated moral panics. Conversely, spontaneous order can be understood as an authentic site of resistance because it involves direct relationships that undermine state control. It is argued that creating the conditions to expand autonomous activity may sometimes entail tactical engagement with the state in disasters but this requires political consciousness and autonomous desires in order to resist co-optation. The next chapter will examine how these dynamics play out empirically and whether disaster movement participants' experiences confirm the implications of using a social/political distinction.

5

Occupy Sandy Mutual Aid, New York, 2012

INTRODUCTION: DISASTER ANARCHY IN ACTION

In this chapter, I offer an account of how anarchist approaches to disaster work in practice, drawing on the case study of Occupy Sandy. Over the last decade and a half, many grassroots social movements espousing broadly anarchist values and organising principles have begun to mobilise around disasters. They provide practical relief to survivors in a spirit of solidarity and mutual aid, underpinned by commitments to social and ecological justice. In this chapter I continue the argument that this movement should not be understood independently of their political content, nor as a form of 'social capital' compatible with the state. The chapter draws on interviews with activists, published participant accounts, activist texts, and documentary analysis of websites. I also occasionally draw on narratives around the mobilisation of the Common Ground Collective after Hurricane Katrina in New Orleans in 2005 because it was the first movement to visibly mobilise grassroots disaster relief with radical social and ecological principles in the US and because the state behaved very differently in this case compared to Sandy.

ORGANISATIONAL FORM

Occupy Sandy (OS) was, even by statist standards, a highly effective disaster response. OS volunteers mobilised rapidly at a time when established NGOs and state agencies were paralysed. This shows the advantages of grassroots activism. However, it is important to distinguish two ways this effectiveness can be understood. In itself, effectiveness is compatible with an associationalist view, in which the creative energy of movements can be mobilised in pro-systemic ways and integrated into state responses.

OS seems to display the neoliberal virtues of 'resilience' and 'social capital'. This section will seek to show instead that OS's activism is an instance of the social principle. It is juxtaposed to state management of disasters, not supplementary to it. Even when its approach was pragmatic and it worked with state agencies and NGOs, OS embodied a different logic and was resistant to subsumption in authoritarian structures. As an anarchistic form of social organisation, OS supports the hypothesis that the social and political principles are contradictory, not complementary.

OS did not initiate mutual aid in a vacuum. Mutual aid was happening in communities anyway, but OS acted as a network through which mutual aid relationships involving outside volunteers and resources could be sustained and coordinated. In disasters, non-hierarchical self-organising is not exclusive to anarchists, and many Occupy participants did not necessarily see their involvement as political. One interviewee informed me that churches, synagogues and mosques were just as involved as explicitly political groups,[Q5] while another distanced himself from what he saw as more conflictual aspects of politics: 'We do our own thing as people, and it's not something to compare with what the politicians do … it's inherent in what we do and how we speak about it is different and how we project that out to the world, our efforts, it's then that it becomes politics.'[Q5] The interviewee seems to point to a certain congruence between everyday life beyond and against official politics. This resonates with the anarchist approach that sees the social principle as a form of anarchy.

Connecting volunteers and communities with resources was organised through distribution hubs, initially set up in two churches in Brooklyn, the Church of St Luke and St Matthew, and St Jacobi, which operated as warehouses for storing donated goods and as volunteer training centres. The effort then spread, with more hubs opening, particularly in the worst affected areas including the Rockaways, Staten Island, Coney Island and the New Jersey shore.[1] Occupy Sandy ascertained the needs of the affected communities through door-to-door canvassing and organised direct distribution of food and supplies.[2] Transport was organised through a motor pool and through bike rides facilitated by the group Time's Up![3] Volunteers included self-organised groups of medics and public health workers, Legal Aid volunteers, experienced kitchen crews, web designers and construction workers.[4] Occupy Sandy mobilised the latent skills, networks, activists and wider popular support of the Occupy movement into an effective relief effort, encompassing around 60,000 volunteers and

$1.36 million in donations.[5] The movement distributed food, blankets, clothing, medical supplies and construction materials, coordinated the transport of supplies, repaired communications networks, restored properties, and effectively mobilised technology, including internet and social media sites, to coordinate donations and recruit volunteers.

The structure was anarchistic in that it relied on voluntary 'plugging in' rather than assigned roles. Activists praised the ease with which they were able to find a role within the organising model of Occupy Sandy: 'It was so simple if you plugged in they'd say what do you wanna do? How can you help?'[Q2] The idea of 'plugging in' was echoed by another volunteer who emphasised the importance of the movement's social media infrastructure in her journey: 'we were just people that were coming together and happened to have like a pretty good infrastructure. A pretty quick, you know, open-source infrastructure for anybody to be able to plug in.'[Q3] The ease of plugging in was thus a motivation for choosing Occupy over other response agencies. Another interviewee had originally travelled to New York to volunteer with the Red Cross, but despite his efforts was unable to do so effectively: 'I volunteered for the Red Cross for about a week. They sent me out to Long Island and it was disorganised. I was only meant to go for two days and they just never picked us up. So eventually we hitchhiked back.'[Q4] He went on to volunteer at the Church of St Luke and St Matthew, initially just for one day, yet 'The next day I had nowhere else to go. I hadn't heard from the Red Cross. Came back to the church. Started messing with the donations and it was like "oh so you're managing the donations?" I'm like "aaah, yes". So over the course of like a week that went from like one corner of the church to the entire church'[Q4] The informality of the process enhanced his opportunity to volunteer, while at the same time being enjoyable and providing social benefits: 'it was a place I could come and there was food there every day and you could just, you know, work all day and make friends. Have beers after come back the next day and do it again.'[Q4] Both the effective organisation and the ease of involvement thus encouraged sustained participation.

Another interviewee expressed frustration with established relief organisations, arguing that 'people who don't have church or religious institutions to plug into and were on waiting lists to volunteer at the Red Cross or for the city just were able to show up to a thing', though it also differed from the spontaneous disaster communities because 'it gave an interface to relief'.[Q6] While Occupy Sandy has been referred to with seemingly vanguardist language as a 'brand'[Q6] or a 'platform',[6] there were no leaders and 'nobody was waiting for marching orders, we just went where we were needed. We're letting the community dictate what their needs are then we facilitate and connect them with resources.'[7]

Occupy Sandy illustrated in practice that self-organised networks with low bureaucracy create faster and easier connections than bureaucratic organisations, giving them greater speed, flexibility and connectedness. Occupy Sandy was widely recognised to have organised relief more quickly and effectively than the official relief effort of FEMA and NGOs, particularly the Red Cross.[8] These agencies were widely perceived to have failed communities, provoking widespread public anger.[9] FEMA was perceived to do very little at all, which one of my interviewees argued was largely due to communities' misunderstanding FEMA's role and obligations,[Q1] which do not extend to providing immediate relief.[10] The Red Cross came under criticism because their burdensome bureaucratic procedures impeded the speed with which relief could reach communities,[11] which one interviewee attributed to the corporatisation of their model.[Q4] The size of hierarchical organisations means they were not in touch with communities' needs in the same way as Occupy Sandy, which had local connections: 'the Red Cross had no idea what to do with all their food. They had a ton of food and they just did not know where it was needed cos they'd never developed a system to figure it out.'[Q4] Similarly, scott crow recounts how, after Hurricane Katrina, the Red Cross arrived in the Algiers neighbourhood of New Orleans four weeks after the storm had struck, guarded by Homeland Security, with a van full of nothing more than plastic cutlery and napkins, but with no food or water. His Common Ground Collective had arrived much earlier.[12]

In Chapter 2, I outlined some mainstream theories which view networks and hierarchies as compatible. It is clear that non-hierarchical networks do indeed have many advantages in terms of organising structure, which can be mobilised in the service of the state and capital. During Occupy Sandy's relief efforts, the state engaged in heavy surveillance of the movement through the DHS and other agencies. The DHS published a report: *The Resilient Social Network*[13] which praises Occupy Sandy and other emergent relief groups, proselytising certain features of anarchist organisation as 'success drivers'. The report suggests that the government learn from and facilitate such groups in the future, integrating the efforts of such 'emergent grassroots entities' into FEMA's 'Whole

Community approach'.[14] The document presents groups such as Occupy Sandy as 'filling the gaps'[15] left by traditional state and NGO relief entities. The social capital terminology seems to be tied up, in the DHS document, with attempts to co-opt/use social networks, on the assumption of a basic compatibility between networks and hierarchies. Such co-optation would, however, kill the goose that lays the golden eggs; Occupy Sandy was agile and effective precisely *because* it was not bureaucratised or 'managed', and was driven by direct, prefigurative political approaches. In the next section, I will consider how mutual aid operated as a motivating value for volunteers involved in Occupy Sandy, and the extent to which this was understood as fulfilling a prefigurative, utopian and/or revolutionary function.

MUTUAL AID AS A RADICAL VALUE

Previously, I contrasted the conservative idea of a *temporary* disaster utopia with an anarchist theory of disaster based on wider ideas of mutual aid. A key phrase of Occupy Sandy, repeated on signs outside distribution hubs, was 'Mutual Aid, Not Charity'. Mutual aid as a value is strongly associated with Occupy Sandy, and is cited across activist accounts,[16] government reports,[17] and academic writings,[18] with five of seven interviewees also mentioning it as a core value of the movement.[Q2, Q3, Q4, Q5, Q6] The term had not entered everyday parlance or mainstream media at the time, which we shall see it does a few years later in the following chapter. Mutual aid as an explicit value links Occupy Sandy with Kropotkin and others in the history of anarchist political thought, outlined in Chapter 4, and also with practical disaster relief movements that came before and after, including the Common Ground Collective, Mutual Aid Disaster Relief (MADR)[19] and, later, the Covid-19 Mutual Aid movement as well as more antagonistic movements which do not fit into an associationalist model.

It is worth taking a minute to consider the history of Occupy Sandy's radical cooperativism in Occupy Wall Street, itself composed of prior radical groups which composed the New York General Assembly.[20] OWS also took inspiration from international anti-austerity and direct-democracy movements, including encampments in central squares in Spain, and the occupation of Tahrir Square during the Arab Spring.[21] Occupy was a pragmatic movement with an ambivalence towards prescribed values and 'politics'. Nonetheless, its organising model observably echoed anarchist themes such as consensus decision making, non-hierarchy, direct democracy, prefigurative politics, autonomy, and non-vanguardist knowledge production.[22] Although the movement was broadly anarchist in structural terms, it encompassed an entire spectrum of dissident opinion, including liberal and social democrats, revolutionary communists, and even some right-wing libertarians and conspiracy theorists.[23] While OWS did create outward statements of values arrived at by consensus,[24] the urgent and dispersed nature of the emergency situation in which OS emerged did not create the same kinds of spaces for prolonged discussions, decisions and consensus that formed the backbone of OWS. This was similarly the case for Common Ground during Katrina, and scott crow argues that a looser definition of consensus is needed in an emergency.[25]

In both OWS and OS, the reliance on the social principle rather than an explicit ideological 'trunk'[26] led to perceptions of the movement as apolitical and as social capital building. For example, the DHS report praised the mutual aid 'model', reporting that it empowers vulnerable populations without fostering 'dependence on aid'.[27] Aside from the amusing ambiguity of posing 'mutual aid' as an alternative to 'aid', this is a very explicitly neoliberal argument for mutual aid to encourage the preferred kind of entrepreneurial subjectivities. State recuperation of the idea of mutual aid has a long history in America with the idea of the deserving and undeserving poor.[28] Such recuperation attempts caused unease among participants who do not *want* to be functional providers of social capital, a position reminiscent of Marxist critiques of NGOs. One interviewee expressed concern that Occupy Sandy in some ways was 'like a neoliberal's wet dream' because 'it's something where the state doesn't have to provide services. The regular people are gonna provide this mutual aid service. If Occupy Sandy can come do it there's a feel-good story that's gonna take us away from having to think about what they're not doing.'[Q2]

Another interviewee argued that the early pragmatic needs-focused response falls into the standard 'disaster relief recipe'. However, the political background of OWS was a distinct undercurrent.[Q3] In contrast, some interviewees are themselves ambivalent, using neoliberal concepts such as 'resilience', 'individual transformative experience' and 'empowerment' interchangeably with terms such as 'mutual aid'.[Q1, Q6] One was also unhappy that OS was too 'political', trying to 'make the city look bad' whereas he would have preferred 'mutual aid and solidarity as a long-term thing'.[Q5] There was in fact a real division in the movement, recounted in detail in participant accounts,[29] between those who would have liked the movement to have been more explicit and radical in its politics and those who were afraid of unsettling fragile relationships with affected communities, the state and mainstream organisations like the Red Cross through confrontational political language. This led to many volunteers boycotting public actions, such as marches in affected communities and a protest in front of Mayor Bloomberg's house.[30]

Even when explicit politics is avoided, mutual aid may have political effects. One way in which mutual aid functions as a radical value is that it operates as a means of *social recomposition*. Mutual aid differs from charity because it involves acknowledging and critiquing unequal power relations. Unlike charity, it does not just 'put a bandaid on the problem, while leaving capitalism still in place'.[31] Rather, it recomposes social relationships that oppose and resist the alienating and extractive logic of capitalism. 'The inherent atomisation of capitalist society means that many people are afraid to accept assistance because they think that something will be expected in return or they do not want to feel that their self-reliance has been undermined. Charity assumes hierarchy; a giver and a taker, whereas mutual aid involves sharing amongst equals with different needs.'[32] Mutual aid in disaster relief disrupts neoliberal certainties about individualism, competitiveness and selfishness by showing that cooperative being and relating are not only possible and desirable, but in fact already exist and are an effective way to solve problems.

A second way in which mutual aid functions as a radical value is through *prefiguration*. As outlined in Chapter 4, prefiguration refers to action that seeks social change through direct action, bringing a desired future into being in the present through reconstructing social relations, rather than appealing to governments or external organisations. One participant in OS cited the movement as an experiment in 'putting theory into practice' through non-hierarchical processes of peer learning, exchange and reciprocity.[Q3] Other interviewees raised the idea that OS mutual aid prefigured social relations in the context of the state becoming less functional, and that as the state continues to withdraw support from poorer communities social movements like OS and communities will increasingly form connections, learn from one another and provide mutual aid support to one another. The interviewee elaborated that if the state and mainstream organisations continue to ignore mutual aid organising, 'They're gonna be running round like chickens with their heads cut off just like "oh where should we be delivering aid?" like the Red Cross was doing this past time. We were the largest relief effort at times and to not hang out with us, to not like figure out what we're doing is A) to cut off a really valuable source of information but B) to be on the losing side of history.'[Q6] There is a utopian aspect in the sense that forming strong social bonds can create 'alternative lifeworlds'.[33] For example, one interviewee recounted how, in one of the relief hubs in Queens, there was a full room of people bringing supplies, wrapping presents and cooking food 'and the only table that was empty was the FEMA table', while everyone else, including volunteers, activists, and community members were 'bringing their kids, helping out, right, and having fun. You feel good. It was a great way to spend the day. And so I think it was also a way for people to build community.'[Q2] The roots of OS in OWS were not ideological, but drew on a 'tribe that was already in place. And we see each other all the time ... I see the networks.'[Q2] Rebecca Solnit describes the idea of disaster collectivism as an emotional, affective experience, acknowledging the paradox of using the term 'enjoyment' in the context of disaster she articulates 'that sense of immersion in the moment and solidarity with others caused by the rupture in everyday life, an emotion graver than happiness but deeply positive. We don't have a language for this emotion, in which the wonderful comes wrapped in the terrible, joy in sorrow, courage in fear.'[34]

A third way in which mutual aid functions as a radical value is through *structural critique*. Mutual aid is a form of direct action that offers a buffer of immediate relief for the vulnerable from the worst effects of disaster, but, furthermore, participants also saw it as offering a broader structural critique, raising awareness and creating conditions to resist disaster capitalism:

it's a perfect gateway to show people what's really at work with our systems. Like this is what happens. This is what is real, you know, like you're in, the government is not helpful actually in this context and you are not safe in your home that you bought for this much money and, you know, you should not have all of the public housing in New York

City should not have their heaters and electricity and everything in the basement where it can flood.[Q3]

In the context of an atomised and fragmented society, 'environmental threats are a convenient way to keep the public scared and dependent on established institutions'.[35] This means that strengthening constituent power is a radical act that illustrates the possibility of an alternative lifeworld beyond the unequal and exploitative relations of the status quo. Ryan Hickey, a journalist and participant in the movement, argues that mutual aid 'formalises and sustains relations that run counter to the very existence of predatory capitalism, in contrast with NGOs/charities'.[36] This is revolutionary because 'revolution means we need each other'.[37]

A fourth way in which mutual aid operates as a radical concept is linked to its rejection of mediation through *direct action*. Direct action refers to social change through direct intervention, without appealing to an intermediary or external agent.[38] In the context of OWS, this was often interpreted as 'demandlessness', a refusal to make demands on authorities.[39] Rebecca Manski argues strongly for a continuance of values between OWS and OS. OWS was a 'metaphorical relief movement' with Zuccotti Park both a kind of disaster zone as well as 'an expressive space of refuge from the economic meltdown'.[40] OWS also provided services and care through mutual aid within the camps, including advice, temporary housing, and food.[41] OS is the same movement 'coming into its own' by highlighting enduring links between climate disasters like Hurricane Sandy and capitalism as an ongoing disaster.[42] At the same time, this form of demandless affinity belies the need for sameness and identity; people have different needs in a disaster that cannot be universalised or represented as demands in the way that conventional charity, state relief or populist politics would require.[43] Preston et al. argue that disaster-struck communities who share collective values and engage in direct action that is creative rather than merely oppositional employ a form of learning which 'rejects the very terms of the disaster'. Rather than seeing it as a problem to be navigated or resisted, they are able to 'reframe the disaster as having its origins in social and power relations'.[44]

A great example of direct action comes from Time's Up!, a New York direct-action, DIY environmental group that originated 30 years ago in the squatter movement, building links with local community organisations and global social movements such as Occupy. The group fights to reclaim public space from private capital by organising group bike rides and supporting community gardens. It also raises awareness of climate change.[45] During the Hurricane Sandy relief effort, Time's Up! mobilised alongside and under the banner of Occupy Sandy. Cyclists from Time's Up! had been involved in the OWS Sustainability Committee, using bicycles to transport food from community gardens in the Lower East Side to the occupation and using bicycle-powered electricity generators to supply the camp.[46] When Hurricane Sandy hit, Time's Up! organised relief bike rides to deliver blankets, food, bike-powered mobile phone charging stations and mobile bike repair units to geographically isolated areas in need. This was a highly pragmatic move at a time when public transport was frozen and roads congested, but also an ideologically consistent critique of the view that disasters are neither wholly natural, nor are the devastating consequences inevitable: bike-powered relief illustrated this through practice by delivering 'sustainable solutions to the devastation caused by climate change'.[47]

I believe that the general criticisms of anarchism as impossibly idealistic and the assumption of hierarchy as natural are deeply flawed. OS clearly manifests a pragmatic type of anarchy in action. While hierarchy is not necessary, however, mutual aid and non-hierarchy (social principle) are often easier to practise in homogeneous groups, and anarchist movements are often demographically specific. In disaster relief movements, this can manifest in separations and differences in both the *values* and the *social and economic status* within and between activists and communities. Bondesson highlights the contradiction inherent in the fact that 'emancipatory projects are often initiated and steered by privileged actors who do not belong in the marginalised communities they wish to strengthen, yet the work is based on the belief that empowerment requires self-organisation from within'.[48] Some thinkers view this as a fundamental obstacle to anarchist organising.[49] It is common from this perspective to call for formalised institutional structures in movements to ensure more transparent and democratic distribution of power.[50] Radical social movements in general, and Occupy in particular, have also been accused of being predominantly white and middle class.[51] This is probably true, although there is also a evidence to suggest that both are a lot more diverse than is often assumed.[52] It is also true that individuals who are committed and contribute to movements with a degree of longevity tend to be present when more decisions are made. However, it is also important not to overplay this and argue that the replication of domination on a small scale delegitimises the anarchist viewpoint per se. Horizontalism expressed in mutual aid is simultaneously a practice and a normative value – one can work towards it without always needing to see it achieved perfectly.[53]

Interviewees cited issues of conflict, oppression and exclusion within the movement that replicated those of the wider society. 'We're a very stratified culture, and the media started writing horrible stories about some of the Occupy activity and if you're gonna have a microcosm of our society there's plenty of flaws.'[Q2] Another interviewee stated that, with a few exceptions (working with churches and the Yellow Boots group), they experienced very little collaboration with working-class or non-radical relief organisations, who tended to join the mainstream effort instead.[Q4] Other interviewees cited a lot of collaboration with local groups, churches and other spontaneous disaster communities, but some expressed concern that Occupy 'hijacked the local efforts'.[Q5] Mutual aid was happening in communities anyway, even if they were not calling it 'mutual aid' and certainly not 'anarchism'. One interviewee stated: 'you talk about co-option by the state, but Occupy Sandy co-opted a lot of local mutual aid things. Cos there was a lot of people who just said bring stuff to my garage and we'll hand it out. And Occupy Sandy would find these or hear about them because of Facebook and Twitter and they would direct people to those places or we'd collect at the hub and take it to those places.'[Q4]

There are issues involved in attempting to impose or introduce political values and beliefs that could be perceived as vanguardist or colonising and at odds with anarchist values. Some interviewees were keen to emphasise that Occupy Sandy was not the only group engaging in mutual aid; communities were doing things anyway before the movement arrived. This included many community churches and religious organisations doing relief work. Some of these churches, particularly in North and Middle Brooklyn, were radical, insofar as they were open to progressivist and even anti-capitalist ideas, but churches in more peripheral regions were not. Kieran recounted how community members working in the field included 'firefighters, police, a lot of conservative people', who were 'not particularly radical people'. He attributed the source of their mutual aid to their working-class position rather than radicalism, and described how they 'were wary of Occupy initially, because they didn't know who we were or what our goal was'. The interviewee described processes of 'mutual learning' and 'affinity building', and 'compromises made by both parties'.[Q4] There were many examples of anarchists negotiating and compromising deeply held principles in order to accommodate or incorporate local and community values, for example 'Rainbow Rapid Relief ' – deviated from their vegetarian principles to accommodate local tastes, for example offering hamburgers and pork-roll sandwiches in New Jersey.[54]

Another difficulty is whether to require particular principles as conditions to participate. Kieran raised the tension between openness, inclusiveness and having shared principles. 'We're much more inclusive if people don't have to agree to any principles before they join. However, inclusiveness was seen to limit stability and persistence: 'the longer you're around, the more difficult it is to stay organised without shared principles'[Q4] Emily cited a delicate balance between remaining connected as a network without stemming the flow of resources. For her, the question was: 'how can we use a really informal but real network to facilitate the flow of resources? And I think that was a challenge because we didn't wanna put up walls and say you're in you're out.'[Q6] OS thus tended to adopt a broad view of mutual aid, similar to that of Colin Ward, outlined in the previous chapter.

Interviewees drew attention to the fact that (some) social movement activists, who are often more educated, with greater access to economic and cultural resources, can move around their city and country more freely than underprivileged, racialised or poor members of affected communities. On the one hand, groups like Occupy Sandy are able to critique this and raise awareness through their direct action. William Conroy suggests that Occupy Sandy's praxis makes racial liberalism 'visible as an *infrastructural* mode of governance that perpetuates and obscures a range of contradictory (dis)connections between people', in relation to material, resources and information.[55] On the other hand, the greater freedom of movement enjoyed by activists means that they will almost always leave communities eventually, often unintentionally abandoning them without having made substantial changes;[56] or, even worse, people with the best intentions may start programmes that communities come to rely on and then drop them. scott crow therefore argues that consistency and commitment are important values, and that it is also important to encourage the proliferation of alternative projects rather than any single group attempting hegemony.[57]

In summary, mutual aid is a political concept that implies a lack of separation between helpers and helped. It implies attempting to overcome alienation and form unmediated social bonds through direct action. It prefigures a disalienated society beyond the state, and which operates through mobilising emotions and affects such as joy, hope and connection in the midst of the fear and insecurity of a disaster. It also offers a structural critique of capitalism. Nonetheless, there are difficulties practising mutual aid in communities that are diverse, unequal or structurally alienated, and between people who hold different political values and beliefs. These are contingent rather than essential difficulties, and mutual aid does not preclude other forms of action, such as raising awareness of structural causes of disasters.

ALTERNATIVE ECONOMIES AND THE COMMONS

In Chapter 4, I considered how anarchism and associated theories of communisation and commoning have started to think through conditions for social change in the context of ecological and civilisational collapse. Both OS and OWS are clearly commoning initiatives. OWS was an attempt to reclaim public spaces; Halvorsen speaks of the use of territoriality as an offensive weapon against the financial elite.[58] This kind of tactic can be seen as a direct assault against the status quo and, it could easily be predicted that the state would not react kindly. Mayors and police coordinated the use of 'strong arm tactics to force Occupy to abandon most of its public spaces'.[59] The result of this was the emergence of smaller, more localised groups in 2012, including Occupy Sandy, Occupy the Hood, Occupy our Homes and Occupy Debt. In OS, the movement took on a more dispersed spatial strategy compared to OWS, yet also more localised in that it was not linked to a global movement like the 2011 wave of protests.

One major aspect of commoning in OS was the provision of organising infrastructure. Commoning and communisation were seen as an alternative, rather than complementary, to mainstream views of resilience and risk management. Horizontal social movements were seen to play a key role in tying together community efforts, which are 'just too big and there's no community that's gonna be able to deal with a disaster that big on its own.'[Q4] One interviewee articulated OS as a 'network infrastructure' which 'was a place to put all that mutual aid-y energy under a brand that was still hot, that could still bring resources in.'[Q6]

This idea of social movement 'branding', though predictable enough today, is also rather out of synch with the anti-systemic aspects of the mobilisation. It reflects the growing importance of social media networking and public visibility, in which social movements tend to emerge as cascades from initiatives which 'go viral' online. This has been theorised by Juris as 'emerging logics of aggregation' – that is, the use of virtual spaces such as social media to organise assembling of masses of individuals from diverse backgrounds in physical public spaces.[60] Pickerill and Krinsky speak of 'the importance of crafting and repeating slogans' in the context of 'the core claim to space', which is linked to ritualising protest and confronting the police.'[61] However, it is also a controversial aspect of contemporary protest. Goyens[62] and Halvorsen[63] have argued that the Occupy movement illustrates both the potentials and the limits of the 'Facebook revolution',[64] demonstrating the need to be grounded in space and territory that has long been observed in autonomous and utopian politics.

Although the organising model is anarchist-inflected, OS involved participants with a range of political positions, which often echoed the other radical critiques of mainstream disaster responses discussed in Chapter 3. Most of my interviewees touched on ideas that governments and corporations can use disasters as a premise for profit, akin to Naomi Klein's idea of 'disaster capitalism' or Harvey's ideas surrounding 'accumulation by dispossession'. The interviewee cited earlier on public housing is a case in point. The same interviewee later stated explicitly that she would love to see more research done around 'disaster capitalism', arguing that 'at the beginning it comes down to economy and access to land, food and basic resources. And a lot of this we already have information about but something about the tipping point of how a natural disaster really exposes the real disasters and how we can make those direct correlations easily digestible and understandable by the public.'[Q3] In some cases, techno-optimist orientations intersect with a politics of mutual aid networks in ways which lead to framings of technology itself as a pathway to communisation. One interviewee sought to 'turn the NGO sector into a non-coercive anarchist-organised kind of network.'[Q1] For this interviewee, the core purpose of Occupy Sandy was one of reshaping material infrastructure, and he was keen to discuss the ways in which technologies like Bitcoin would take away the state's ability to produce money and open-source software would enable people to organise non-hierarchically without government structures and control.

Interviewees also stressed the importance of urban geography for facilitating political organising, participation and democracy, especially in the context of securitised and militarised space of disaster capitalism. One interviewee highlighted a visit to Madrid, Spain: 'in Madrid it's really cool cos the way the city is set up is perfect for organising'. They cited the way in which barrios have their own spaces of assembly, and can combine in a more central space of assembly in the centre of the city, concluding that 'they know a lot about how it's to do with geography, it's really interesting'.[Q3] Another interviewee cited the importance of similar efforts to open up public space in New York, both for facilitating community building and also for creating infrastructure that can spring into place in the event of a disaster, using the example of community gardens: 'this was a safe space where their kids could play, and people started growing food here, and they started composting, recycling, coming up with ideas that aren't corporate ideas, then if a tragedy happens we can use these spaces to organise'.[Q4]

Storms and emergencies have been interpreted as opportunities to repurpose the capitalist-oriented infrastructure of the city for new, ecological, socially just ends. This ethos of commoning and repurposing is reflected in some of the longer-term projects initiated by Occupy Sandy, including small projects, worker cooperatives, and social businesses, many of which used non-hierarchical and inclusive decision-making processes inspired by Occupy Wall Street and followed its aim of creating sustainable and socially just neighbourhoods.[65] Examples included Rockaway Wildfire, a community organisation, Staten Island Tool Library, inspired by similar projects after Hurricane Katrina, a community-led project providing free access to tools and support for people and groups involved in rebuilding after the storm,[66] several mould remediation skill-shares and volunteer projects, including Respond & Rebuild,[67] Worker-Owned Rockaway Cooperatives, an initiative that aims to 'equip Far Rockaway residents with the skills and financing to launch small, worker-owned businesses that fill a need in their community'; FLO Solutions, a project that trains New York City based disaster relief groups in free/libre/open-source tools and techniques; and Sandy Storyline, a collaborative documentary and website to share experiences of Sandy and the relief efforts.

The longer-term projects were funded through the Occupy Sandy Project Spokes Council, which provided grants to grassroots projects using a participatory budgeting framework. Fundraising was a sometimes uncomfortable and controversial aspect of the movements' activities. Longer-term projects needed money to pay volunteers and rent for spaces. It also required time, effort and compromise to forge relationships with civil society organisations and government agencies and officials. This raised tensions within the movement between resisting NGO-isation and state control. One interviewee mentioned that, for many members of the movement, money 'ruined everything',[Q4] and another said that if you begin to grow too large and provide funds to groups beyond the immediate network, it removes the direct relationships needed for accountability and would make the organisation more like a traditional NGO/charity.[Q6] There were also divisions in the movement in cases where local projects sought to combine Occupy Sandy's financing with state or NGO money[Q4] Another interviewee defended the movement's fundraising capacities, and even suggested that the movement should do more to appropriate federal funds, since 'a disaster capitalism world already has all that shit like locked up really quickly cos they have people who are employed full-time that know exactly how to write a proposal or exactly how to get the money'.[Q3] Corporations either appropriate the money or redistribute it to victims as debt through individualised loans.[68] The movement sometimes came under criticism in the press for managing money badly and losing track of funds.[69] Still another interviewee was concerned that the focus on volunteering left some participants impoverished and in debt. They pointed to dilemmas regarding recognising the value of labour and whether to funnel resources to volunteers or affected communities. One interviewee mentioned 'a lot of opacity around like what was happening with money' in both OS and the earlier OWS 'as very much a thing that drove a wedge within the movement, I mean wedges, wedges aplenty'.[Q6] Nevertheless, it is widely accepted that the movement was incredibly successful at raising money. Despite initially modest ambitions to de-prioritise monetary fundraising efforts and raise only $10,000 for blankets, the movement eventually collected around $1,377,433.57 from online donations,[70] in addition to even greater non-monetary donations which one interviewee estimated at almost treble the worth of monetary donations.[Q4] Thus, while the use of money, traditional fundraising methods, and even the appropriation of federal funds might seem at odds with ideas of reconstituting the commons, for many members of Occupy Sandy this was vastly preferable to the money going to organisations that would further exploit communities.

From the perspective of the movement, the relationship to NGO-isation was slippery. One interviewee spoke of trying to take over and transform the NGO sector into more of an anarchist-organised network, but added: 'they're gonna be like hey, it's great being an NGO professional and they're gonna get co-opted.'[Q1] Another stated that the organisational autonomy of the early stages of mutual aid was helpful, but unsustainable in the longer term; 'then you get into, if you form non-profits out of this it becomes slower and messier with grants and things'.[Q2] One interviewee suggested that the topic of money created a split in values both within the movement, and between the movement and potential funders, since 'they want to hear that everyone are volunteers but the reality was that everyone needs resources to survive and some people don't have equal access to resources'. He recounted debates over whether OS activists should be paid, and gave an example of 'one woman who was very against people getting paid', who had made a huge amount of money selling a condo in New York. He recounted that she argued money should only go to affected communities, while her fellow activists were living on food stamps and sleeping on couches.[Q4] While he supported the position that the movement should take money to support activists, he expressed frustration with wasted overheads and corruption in NGOs. There were also questions from within the movement as to whether providing relief was always-already a recuperated action since 'recipients often did not see it politically' and OS volunteers were sometimes accused by other volunteers of 'seeking personal reward through jobs or consulting contracts'.[71] Further tensions in the movement included whether to work with police. While some believed this was essential for the 'security' of affected communities, others found it hard to befriend community members then open conversations about working with the NYPD, whom many in both the movement and the housing projects perceived as their enemy.[72] Tensions over whether to work with the city council and police led to volunteer walk-outs.[73]

Questions of autonomy versus centralisation overlapped with those concerning the need to adapt to the diverse and ever-changing needs of affected communities while attempting to maintain OS's own values and organisational principles, and Smith reports that 'the debates surrounding these issues were very complex and occurred in the late evenings after volunteers had worked upwards of 14 hour days for weeks on end'.[74] One interviewee spoke out against purism and 'a trend of dogmatism' based in a desire to clarify 'absolute principles' which she felt was incompatible with the need to run a relief effort: 'do your politics say we need to wait six weeks to have this conversation? Fuck you. There are people who are not in their homes right now and there are other people who are doing mould remediation on their homes, and your process is just not the most important thing right now.' In the end, she argued that 'the do-ocracy won out' and the political aspect of this was 'a move towards more community-based processes'.[Q6]

Groups like OS cannot simply be integrated into state-led relief efforts because many of their activists are averse to working with the state and value mutual aid partly as a means towards social change or a way of living differently in practice. Three interviewees explicitly rejected the associationalist view that democratic governance and social movements are mutually complementary, and they tied this to a perceived continuum between recuperation and outright repression. For example, one stated that 'police are very hostile to social movements' and 'have one role which is to keep down the poor'.[Q2] Another expressed a strong desire for the movement to move in a more autonomous direction, arguing that 'we need to be really strong in our political analysis' in order to develop 'autonomous yet connected alternative ways to organise that we're not dependent or involved with the government at all'.[Q3] Another interviewee said the government gives the impression of preparedness, but when a disaster happens: 'The government never shows up, it's just a crazy thing. I mean if they do come, they come with weapons, they're not gonna come with food or anything, they always just want to, you know, come with weapons and demand order, and the media will focus on "RIOTING WILL TAKE PLACE! WITHOUT THE GOVERNMENT IN CHARGE" and they start their propaganda and stuff.'[Q7]

These comments throw light on the limits to behaviourist and structuralist views, and their focus on managing human responses to disaster and controlling media narratives. In addition, activists seem to have longer memories than state agencies, and past repression continues to affect perceptions of the state. Some activists remembered clearly the violent repression of OWS, saying it was 'very sad to watch the greatest movement of my lifetime be crushed'.[Q2] Others drew parallels with the repression of grassroots and community responses to Katrina, which they said relied on 'command and control, you know, preserving the authority, you know, preserving the command and control structure at all costs before anything else', which leads to 'creating an increasingly brittle society that ... can't withstand stuff'.[Q4] In some interviewees' accounts, therefore, authoritarian disaster management is seen to conflict with goals of social resilience, rather than to mesh with them.

TECHNOLOGY AND INFRASTRUCTURE

Occupy Sandy utilised a dazzling array of technology for multiple uses during the relief effort and in longer-term recovery. Indeed, it is likely the movement would not have existed beyond localised projects were it not for internet technology. One interviewee argued that the combination of mutual aid and global technology was particularly powerful and a 'game changer' not only for 'humanitarian aid space' but also 'as communities of interest in education and healthcare and all that stuff kind of come together like it's really this question of like how do you leverage that global knowledge resources for local, pretty local solutions?'[Q1] Another argued that this distinguished OS from traditional disaster communities: 'I do think that's a big difference from your very hyper-local traditional mutual aid things. Because we had access to [technology and social media] and we knew how to use it.'[Q4] Social movement use of technology has been theorised as 'peer production',[75] which refers to the production of goods and services by self-organising communities. Speaking to activists in interviews and reading online accounts gave a very wide spread of attitudes towards technology, ranging from straightforwardly techno-optimist, including a technological determinist who believed technology had the power to emancipate humans and revolutionise society, through positions for tactical media and those advocating selection among technologies, through to relative pessimists who were prepared to make some pragmatic compromises.

The relationship between Occupy and social media is widely discussed in the academic literature, with views ranging from associational to radical. In the context of OWS, crowd organisation has been theorised as a form of peer production, and it has been argued that social media such as Twitter, Facebook and YouTube enable the activation, structuring and maintenance of large crowd-based protest movements without the need for recognised leaders, common goals or conventional organisation. Peer production in this context involves the production, curation and integration of information and organisational routines.[76] Some theorists of the uses of social media and communications technology in social movements view the relationship in associationalist terms as facilitating the creation of social ties that enable civic action within conventional structures.[77] For example, groups formed through shared experiences began to move beyond mere 'crowd' formation via social media towards peer-produced platforms, spreadsheets, communication networks and listservs, ultimately coming to resemble 'full-fledged advocacy organisations, complete with board meetings, fundraising deadlines, and coalition partnerships'.[78] Other theorists emphasise the radical potential of OWS's and OS's use of social media, for example, in drawing links between disasters and climate change.[79] Social media can have a consciousness-raising and politicising function, drawing communities into mutual learning about structural problems.[80] Some interviewees referred to OS as a 'brand' or 'meme',[Q4, Q6, Q5] referring to the fact that following OWS, people often recognised Occupy as 'a brand that's still hot, that could still bring resources in'[Q6] through online platforms, which further encouraged them to join the movement in person, or to donate. This illustrates how social media draws crowds into an emerging logic of aggregation, troubling the distinction between spectators and participants by drawing the former into the latter.[81] Social media and communications technology can also allow space for resistant movements to articulate their opposition to capitalist modes of production, express alternatives and create new spaces of everyday action and meaning that are opposed to the dominant order (despite operating within it, actually and virtually).[82] However, criticisms also arise regarding the reliance on massively monetised platforms, vulnerability to surveillance and censorship, degeneration of movements into 'clicktivism', and criticisms of technology as such. The novelty of computer-mediated activism is also starting to fade. As Karatzogianni notes, digital activism is becoming a part of 'politics as usual'. It is both 'mainstreamed by governments through collaboration with corporations, the co-optation of NGOs and the resistance of new socio-political formations'.[83]

The OS movement began when it used social networks, particularly Twitter and Facebook, to mobilise volunteers and garner donations. Social media had not been used to the same extent by movements in previous disasters, such as Hurricane Katrina. It took on many different organisational functions. Interviewees mentioned social media as the primary way that they 'plugged in' to the project in the first place: 'I saw through my social network, social media primarily, that folks were getting involved. I saw there was this thing on Occupy Sandy and I was already closely connected to the Occupy network. I was involved with Occupy Wall Street so these were my people.'[Q6] Social media was also used to get volunteers to where they were needed during the relief effort: 'people could use the Twitter feed to Occupy Sandy to say hey we need some people to show up in Red Hook housing and do some clean up.'[Q2] Social media was also useful for making very specific requests: 'You know people would be out knocking on doors in projects that had no elevators and like there's a lady here who speaks Polish. We need someone who speaks Polish. We understand she needs medicine but we can't figure out more. So we'd tweet that we need someone who speaks Polish and two hours later there's somebody speaking Polish in Coney Island.'[Q4]

Occupy Sandy was the first movement to use an online register to canvass donations from worldwide donors via the internet. They used the Amazon Gift List, usually used for wedding gift lists, to create a call for needed items, such as dehumidifiers, torches and cleaning supplies, which donors could then order directly via the site for delivery straight to one of the OS distribution sites. One interviewee lauded the use of Amazon as 'revolutionary', in a situation where 'you could not buy flashlights, batteries or candles anywhere in New York City by like two days after the storm when everything was sold out', and 'people all over the world were buying stuff and you could send directly to us'.[Q4] An article in *The Atlantic* described the process in its headline: 'Occupy Sandy hacks Amazon's wedding registry (in a good way)'.[84] In some ways, this exemplifies the tactical uses of mainstream technology and infrastructure listed in the previous chapter.

Occupy activists also developed FLOSS solutions for use by grassroots groups during the relief effort and in long-term recovery coalitions. FLOSS solutions used during Sandy included programmes for volunteer management and case tracking systems, inventory management and assessment tracking, request fulfilment, databases helping community-based recovery groups make information about critical services accessible to the public, and website content management. One interviewee cited open-source as 'an important part of what we do' and information-sharing software as 'the essential building blocks of what we do well'.[Q6] Information management involved a lot of spreadsheets, shared through online services like Google Drive. OS also created the most comprehensive searchable directory of services for victims of Sandy. One interviewee recounts: 'as it happened and like not accidentally I ended up making spreadsheets. Which didn't have that same sort of like deep resonance but I came to realise as time went on was like really the crux of what we did well. And like the value add of the Occupy network was information management in a lot of ways.'[Q6]

In terms of creating autonomous infrastructure, interviewees discussed localising energy production during the disaster, for example using the Occupy Wall Street Energy Bicycle (described later in this section), as forms of commoning.[Q7] Interviewees also discussed the importance of sustainable food production and public housing for long-term recovery,[Q3,Q4] the importance of grassroots education and knowledge production[Q3,Q7] and the importance of a politicised grassroots arts and culture, as well as solidarity between artists and labour.[Q5] There was also an emphasis on communisation of knowledge in order to create connection to social movement history: 'personally I think the most important thing is getting all of our shit archived and so we can, so I can be like talking to you and have the whole thing to show you exactly what happened.'[Q3] Occupy Sandy also set up 'tool libraries', giving communities access to a wider variety of tools, and gave workshops and skill-shares under the terminology of informal learning and capacity building: 'And so we actually use open-source software we build from a bunch of movements with these capacity building moments our software gets better and better so it's real and open information-sharing practices.'[Q6]

What is framed in mainstream accounts as an uninvited assault on disaster sites by unprepared volunteers,[85] is seen by interviewees as a productive, empowering, and emotionally inspiring attraction. Emily stated that 'people like disaster' because they 'like to see the grassroots response thing'. She elaborated that she was aware of people who travel around to attend disaster scenes through a desire to be close to self-organised efforts. This means that grassroots capability was increasing at the rate of 'you could call it consumer technology or network communication infrastructure', citing examples such as smartphones and laptops as well as communications, spreadsheets, collaborative documents and open-source software. It is precisely the fact that OS is *not* 'coordinated' by central disaster agencies that enables it to make effective use of such technology. This is because the rapidity at which both consumer and open-source technology develops means it is a 'self-trained endeavour' so 'grassroots effectiveness is going to be hugging that curve, because it's the effectiveness of individuals empowered in this techno-future we live in'. She suggested that technology endows grassroots movements with 'situational awareness' to document needs and deliver information to people with resources. Government agencies and NGOs were hindered by their bureaucracies, technological procurement and training processes, and their institutional information management flows, leading to massive stockpiles of resources and lack of information on effective means to distribute them. Despite her faith in grassroots technical learning, Emily was concerned about differential access and competence with consumer technology, but focused more on its progressive impact.[Q6] Similarly, Daniel argued that although consumer tech meant the public is better able to respond than institutions, it has also led to what he called the 'kickstarter problem', where 'the middle class keeps hitting each other up with fundraising requests' while publicly funded government stockpiles go to waste. If this keeps happening, 'it's gonna hurt people'. He further expressed concern that certain of the platforms used, such as Amazon, were ethically and environmentally dubious and unsustainable, mentioning in particular that the orders are fulfilled far away and come individually packaged. The solution he offered was that movements like OS need to be 'not just appealing to the state, but providing the state a managed process whereby they can mobilise the resources they have during disasters'.[Q1] In this case, tech-optimism overlaps with sympathy for other potential lines of capture.

Nobody I spoke to was straightforwardly tech-pessimist or primitivist. It is possible such people self-selected out of OS. Nevertheless, some were tech-critical. Fiona linked the idea of technology to the larger-scale infrastructure of a fossil fuel-based economy and emphasised the need for divestment from unsustainable technologies.[Q3] Daniel, who appeared tech-utopian in his earlier quote, also expressed fears of another possible tech-dystopian future, where technology was used for surveillance and social control.[Q1] Others, such as David, had little or nothing to say about digital technology or media despite explicit questioning,[Q5] while Blake and George mainly advocated sustainable technology, specifically bicycles, sustainable energy production and permaculture.[Q2, Q7] George recounted a notable incident involving 'hacking' non-digital technology and infrastructure in the form of the 'Occupy Wall Street Energy Bike', which at the time of Hurricane Sandy was an exhibit in the Museum of Reclaimed Urban Space in the Lower East Side of Manhattan. When the basement of the museum was flooded, there was a pump at the museum but no electricity, so volunteers from the museum and wider neighbourhood began to use the bike, generating energy by taking it in turns to 'cycle', in order to pump out the basement. When word spread that the museum was able to generate electricity, people brought their cellphones to be charged and, by coincidence, the museum was one of the few areas with any mobile reception, since the antennae were brand new and still working on batteries. In this way, the museum and nearby community garden became a really important organising hub, with many people coming to drop off donations, which were then distributed by bicycle.[Q7, 86] The use of bicycles as transportation was particularly important because many of the subways and other means of transportation had stopped working due to the storm. On the other hand, the issue of weapons and counter-power technologies barely came up in OS, in contrast with Hurricane Katrina.

When OS mobilised, it was the first movement to use social media to such an extent for disaster relief, but this is now common. What is thus worth noting, rather than the novel uses of technology, is the ways in which OS integrated technology into a radical politics and existing place-based politics and networks, using technology to mobilise people and resources and as part of a much wider reappropriated infrastructure that attempted to carve out an alternative lifeworld within and beyond the reproduction of capitalist social relations. More recent movements, specifically Mutual Aid Disaster Relief, have created a stable, consistent and up-to-date web presence on their website and on social media platforms.[87] MADR provide hope that disaster anarchism will be an ongoing presence in the frightening future of ecological collapse and climate catastrophe faced by many. In the next section, I am going to think through how, and under what conditions, anarchist disaster relief movements are able to remain radical and anarchist, compared to circumstances under which they might be (violently or otherwise) repressed, or alternatively recuperated into the de-radicalised non-profit-industrial complex.

RECUPERATION AND REPRESSION

The state attempted to recuperate the creative energies of Occupy Sandy into a neoliberal discourse. Sandy was, so to speak, a PR coup for horizontalism and a PR disaster for the state. Agencies of the state, and FEMA in particular, were widely criticised after the storm by a very wide array of actors, including other authorities such as the NYC Housing Authority, governors and mayors.[88] This illustrates, as argued in the previous chapter, that the state both *needed* the creative energies of the grassroots for the practical recovery efforts yet at the same time was threatened by them. The DHS report cites 'rising public distrust of hierarchical institutions', while musing on ways that grassroots entities and their 'personal relationships and deep local knowledge and caring for the community' might be incorporated and controlled.[89] The report praises the 'volunteer army of young, educated, tech-savvy individuals with time and a desire to help others' that emerged from 'seemingly out of nowhere'.[90] The idea that all of the participants were 'young' belies the diversity of the movement,[91] that they emerged from nowhere belies the strong basis in radical movement heritage, and the idea that they had disposable time was belied by the fact that for many participants, time and education were bought through debt – for example one interviewee lived off food stamps, slept on couches, and lived off the remnants of a graduate loan for the duration of the effort ('I intentionally took too much loan money to carry me through').[96] The DHS seems determined to exaggerate both the spontaneity (and thus, social media dependence) and the privilege of OS participants.

Again, from the perspective of power, and highlighting the complicity between state and traditional relief organisations, the report states: 'it was not uncommon for individuals to make a disparaging remark about traditional relief organisations in public settings, which did besmirch the network's reputation.'[92] In the words of Easton Smith, whose article offers the most comprehensive radical analysis of the document I have been able to find: 'It is only from the perspective of the state that an increase in grassroots responses to disaster necessarily implies a needed increase in "unity". In fear of losing its control over local organisation and its ability to "read" its own peoples' [sic] forms of organisation, the state opts for unity, and leverages its historical legitimacy to bring groups together.'[93] The media – both mainstream, and some activist factions – also misread, misinterpreted or downplayed the radical aspects of OS. Several media sources echoed the DHS's surprise that the movement seemed to appear out of nowhere, neglecting that it had grown out of networks established by OWS, which had continued to operate as a radical network despite violent eviction of the camps by police and severe ongoing repression.[94] Other sources accused them of legitimating the neoliberal rollback of welfare.[95]

A further force of recuperation is NGO-isation. The DHS document encourages the NGO-isation of grassroots movement, saying that being affiliated with a known NGO or FBO 'affords volunteers special rights and privileges to enable them to serve'.[96] Smith argues that when Occupy Sandy met the state, whether in the streets or in meetings, the representative always understood OS as a tool to be utilised. It was either to be brought into the existing NGO apex body or ostracised.[97] Even when it is not repressing a movement, the state operates in an authoritarian manner. An interviewee echoed this view of the state:

> I think that they need to work a lot more on dialogue and learning from community-based responses. If they wanna fund them and support them you can write your cheques but please, it's very difficult. The state has its punitive means and that's a problem. And I've seen the state relax and talk about being community based but I've not seen it always be a good collaborative partner. And that's the problem.[Q2]

It is undeniable that the state's reaction to the social movement and community responses after Hurricane Sandy was very different to that which occurred after Katrina, which was a vivid illustration of Out of the Woods collective's proclamation that 'the state sees localised self-organisation, collaboration and mutual aid as a threat to be crushed. Which is why the state is often quicker to provide its own citizens with hot lead than fresh water: order must reign.'[98] Accounts of the aftermath of Katrina by Clark, Solnit and crow all recount, in harrowing narratives, how the state response criminalised community responses, often reacting with extreme violence, and actively repressed social movement efforts.[99] It does not seem convincing or appropriate to argue that the state had 'learnt lessons' since Katrina. This would imply that the state would not use repression as a tactic in any future disasters, which seems unlikely. Indeed the state used violent repression, intimidation and armed enforcement against movement activists in Puerto Rico after Hurricane Maria.[100]

Rather, in light of OS's effectiveness and its own ineptitude, the state made a strategic decision to attempt recuperation rather than repression.

From an anarchist perspective, one might uncover a range of reasons behind the state's choice of whether to repress or recuperate. It has been argued throughout that the state has a conflicted relationship towards the grassroots, which it needs in order to survive but which it can also perceive as a threat. In the case of Katrina, compared to Sandy, the racialised and classed nature of the communities and movements is very obvious.[101] Another factor that may have come into play in ameliorating more visible forms of repression in the case of OS is the visibility of New York on the global stage compared to New Orleans, and also the visibility of the Occupy movement at this point in time (one year after the eviction of Zuccotti Park).[102] However, it is important to note that recuperation and repression are not mutually exclusive. Rather, I would argue, they are very much a continuation of the same: social control, and the logic of the state as such. For example, one might note that outright and violent repression *did* sometimes occur during Hurricane Sandy relief efforts, even though it did not play such a large role as during Katrina, and repression was more prevalent in working-class and black communities in New York.[103] Some interviewees also mentioned they were very aware of police derailing important conversations in meetings, while others mentioned that internalised repression and self-censorship came into play when they felt that the FBI were watching, which may have prevented the movement from moving in a more radical direction. It will also often be the case that different agencies or bodies within the state have different functions or agendas, with some preferring recuperation and others repression.

CONCLUSION

In this chapter, I have attempted to exemplify and build upon the anarchist approach to disaster outlined in Chapter 4 by drawing on the case of Occupy Sandy, using interviews and published/online activist accounts. The accounts show that OS's reliance on the social principle is compatible with a range of ideological positions, and with mutual aid support for communities that are not necessarily anarchist. The state's choice to recuperate rather than repress is probably conjunctural and not dependent on the success of OS itself. The state has also 'learnt' from

OS and has been more careful to channel or censor social media flows in subsequent 'emergencies'. OS does, however, seem to count against purist approaches: OS was able to work with state agencies without being co-opted, and at least some interviewees retained anti-authoritarian intentionality throughout. In the following chapter, I will turn to a very different, and more recent disaster in which mutual aid came into play – the Covid-19 pandemic and mutual aid groups in London.

6
Covid-19 Mutual Aid, London, 2020

INTRODUCTION: MUTUAL AID UNDER LOCKDOWN

In this chapter, I develop the account of how anarchist approaches to disaster work in practice by drawing on a very different case study in mutual aid: the groups that mobilised during the first Covid-19 lockdown in London, UK, in the spring and summer of 2020. I have covered the UK context and critically engaged with the government response in more detail in work published elsewhere,[1] but suffice to say that the policies employed in the UK were underpinned by many of the same neoliberal policies and cybernetic management as those in evidence in the crisis that followed Hurricane Sandy. If anything, techniques of population-nudging and the co-optation of radical mobilisations have become even more well-honed.

The virus was first thought to enter the UK towards the end of January 2020, although some estimates place this earlier.[2] In England, public health messaging started in February and mandatory lockdown on 23 March. This included 'stay at home' instructions backed by legislation, allowing only 'essential' work, shopping and travel. Infected people and the most vulnerable were advised to 'isolate' and 'shield' respectively by not going out at all. Obviously, these guidelines, which were general and sweeping in nature, had different effects on people depending on their situations and resources.[3] The distinction between advice and legal restrictions was not always communicated clearly. Degrees of enforcement and obedience also varied. These measures were backed up by heavy securitisation, but in many places a notable absence of police on the streets was substituted with diffuse social pressure promoted by government and media, with neighbours being encouraged to spy upon and report each other for having guests around, and to intervene in one another's behaviour in public in a kind of crowd-sourcing of policing through a heavily classed moral discourse.[4]

This chapter focuses on mutual aid activity that occurred during the first lockdown (23 March to 10 May). The interviews were conducted between May and August 2020, with people identified through personal networks. The interviews were conducted virtually (Skype/Zoom/Jitsi, depending on interviewee preference). As in the last chapter, the names of interviewees have been anonymised. This chapter also draws on my own participation and on accounts, activist texts, media and academic analyses, government policy documents and websites of mutual aid groups and activists. So far, there is little published work on the mutual aid groups (Covid-19 Mutual Aid Groups, or CMAGs).[5] Much of the emerging work on the movement takes a civil society, social capital perspective, consistent with the mainstream orientations of many of the non-anarchist participants.[6] I therefore feel it is a valuable and not only pragmatic exercise to explore the views and experiences of my interviewees in depth.[7]

Continuing the emphasis from the previous chapter, I draw on the anarchist theory constructed in Chapter 4 in order to understand mutual aid as a process of constructing autonomous lifeworlds, which is often in danger of being recuperated by statist logics, yet is not essentially co-opted. I continue the argument that mutual aid should not be understood independently of its political content, nor as a form of 'social capital' compatible with the state. Most of the people I interviewed identify as anarchists and other anti-capitalist radicals. This is *not* representative of the CMAG-UK movement as a whole, which was composed of a confusing and contradictory mixture of left-liberals, leftists and anarchists. The reason I chose to speak mostly to anarchists was due to the focus of this book, which takes a unique anarchist perspective of maintaining the radicalism of mutual aid.

The Covid-19 crisis was not only national, but international in scale, as was the anarchist response. The communities most likely to need mutual aid were those officially euphemised as 'vulnerable': impoverished, deprived people affected by austerity and inequality, and often also by race, class, gender and other discriminations. Mutual aid arose spontaneously in communities, alongside and in cooperation with actions organised by politicised activists. The crisis was challenging for mutual aid activists due to prohibitions, discouragement and risks associated with face-to-face contact, with heavy pressure for physical distancing and avoiding meetings in person. Previous movements have frequently conflated physical and social closeness. Anarchists and others involved in mutual aid had very diverse reactions to this context (ranging from critical support for 'stay at home' measures based on solidarity with the vulnerable, to opposition to a control regime perceived as dystopian and totalitarian).[8] In practice, all groups studied here worked together mainly virtually, and so communication technology played an even more central role than during OS. It has also been noted that the pandemic was more slow-burn than most disasters, with the slower pace allowing more time for critical discussions.[9]

ORGANISATIONAL FORM

In the previous chapter, I considered how the Occupy movement made it possible for people to 'plug in', choosing roles on an informal basis depending on what they wanted to do. The Covid-19 Mutual Aid UK network started very differently, as a UK-wide website offering a platform for groups (which were already organising spontaneously from the grassroots) to connect and to recruit members and access resources.[10] The network claims not to be affiliated to any charities or governmental agencies, and also does not claim affiliation with, or accountability for the activities of the local groups that use its resources.[11] They stipulate that they do not work directly with the police, councils and local authorities, political parties, NGOs and government bodies and departments, including the Home Office. They define 'a mutual aid group', without reference to its history in anarchism and radicalism, as: 'a volunteer led initiative where groups of people in a particular area join together to support one another, meeting vital community needs without the help of official bodies'.[12]

The main resources the website offers are a directory of local groups, resources created for local groups,[13] as well as materials created for wider communities 'not just defined by geography', including migrants, disabled people, LGBTQ+ people, autistic people, and people suffering domestic abuse.[14] They also link to NHS public health advice and 'recommend that everyone listen to government advice surrounding social distancing and limiting non-essential contact with others'.[15]

The website's relationship to local groups is not entirely clear. The website recommends a spatial strategy to groups, focused on the small 'really local' scale, 'for example just on your street or apartment block and surrounding area,'[16] which many groups did follow. An interviewee informed me that the founder of the website and national network claimed that they had started the first mutual aid group, 'or at least they think that they did' in Lewisham, and that they then received television and further publicity, through which exposure they began to 'feel a bit responsible for how this national network pans out', which led them to set up various training sessions alongside the website. The interviewee stated that the founders were 'a bit NGO-ish' and would not call themselves anarchist, neither would the interviewee 'call them anarchist or coming from the anarchist tradition' but they were 'radical, anti-colonial, feminist, queer, NGO people.'[S1] In London there was a complex 'nested' structure with a national network, borough-level groups and others divided more locally. This structure appears to be recommended via the website on a National Food Network Safeguarding document, recommended as reading for all groups.[17] There were also London-wide groups, such as a more politicised London Radical Assembly group.

While organisation was partly autonomous and localised, there was not a consistent orientation to anarchist/social principle approaches, but a tension between such approaches and a social capital or resilience orientation. As in OS, there was a widespread understanding of non-hierarchical organisation as being more efficient and effective than rigid bureaucratic structures. For some interviewees, this was the primary value of this type of organising: 'there were about 10 of us and we worked along non-hierarchical principles. We're not political people by any stretch of the imagination but just wanted to help out, and a lot of mutual aid went on between members of the group anyway, if any of us were self-isolating, we would get food for each-other.'[S5, 18] It is thus clear again that, with inadequate state/NGO support, people turn to mutual aid as a matter of survival, taking approaches consistent with anarchist methods without necessarily having political reasons to do so. Another interviewee emphasised ethical values in organising. He found the larger groups unwieldly, and his group set up a smaller 'solidarity fund' independent of the mutual aid groups: 'there's four of us, we do consensus, we've all met each other, we went social distance flyering, we use an online platform, so all the information we use is public – the money going in and out, who's applied – it's easier for us to be accountable'. In the larger groups, the problem is not a 'cabal of elites' but the lack of energy for reflective processes. This interviewee was part of one of the more radical local groups who had adopted a constitution and ethos based on anarchist principles (adapted from the Green Anti-capitalist Front). They found that in the smaller solidarity fund group, 'We're not dealing with hundreds of volunteers, so that makes us more agile – each of us who's signed up for the constitution has more autonomy, each of us to reply to people, also a result of trusting people.'[S2] Informal trust thus largely takes the place of formal checks, but this is not scalable beyond small groups. Other local groups handled scale problems by dividing into multiple WhatsApp groups, also divided into sub-groups, but across different lines; for example, one group had several functionally differentiated WhatsApp groups.[S4]

It seems that the scene in London was thriving. However, there were problems sustaining activity on the ground and bridging differences. Nicole, who was originally from London but organised in a group outside London, regretted that the group was very small and not very active. She was also concerned that 'we haven't transformed into anything', despite the impending second wave.[S5] Some groups explicitly organised using anarchist and consensus principles and Rich found that: 'Some people left because they weren't comfortable with that way of organising, not many, we only lost about 10 people because of that.' He had considered in great detail the advantages and disadvantages of non-hierarchical organising. The advantages he described were in terms of speed and flexibility in organising, saying that the local nature of organising means 'you can step it up very quickly', which he compared to work he did professionally, which is profitable but slow in delivering services, with a user/provider split. He adds: 'mutual aid on an anarchist understanding is about the people with needs and people with resources being the same people'. This led to a second advantage, that 'the needs are very well understood', and gave the example that 'one of the things we had to do was food collections and deliveries for a group of teenagers living without adults, and one of the discussions we had was: Do we give them condoms? Because the last thing you want is a teenage pregnancy at a time like this. It was eventually resolved by us asking them, and they said no they didn't [want them].' He argued that an organisation with traditional or restrictive morality like a church organisation, or with a more alienated and hierarchical structure, might have avoided these discussions, whereas anarchist mutual aid 'allows people to talk about things that people need that you might've thought they wouldn't've thought they need, or that you thought they'd need but they didn't.'[S7]

During the first wave, most participants were furloughed: that is, on a job retention scheme whereby the government paid 80 per cent of the wages for people unable to work during the crisis. They thus had a non-activity-contingent income and more time to spend on activism. However, this led to dropping out when work resumed. This is a recurring problem in anarchist organising: the inputs of voluntary activity and energy needed for vibrant movements are difficult to sustain in conditions of precarity and generalised depression, and/or for people in full-time work, with families and so on. The second problem was that anarchist organising required 'consent as an adult' as well as trust and good faith, while due to the group's inclusive ethos 'we had a couple of people who were Tories', they were 'very angry people' who 'didn't understand the concept of coming to a negotiated, agreed, mutually consensual decision and wanted to be all "tough guy"'. Rich argued that: 'For mutual aid to work, for any system to work, it has to be able to work when most people are not radicals. Communism must work when most people are not communists. Capitalism must work when most people are not capitalists. They both do it by force. Anarchism needs to work when most people aren't anarchists, but because we don't have recourse to force, anarchists need to think carefully about how we can get anarchism to work for non-anarchists.'[S7]

The affective differences between horizontal and organisational approaches are also apparent in the interviews. Interviewees offered as advantages of anarchist organising that 'people feel empowered, I think they feel like they are valued, their position counts, and it leads to better outcomes because they can talk through issues to reach consensus, you have more perspective and more viewpoints', but that the dangers included turning into a 'talking shop' with no action, and also that 'radical ideas can get sidelined by a conservative majority position.'[S5] While the emphasis here is on the effectiveness and inclusiveness of anarchism as an organising principle, another interviewee maintained that the ethics of anti-authoritarianism should not be forgotten: 'It's not only a practice but a commitment to fighting these authoritarian institutions so mutual aid can be fully realised.'[S4]

There were also accounts of a drift towards mainstream approaches as energy faded. Interviewees mentioned a problem that hierarchies set in over time,[S5] or that people accustomed to workplace hierarchies are seeking leadership and may push experienced activists into taking that role.[S6, S7] While a previous interviewee had lauded the system of having a separate, smaller core of more active people as creating more trusting and open relationships, another interviewee criticised this model as a 'central organising committee' which magnifies 'inequality in knowledge and power'.[S6] Another interviewee stated that some members of the communities they worked within expected them to fulfil a state services role which was very different to mutual aid; for example, to help a very vulnerable person who expected almost constant social care was beyond the capacities of the mutual aid group.[S1] Members of the group were not comfortable taking on this responsibility, as they did not have training.

MUTUAL AID AS A RADICAL VALUE

The movement adopted the term 'mutual aid' in their website, communication channels such as WhatsApp and social media groups, in their general communication with one another, but may not have had mutual aid as a core value in the same way as Occupy Sandy did. The use of the term by initiators did not imply any common understanding of the term, and this issue was the basis of disagreements and splits. OS's radicalism stemmed partly from their roots in OWS and NYC General Assembly. But in the case of CMAG-UK, the movement encompassed a complex configuration of different movements with different values. These included radical groups like London Radical Assembly and all kinds of other groups.[S1] As with OS, many radical interviewees in my sample also reported their involvement in previous movements, for example in Extinction Rebellion (XR), animal rights protests, and social centres such as 56a Infoshop in South London and Common House in East London.[S2] Another activist joined through their existing activist networks but expressed concern that mutual aid was sapping energy from other movements, such as London Anti-Fascist Action (LAFA) and the International Workers of the World (IWW).[S7] Another had previously been involved in 'student stuff at university' as well as 'migrant rights, stopping deportations and closing detention centres'.[S6] Another was alienated from formal politics through involvement in People and

Planet, an environmentalist group active within the National Union of Students (NUS): 'I saw the horror and shit-show that is the NUS. The president was a New Labour slimeball. I became really disillusioned and decided not to become involved in formal politics after that.' This led them to get involved in several small radical/prefigurative groups like Queer Mutiny, International Organization for a Participatory Society and an autonomous social centre.[51] Another interviewee cited no prior organising or movement membership, her only political affiliation being membership in the Liberal Democrat Party. She had, however, attended anti-war and anti-Brexit protests, described herself as a 'sofa activist' and was on the lookout for a feminist group to join. She spoke passionately about how easy she had found it to get involved in mutual aid and how impressed she was with her group and the people in it.

Similarly to OS, CMAGs in large part cohered around reliance on the social principle rather than an ideological 'trunk'. This orientation to action and relation rather than ideology led to an inclusive movement, but one that was easily mistaken as purely apolitical and recuperated by middle-class values. There was a pragmatic needs-focus, with mutual aid acting as a form of direct action oriented to helping people meet their needs directly through the community rather than seeking aid from the state. However, even more than with OS, there were splits between factions desiring an explicitly radical movement and those who wanted it to be less outwardly political. First, some participants with mainstream liberal or social democratic positions close to hegemonic 'common sense' perceived their own viewpoint as apolitical despite its constitutive exclusions. Since I accessed my interviewees through radical networks, I did not speak to many people with this viewpoint, although there was one interviewee who was close to this approach.[19] Second, there were politicised anarchists and other radicals who saw a strategic (or ethical) need to allow politics to take a backseat to ethical and organisational concerns in order to build relationships and affinities.[20] Third, there were anarchists who viewed anarchist ideology and principles, or at least the ability to openly discuss these, as essential to anarchist organising and values; that is, they did not feel that 'mutual aid' was worthy of the name, unless it was explicitly anarchist to some degree.[21] Radicals included not just anarchists but XR, Labour-left and Marxist-communist activists.[52] Despite this seeming lack of ideological coherence, the organisational features of mutual aid can have radical effects, and similarly to the previous chapter,

I will consider how CMAG expresses radical, anarchist values such as social recomposition, prefiguration, structural critique, and direct action even in the midst of ideological diversity and conflict.

The concept of *social recomposition* is sometimes posited as the goal of mutual aid and community building in approaches influenced by autonomism and open Marxism. Social recomposition is different from social reproduction because it does not simply fill gaps for the state in anticipation of a return to 'normal' or 'new normal'.[22] Instead it aims to increase active connections and reconstruct a source of counter-power in people's lived activity. In CMAGs, it is a fundamental aim that the aid is mutual, and interviewees frequently mentioned that anyone could become a recipient should they catch the virus, undermining provider/client binaries. There is also recurring concern in the interviews when the mutual aid and provider/client structures begin to overlap. Ronny argued that wider acceptance of giver/receiver divisions as a neutral and apolitical position is probably socialised from a young age. Although mutual aid risks upholding this 'model of charity volunteer', even just by helping people you are 'helping to establish connections and getting them familiar with these ideas, and getting them familiar with you, and seeing anarchist flags in the neighbourhood and talking about it', and that the way to really make change is 'to get people involved in not just taking from you, but helping others and helping themselves and trying to instil autonomy in them'.[54]

Mutual aid also functions as a radical value through *prefiguration*, attempting to spread social change through grassroots practice by providing alternatives rather than through top-down directives. While CMAGs partly realised this, there were concerns that its practices were insufficiently prefigurative. Bobbie feared there was a conflict between the altruistic hope that their activism was driven by concern for their neighbours, and their potentially vanguardist desire to involve their neighbours in radical politics: 'it just seems more noble to see suffering and wish to help it than think "I'm an anarchist who's trying to organise global insurrection and this is my opportunity to further my political aims."' This reflected a series of concerns among interviewees over colonising local efforts with anarchist ideals and whether this is vanguardist. On reflection Bobbie modified this position to reflect a shift in perspectives between short-term action and long-term vision, where the 'helping' function of mutual aid prefigures the more 'equal, liberated and humane' society Bobbie would like to see in the long run. This only need be perceived as a conflict in a mainstream internalised liberal narrative of inequality and self-sacrifice, yet Bobbie was reluctant to let go of the idea of a specifically 'anarchist global insurrection'.[51] Bobbie went on to define mutual aid as 'when people organise together to see to people's needs in an egalitarian way. Usually without payment, ideally without hierarchy, and as an explicitly political act; deliberately political act.'[51] For Bobbie, differences in the movement led them to question whether mutual aid was distinctly political or anarchist. They concluded that values matter but people are capable of illogical disjunctions of theory and practice: 'It's important therefore to make your analysis explicit and use words like "anarchist".' They added that the main difference between anarchist and liberal approaches is the 'structural analysis of what's wrong.'[51]

Ronny took a somewhat different position, arguing that 'you don't need to turn people into anarchists ideologically, you don't need to get them to read Kropotkin or make them act in anarchist ways … they see it work for them and have a positive impact, you don't need to convince them ideologically because they've already seen it.' However he admitted that some people are harder work than others when 'they still think they need the government and the council, even if they take a more critical look at it', and he argued that this was in large part a problem of the left in the UK because 'they are really divorced from everyday people's lives and needs, and you need to put in the effort of getting out there.'[54] This view sees the radical potential of mutual aid in its ability to prefigure and enact alternative relations and lifeworlds at an affective level rather than through ideological vanguardism. Although anarchism is one road to developing autonomous organisations, Ronny also believed that people develop these principles on their own. Anarchists bring greater experience and longevity, but with some risk of co-opting/colonising existing initiatives by marginalised communities. After all, groups like homeless people and food-insecure British African-Caribbean parents already engage in mutual aid.[54] Ronny continued that: 'The only way mutual aid can be fully realised is in an equal society and a free society, so mutual aid is not only trying to deal with symptoms, it actually has to aim to destroy the systems of oppression and the root causes of suffering.'[54]

Another interviewee, Matt, made similar claims that the participation of people who identify as apolitical or non-radical strengthens prefiguration in practice. He expressed awe that even after 40 years of neoliberalism people 'still have a heart' and will take action in solidarity with others, and saw this as evidence that the anarchist faith in mutual aid as an expression of human potential is not misplaced.[52] Rich suggests that, while most mutual aid groups do not embrace anarchism, anarchists 'do mutual aid well because we think about it a lot'. He continued that 'If there aren't any orders coming from government, then everybody has to do anarchism, even if they're not anarchists' and that 'in some ways it's good that anarchists don't lay down a template', although simple instructions would be helpful.[57]

We have seen in previous chapters how dominant framings either treat disasters as events arising from outside (behaviourism) or at most as differentially impacting on social groups (structuralism). Radical critiques focus on showing the systemic causes of disasters, or *structural critique*. In the case of Covid-19, such critiques range from the issue of health service cuts to patterned inequalities in health risks and ability to 'stay at home' to the various speculations as to the causes of the pandemic and responses to it. Many of my interviewees were committed to structural critique on some level, usually in relation to capitalism. Where OS was focused on linking hurricanes to broader climate change, CMAGs seemed more focused on class, wealth inequality and austerity, as well as the differential effects of securitised lockdown policies on different groups. For example, one interviewee recalled growing up in the same area where he is currently active, saying how it used to be a heavily working-class area that has now been gentrified, but which still has a lot of inequality and diversity. He emphasised classed differences between homed and homeless, with the latter unable to follow lockdown guidelines and at more risk both of criminalisation and Covid-19. He also suggested that middle-class activists need to undergo un/re-learning, for example regarding the role of the police as the 'armed wing of the state', a task he conceived as difficult but possible. He said that at the beginning there had been a lot of arguments within his group, for example, over calling the police to a window cleaner who they believed was not adequately following 'stay at home' guidelines, yet who 'is clearly just someone trying to make a living'.[52] Incidents of this kind potentially drive a wedge between radical and conformist participants.

A fourth way in which mutual aid operates as a radical concept is that, by definition, it is a form of *direct action*. As such, it eschews mediation by the state or professionalised charity structures, working to meet needs directly through solidarity rather than charity.[23] Similarly to OS, participants in CMAGs contrasted their efforts with professionalised charities and NGOs through the lack of separation and alienation 'between the professionals and the vulnerable people'.[54] Ronny argued that the main difference is that 'everyone who participates in mutual aid are equals'. This involves people acknowledging their own vulnerability rather than 'seeing themselves as good Samaritans' and it also involves letting go of the urge to control others. For example, 'If people have drug abuse problems [the charities] say you can't do drugs', which individualises responsibility for the problem, whereas 'mutual aid is part of a wider programme of liberation', which involves identifying and dealing with the causes of a sick society.

If the anarchist understanding of the state outlined in Chapter 4 is correct, then the state will always seek to dispossess and commodify the community and infrastructural building achievements of mutual aid groups. The specifically anti-capitalist nature of mutual aid inevitably brings it into contact with the state, particularly if this activity extends to squatting or fighting evictions. These actions are similar to mutual aid insofar as they follow the anarchist ethos of 'ask nothing, demand nothing'; yet, with the added concomitant to 'occupy and resist' they involve seizing 'property' and therefore bring anarchists into a much more direct confrontation with capital.[24] For example, during the pandemic, informal unions called for new members to join to support rent strikes during the pandemic, when many precarious workers were left unable to pay rent.[25] On Mayday, squatters from across the UK coordinated a series of decentralised actions to highlight their plight and to address their needs; actions included occupying commercial and residential buildings, banner-drops in support of squatters facing eviction, and occupying land to repurpose as open public space and to grow food.[26] Casting an eye on international examples, one finds a wider array of actions. Examples include students in Ohio and Massachusetts rioting against police and occupying buildings when evicted from their accommodation.[27] Anarchists have been vocal in their support for wildcat strikes, 'sick-outs' and job actions in response to being forced to work.[28] Anarchists have also expressed support for prison and asylum detention revolts related to Covid-19.[29] Another form of direct action goes against surveillance and identification. Anarchists have encouraged the normalisation of mask-wearing not only for protection against the virus but for anonymity and with a view to facilitating a feeling of security leading to an increased ability to act in public in 'covert and cheerful situations'.[30] Anarchists have also organised or taken part in anti-lockdown or anti-curfew protests in countries including Germany, the Netherlands and Canada, though often with much concern to dissociate from 'lateral thinkers' and the far-right.

Mutual aid runs up against a range of problems amidst authoritarian statism and capitalism, including inequalities among participants. The accusation that radicals were ghettoised and mainly white and middle class was sometimes raised. A survey of 854 participants in Covid-19 Mutual Aid Groups found that participants were predominantly white, middle class and politically centre-left.[31] The majority of respondents in the broader movement were keen to 'keep politics out of the work done by CMAGs'.[32] Several interviewees associated inequality with the fact that mutual aid too often ceased to be mutual due to a provider/ recipient relation. Rich argued that 'people didn't come to us for help, people came offering to help ... We had many more people who wanted to help than wanted to receive it.'[S7] Nicole mentioned that the groups she was involved with were 'very white and middle class', and there was 'this feeling of do-goodism and the philanthropic', which 'wasn't totally disempowering or patronising' but that 'what the white middle-class do-goody people weren't able to do was receive', suggesting this may indicate looking down on those who *do* receive.[S5] Nevertheless, many interviewees lauded the diversity of their groups and the mutual aid model was perceived as less prone to produce class hierarchies among activists than NGO models. Bobbie argued that local, non-hierarchical organising 'caters for people better because you have many different voices making decisions in the group, instead of having people from a particular class, like with an NGO where you have to do four years of unpaid internships, meaning the people are all from a particular inter-section of social groups.'[S1] Matt also reflected how he had been involved in another collective associated with an autonomous social centre for the last few years, which had taught him that working through contradictions with a diverse group of people 'who aren't the same' was possible, and often yielded more creative decisions.[S2] This sense of stability and place provided by the social centre links to the question of creating an anarchist infrastructure.

ALTERNATIVE ECONOMIES AND THE COMMONS

The anarchist position on resources emphasises creating or seizing them from below, rather than applying for funds from state or capital. There is a preference for self-organised infrastructure such as social centres, using participatory horizontal models of the kind referred to as 'commoning' in Open Marxist theory,[33] though free money without conditions is often accepted. An example of commoning among the more radical and anarchist section of London CMAG was the Green Radical Anti-capitalist Social Space (GRASS) in Islington. Having just occupied and been evicted from Paddington Green Police Station,[34] in February 2020 the activists found themselves in a squat in Islington in the midst of a pandemic when functioning as a traditional anarchist 'social space' was no longer viable.[35] They responded to the virus by cancelling their events and transforming their space into a mutual aid centre, storing resources such as leaflets, disinfectant and gloves, and offering free clothes and book donation points. While the activists closed the centre to non-occupiers soon after opening to minimise disease risk, they still built and maintained good relations with the local community, raising awareness of anarchism and overcoming stereotypes about squatters and anarchists while attempting to spread the message that 'we cannot rely on the government to save us, as it will always prioritise the interests of the rich and the powerful.'[36] The squat can be seen as a means of mobilising resources and infrastructure in ways that facilitated the group's mutual activities and helped them build links with their local communities, even where lockdown and social distancing meant that welcoming people into the space as a social centre became illegal and locally unpopular. The social centre aimed to maintain a visible presence without alienating the local community, for example by cleaning up graffiti and giving out free stuff. One activist involved with the squat said it 'made me realise the importance of my anarchism and activism – I couldn't just be on a screen reaching out to other lefty people I had to do something reaching out to people outside.'[54]

Other groups mobilised other non-monetary resources, mainly volunteer time which, however, was underpinned by state-provided furloughs.[51] This affected class composition, as only formal-sector, 'non-essential', mainly white-collar workers were eligible. Interviewees also mentioned 'in kind' donations, including 'goggles, face-shields, clothes donations, headphones ... second-hand stuff, food, a ton of food', which it distributed based on WhatsApp requests. One interviewee mentioned 'we didn't get any money, just time, we perhaps bought bits of food for people as individuals, we also have connections with food banks for very cheap food, a couple of shops that supply food very cheaply, there's lots of ways we had of getting things cheap.'[35] Another interviewee saw the sharing of skills as an important form of mutual aid infrastructure: 'We set up working groups for specific skills – mental health, translators, and people who had had enhanced background checks,[37] and people who had printers, that was a big deal, because when the print shops are shut and you have to go to the library then a printer is a big deal. Other than that, it was just what we had. We encouraged people to buy food for people rather than donating money for us to do it. We wanted to do everything as directly as possible.'[37]

In the previous chapter, I considered how the localised spatial strategy of OS drew on the history of OWS in seeking to make-common public spaces, while linking to a more dispersed horizontal network. The spatial strategy of Covid-19 Mutual Aid UK was also local and linked to wider networks, but somewhat different and, as I shall argue in the rest of this chapter, particularly vulnerable to recuperation in the status quo. The fact that the umbrella website – which claimed not to be a central organisation but is often interpreted as such – defined its boundaries in national terms ('UK'), replicates the territorial and socio-technical strategies of the nation state, as does the assumption that groups will organise by borough and ward, taking the categories of the existing system for granted. I am not sure where this originated, but it seemed to encourage power-grabs and attempts to shut down grassroots organising by local councillors and other officials: 'The local mutual aid groups in our borough mostly map quite closely to the electoral rolls, presumably because when people slice up the population that's a way to do it, and she [the local councillor] was made admin, presumably because it's important for them to be involved.'[37] Radical factions and certain other groups were linked into wider networks, such as the London Radical Assembly, or were more internationalist.[38]

CMAGs mostly did not use churches or community buildings as distribution hubs in the manner standard for OS. This can be attributed to lockdown conditions. However, one interviewee stressed the importance of having the squatted social centre as a space, which made it possible to focus on the redistribution of physical items like clothes, food and books:

'that's another lesson, having a physical space that you control is a really good way to work with people and provide something to people, it's a really important position of leverage'. The same interviewee linked occupation of a space directly to the importance of networked connections:

> The other thing we've used a lot is our network of connections – the people in the social centre are involved in different projects, we have something to draw from, to be able to store the food we need fridges, so when people saw a fridge in the street they would go and pick it up. We might also need something to repair something in the building, someone to print the leaflets – we go to the mutual aid group and we ask and it gives people an opportunity to give something back – you can't just look at it as individuals, a lot of it is about the connections that people are able to draw from – that's a big potential of these kinds of connection.[54]

The movement encompassed a range of positions around the use of resources and infrastructure. The role of money within mutual aid activity is a controversial point. Some public non-anarchist radicals, particularly Eshe Kiama Zuri, have called for much greater emphasis on financial donations, especially from more privileged participants, in order to align mutual aid 'with reparations and redistribution of wealth', in the context of 'new, white, middle-class mutual aid groups launched during the pandemic bulldozing pre-existing networks'.[39] This raises important points surrounding the colonisation of existing classed and racialised local practices by a social capital vision of mutual aid, which has a tendency to attract authoritarians seeking a territory to rule. The use of monetary donations is not new, and OS also mobilised both financial and goods donations, as described in the previous chapter. However, when donations are both financial and individualised, there is a danger of reproducing the patronising saviourist charity model, and commodifying mutual aid, removing possibilities for class solidarity and mutual aid across difference. Even the most generous financial donations by middle-class individuals are unlikely to represent a redistribution of wealth on a significant social scale, but emphasising them risks reifying groups (as privileged donors and oppressed or vulnerable receivers), thereby rendering them easier to co-opt or recuperate.[40] Some of the anarchist mutual aid groups adopted similar donation-based systems, which were discursively linked to ethics of solidarity and structural critique. Rich argued that 'people who are being fucked over by the benefits system understand that they are, we can just make it explicit'. This ethos was linked to a donation-based solidarity fund which was seen as a form of redistribution. The group raised £1,200 from local people. 'We make it very clear that people can give us money and it's a gift, they have no right to tell who we can gift it to'.[52] One major difference between OS and the CMAG's mobilised funds was that the former tended to favour longer-term sustainable group projects and cooperatives, whereas the latter seemed to be directed at individuals in immediate need (OS also helped individuals, but usually with goods rather than money, through the Amazon gift registry system). One interviewee was concerned about lack of accountability and the risk of people 'abusing gifts and donations' in a manner which echoed some of the press concerns over OS's lack of financial transparency outlined in the previous chapter, though this interviewee also suggested her fears might be based on 'an illusion', which she did not want to detract from her positive experiences of this (for her) novel kind of informal organising.[53]

One of the groups associated with a social centre accepted state funding as a registered charity. I was informed that this was an easy decision because they were desperate and there were no conditions attached, so it was felt that this wasn't a co-optation into an NGO structure. It is worth quoting one interviewee's thoughts at length:

> I think it's good to have some redistribution of wealth. I think it's good to have an institution backed up by violence to force capitalists to pay taxes in the unfortunate situation we find ourselves in now. Mutual aid groups are largely funded by people's personal furloughing.... It becomes a problem when you have to explain what you're doing or when receiving the money is dependent on doing different things. I think the state is a less problematic funder than corporate funders.... I don't want the state to exist and don't think state funding prefigures a better way of organising, and when you have centralised funding it can change the structure of the organisation quite a lot if there are conditions attached – the funding structure because of the furloughing scheme is different – some people just have more time and ability and that's fine – because it's inevitable.[51]

Ronny also mentioned working with more NGO-like organisations, such as the Hare Krishna group Food For All. While he would prefer his group to be cooking the food themselves, he saw this relationship as tolerable given that the mutual aid group had independence in distribution.[54] An interviewee from another group cited links to capitalist and state-linked organisations, but in a way which involved commoning in distribution of food and resources without compromise in values (although the same interviewee had earlier mentioned that their own group was somewhat elitist): 'We've also worked away from individual donations to working with organisations, such as food waste charities, food banks, community larders, supermarkets, we've also worked with a university where the colleges have donated a lot of food.'[56]

Another interviewee expressed a desire to increase the longevity of the movement. Although he thought external funding and donor money can be helpful to support activists' time in the short to medium term, he was interested in 'thinking of models that would create long-term structures that are much more autonomous',[54] and gave the example of 'people setting up food cooperatives in their neighbourhoods and streets'. Another expressed a desire for 'something that doesn't yet exist – mutual aid groups as a long-term project', asking 'What would it mean for them to exist in a year?' He argued that mutual aid 'potential infrastructure', had not arrived yet, but that the pandemic groups were a 'germ of something, seeding, a seeding bed of ideology, and potentiality that hasn't arrived yet.'[52] Ronny emphasised the importance of a propulsive, active utopian vision embedded in longer-term and resistant projects, rather than simply reacting to needs: 'the situation has developed and [mutual aid] has normalised, people have become less active as a group ... so I think it's an issue of not giving people an avenue, it's too limited just doing shopping for people. We tried to do that in this group, involve people in long-term projects, we would like to organise more around rental strike or rental issues, or start cooperatives or other projects that people could get involved in, rather than just waiting for requests to come.'[54]

Some interviewees expressed concerns that mutual aid is not as autonomous as they would like, or that it appears merely as a symptom of failing state and capitalist infrastructure, with one interviewee noting that anarchy is much quicker than, for example, workplace organising, and so is well suited for capitalist recovery.[57] Another expressed a worry that mutual aid without explicit politics risks just filling in the gaps for the state: 'They [the state] support mutual aid to let themselves off the hook in preventing people who need help from starving; they probably should be doing more for that, but I think they just support it when it can further their aims and doesn't challenge them.'[S6] One interviewee provided a concrete example where their mutual aid group had supported the NHS by donating equipment to the local hospital, including 'homemade face-shields and goggles. There was a collection in my local area for people to go digging swimming goggles out of their basement, and that is now the equipment they are using in the hospital, and there's been a headphone collection for patients too.' It has been argued throughout the book that the state tries to capitalise on all social relations, and mutual aid is discursively recast as 'social capital'. However, other participants argued that mutual aid is beneficial in spite of letting the state off the hook. 'It's good if we're replacing capitalism – perhaps doesn't matter if we don't get paid for it because it shows that we can exist outside capitalism.' Working with the council was justified on the basis that 'rather than being co-opted by the council, they're trying to co-opt the council – they're anarchists – trying to show we can live without money and bureaucracy.'[S1]

TECHNOLOGY AND INFRASTRUCTURE

Technology was central to the organising of CMAGs. In setting up and running the groups, platforms that proved popular included messaging apps like WhatsApp and Signal for group chats, online office tools like Google Documents and Google Sheets for recording aid requests, arranging assistance and distribution of goods, and free conferencing software like Zoom, Skype and Jitsi for organising meetings. Some groups that engaged in fundraising used the commercial platform GoFundMe or an open-source alternative called OpenCollective. Many of the participants initially learnt of their local mutual aid group through social media platforms like Twitter and Facebook. Only one interviewee widened their definition of technology to include 'bicycles, cars, online shopping, fridges freezers to store food, getting food delivered, and a lot of internet connections.'[S3]

Groups also used technology as a fundamental part of their day-to-day organising, which was essential in lockdown conditions where meeting face-to-face was frowned upon or prohibited. In many ways, however, their use of technology was less innovative than that of OS, who hacked and reappropriated technology in entirely new ways. Rather, the CMAGs used technology in ways that mirrored and replicated how it was being used in mainstream society, translated for radical organising. For example, Skype/Zoom meetings as replacements for face-to-face contact were already widespread, but the CMAGs were using them for political presentations, debates, discussions, and to provide emotional support as an aspect of mutual aid.[41] In the previous chapter, I argued that the use of technology is never apolitical, and that there are problems inherent in using monetised platforms with limiting protocols. This was a point of debate in some of the CMAGs but not others. Rich said that his group did not discuss the issue and defaulted to Zoom and WhatsApp, but 'another group preferred to use Jitsi, which is made by people who are quite uncompromising about their commitment to open-source, but it sucks – it doesn't offer the same level of service'. This came up time and time again, with many interviewees arguing that while they would prefer to use open-source, in reality it was just not as well developed, was 'buggy' or susceptible to crashing. Rich continued that: 'I don't have a problem with Facebook giving me a platform for free that I can use to help people.'[S7] Conversely, another interviewee said they actually switched to Jitsi from Zoom due to technical problems with the latter, but also that they had privacy concerns with Zoom and Skype (many of Jitsi's programs are end-to-end encrypted). The issue of privacy was raised by several interviewees, with other workarounds mentioned, like using disposable phones for organising actions, while Google services like Drive, Documents and Sheets were cited as 'owned by an evil corporation', but in fact satisfactory in terms of privacy concerns.[S4] Fears around privacy seemed to revolve more around making profit for corporations rather than being monitored by police or the state (which was a legitimate privacy concern within Occupy Sandy): 'So yeah all these big, profit-driven, scary software companies are probably logging all our data and turning it into profit somehow, by selling our data to an advertiser somewhere.'[S1]

Interviewees raised several benefits in terms of how the technology and software packages they used helped them to organise mutual aid. In the absence of face-to-face meetings, group messaging freeware like WhatsApp enabled something akin to consensus decision-making: 'It enabled conversations and collaboration. I didn't have to make a decision alone, I knew that we could reach a collaborative decision – it really did enable a non-hierarchical decision to happen.'[S5] The combination of platforms used by a solidarity fund, including a website they built themselves and the fiscal host OpenCollective, was praised by Matt because it helped them to reach out to people, respond to their requests really quickly and send money to them: 'We are giving people tangible help, with far less effort than giving the money physically. We can get through barriers like helping people who have no fixed address, and it makes it easier to organise in the pandemic where none of us can meet.'[S2] In contrast to OS, CMAG participants did not take strong utopian or critical positions on technology, seeing it instrumentally. Nearly every interviewee mentioned that the technology they used was fundamental to being able to organise mutual aid under lockdown, and there was little consideration of what was lost in this context – it seemed taken-for-granted that meeting face-to-face was not possible and using technology was the only alternative. Interviewees did, however, cite several disadvantages and problems with the technologies used, mainly unfamiliarity or lack of access.[S3] This reflected a wider concern in many groups that the dependence on technology might be excluding some people, particularly older generations or people who did not have smartphones. One group that did manage to reach out to several members without smartphones encouraged them to ring or email their requests, but those members were not able to see others' requests or contribute, which undermined the mutuality: 'That's a limitation, some people cannot get involved completely in the mutual aid ethos.'[S4] There was also a tension between the desire to use ethical and open-source technology like Signal, which 'lefties often use' and the desire to reach out in the community, since 'nearly everybody has WhatsApp on their phone.'[S4]

Another interviewee argued that WhatsApp was only good for people who wanted to be involved 'casually' because it had a really wide reach, but that it did not help to encourage people to get more involved in making decisions, and 'it's hard to build relationships in the community just on WhatsApp.'[S6] For these reasons, Amy's CMAG used Slack, which allows sub-groups to use different channels as forums for communication: 'We have the finance channel, support channel, food channel, things like that.'[S6] While she thought it helped to make the conversations less chaotic, Amy thought that the way Slack is designed had the potential to contribute to power disparities, since it is set up to give certain people admin powers and not others, and also encourages the use of 'closed versus public channels, which stops people from being challenged and getting the knowledge they need to contribute'.[56] Bobbie argued that the fact that much of the organising happened through Facebook and WhatsApp plus occasional meetings on Zoom was probably significant, because 'all of these are very large profit-making organisations ... they enable us to organise in a certain way and they shape the way we organise', while open-source alternatives are often 'shit – I mean they're really awful', and simply replicate commercial software's functionalities/formats.[51]

Nicole said that in her group a few people did not want to attend Zoom meetings or felt unable to contribute 'because of anxiety', which she linked to the fact that 'it's a participatory activity, not sitting and watching' rather than a fundamental problem with the technology itself or the effects of lockdown.[55] Another activist did think the technology was fundamentally exclusionary, and compared the CMAGs to OS, citing the problem that the people who needed it most were the ones who didn't have WhatsApp: 'Occupy Sandy, who didn't need to use social distancing, and could speak to people directly, would have been a lot more successful. Social distancing would be unthinkable without smartphones, it's unthinkable we would have done anything without that', however his proffered solution to this was tech-determinist and fatalist; that 'in another generation, all the people who can't use WhatsApp will have died. We exist in an age where technology has moved very quickly. The local council tried to get old smartphones for old people, but it didn't work, the vulnerable people without phones didn't want one or didn't know how to use one or couldn't learn. And that's not a problem that's within our ability to solve'.[57] Another interviewee expressed concern at not being sure of the social etiquette on technology, first regarding privacy/harassment concerns with providing names and telephone numbers, and, second, regarding the acceptability of private messaging among group members.[53] While it was not entirely evident in the people I spoke to, radical social movements in the Covid-19 pandemic did not completely bypass the need for technological hacking. For example two worker-activists created a 'mutual aid tool' for precarious 'gig workers' which provides a map enabling workers to connect with each other to exchange resources, help run errands or for social and emotional support.[42]

RECUPERATION AND REPRESSION

There was not a lot of evidence of visible repression of mutual aid during the first Covid-19 lockdown (visible repression of protests came later). Supporting vulnerable people was a legal reason to go out, and mutual aid in Britain did not face the repression seen in Greece, Australia, China, and the Philippines, which had some of the strictest lockdowns in the world effectively preventing mutual aid from happening. In the UK, many aspects of lockdown were internalised or socially dispersed rather than visibly policed, but there were also instances of visible repression and criminalisation of mutual aid initiatives. For example, several squats were evicted by police or bailiffs during the pandemic, at a time when evictions of rental accommodation were banned.[43] One example was the eviction of the 'Pie 'n' Mash Squat Café' in London, which was at the time attempting to reorganise as a donation and distribution mutual aid centre. It was evicted despite the space being some people's homes, some of whom claimed to be attempting to self-isolate for public safety.[44]

The group associated with the GRASS squat also cited experiences of repression. The original squat in Paddington Green Police Station had been evicted right before the pandemic lockdown, and this experience of repression carried over into the new squat:

> Let's just say the police have taken a particular interest in us – they come here quite often to keep an eye on us, sometimes late at night they come and shine lights in the windows to see what we're doing – on the day after Mayday we had three police vans, including red ones – the armed police – usually used for diplomatic purposes, I've only seen them when we did a protest outside an embassy. We had one occasion where a police van came around the centre and they started to get out from the back, so we all rushed to get our masks and make sure the doors were closed, but they said get back inside and started laughing, I think they were just trying to make fun of us.[54]

Playing with fears of homelessness during a pandemic where people are being told to 'stay at home', seems a particularly ferocious act of repression. Another instance in which an interviewee experienced contact with agents of the state was during a Black Lives Matter (BLM) protest, and he expressed that this was the only contact with police he experienced:

We are involved in the BLM movement – because I'm white I see myself as more of an ally than a movement activist. We organised a local protest rather than going to the large one…. We were standing on a free corner, with masks, there was a group of about 12 of us, 2 metres apart, and some XR people, and mostly people who were local, and we had made our own signs and children had made their own signs, and we were getting lots of support from people driving past us, they were cheering us … and we had some police came to that, but other than that they just ignored us, because I think we ignored them, not in an ostentatious breaking the law way, just that we had things to do and they had better things to do than annoy us.[52]

Given racialisation of policing, the fact that one of the few instances of police presence during the pandemic cited by interviewees aside from the squat harassment was during a Black Lives Matter protest is not without note.

As I have suggested throughout the chapter, mutual aid was not only tolerated by the government, it was often actively encouraged. With OS there was first surveillance, then retrospective recuperation (as evidenced in the DHS document). With the CMAGs, the UK government actively *anticipated* and *encouraged* mutual aid as social capital, using a neoliberal rhetoric that normalised individual resilience and de-politicised community 'helping' functions. These messages came not only from the Conservative government but also from a range of other institutions, including political parties, think tanks and local council networks. For example, New Local is a network of over 60 councils which regularly publishes research reports and hosts events on 'the community paradigm', which encourage ideas around shifting power from government and market-based solutions towards community power. While this might sound innovative and radical, it relies on a social capital model which retains the policing and security aspects of the state but shifts responsibility for recovering from shocks onto the community. They use the language of 'mutual aid' almost synonymously with 'volunteering' in a charity sense.[45] There is minimal focus on more welfare-oriented aspects of public health, such as provision of community education or financial support. Similarly, Public Health England (now ominously rebranded as the UK Health Security Agency), an executive agency of the Department of Health and Social Care, incorporated the expectation of people providing mutual aid in their communities into its official social care policy for 'extremely vulnerable' people advised to completely self-isolate. In official guidance, they are informed that they can have their needs met by taking personal responsibility for reaching out to 'community groups': 'Ask family, friends and neighbours to support you and use online services. If this is not possible, then the public sector, business, charities, and the general public are gearing up to help those advised to stay at home.'[46]

Other ways in which mutual aid during the Covid-19 pandemic was recuperated appear to have come from the grassroots – first of all, through a process of *silencing 'the political'*: from NGO and council workers and Labour Party activists, who got involved within the groups and steered them towards bureaucratic and professionalised models. Deborah Grayson argues that a lot of the impetus within CMAGs arose from the disillusioned left wing of the Labour Party, seeking an outlet for energy after the election defeat of Jeremy Corbyn in the December 2019 election. For many Labour activists, this was a first experience of local organising, and the desire to 'get on' with one's neighbours and foster a sense of community can 'feel particularly arbitrary for transient groups and dispersed minorities' on the receiving end of these efforts.[47] The latter probably includes much of the working-class population in an expensive and rapidly gentrifying city like London, and this may have led to a process of silencing by dominant groups, whereby oppositional ideas and activities were 'constructed as "political" and therefore illegitimate'.[48] Several articles have been written about this by anarchists and other radicals,[49] and almost all the activists I interviewed recounted similar experiences, although some found their groups were more successful in dealing with them than others.

What I found most striking, and touching, in listening to my interviewees was the extent to which they were experienced in exercising patience with others who tried to shut down and silence their ideas and perspectives. This probably reflects its being a depressingly common experience for anarchists:

It's interesting to see how open people are to listening to alternative ideas. If you say you are critical to the police others open up with the same ideas, but some admin stormed off because we said not to advise people to call the police – at the very least we can't take a position on that, but as we go into it people who stick with it are people who are more committed to a line – politicisation of it is really important to make a longer-term commitment. The main reason groups can fall apart is that they haven't got a coherent analysis around the situation as to why they exist, and it becomes reactionary. Like single issue organising, it will only exist for a short time.'[52]

Another interviewee cited experiences of attempts to silence and recuperate radical discourse, but partial success in resisting this: 'In our group if you talked about something that wasn't just getting help – for example resisting evictions or police brutality – there was outrage from people just expecting something else, like charity or a non-political organisation – so we try to not alienate people but explain the principles of mutual aid and I think that people are now more open to change.'[54]

Rich sought to analyse the source of several clashes with 'small c conservatives', who 'may have voted Lib Dem or for Keir Starmer', who were deeply uncomfortable with those who said they were anarchists or used anarchist ideas, and he felt that 'they were uncomfortable that the people who actually knew what they were doing also hate police and landlords'. He spoke of the 'curtain-twitching brigade of property owners [who] didn't want people on their property'. He argued that although he learnt a lot about how to work with people of different positions to his own, 'in particular it taught me that it's exhausting to hide my own affiliation, and it's much more difficult than I realised to work across the aisle with people who actually did not want me to exist – there were many people who were Labour people who would rather work with Conservatives and did not want to work with anarchists, even when we're just doing food deliveries together, and the level of hatred, as a straight white man, is something I've not come across before, and it was surprising and hard to fathom.'[57]

A second force of de-radicalisation was the *acceptance in the movement of rule-based discourses*. The dynamic is also clear within the umbrella website – who claim no overall jurisdiction yet still promulgate an ethos, for example that 'safeguarding' and 'accountability' and 'transparency' are essential.[50] While these may seem like fairly uncontroversial terms – and indeed they were used by some interviewees – they have strong associations with state- and NGO-based social services, such as DBS (Disclosure and Barring Service) checks for volunteers working with recipients who may or may not be 'vulnerable'.[51] The disclosure and proof of ID, residency and criminal history necessary to obtain a DBS certificate excludes many people from ever 'helping' and permanently relegates them to 'helped' status – that is, people such as refugees and asylum seekers, convicts on probation, people awaiting trial, and homeless people. It is therefore a way of formalising a stratified system which undermines the concept of mutuality entirely. Some interviewees also cited pressure from councils to obtain insurance.[56]

Other interviewees cited something intrinsic about the way their group was set up that led to it being like an NGO from the start. For example, alongside practical sub-groups, they had 'an oversight committee and there's a bone of contention about what their role is or should be. It's a group of people who would be legally liable, but that's morphed into people in charge who think they're bosses.'[56] Amy described how 'the pressure came from inside from a couple of individuals who weren't council affiliated, so we still experienced that but internally, which I think had more power than if it had come from the council.' She thinks that the group was 'too polite and didn't want to disagree', which led to a complete recuperation whereby 'what was a more traditional mutual aid group in March is clearly not a mutual aid organisation any more.... I think the term "mutual aid" in the organisation has become completely mean-ingless, because it's only used in the context to stop dissent.'[56] Another interviewee cited experiences in their group: 'There was all stuff with hi-viz jacket, DBS, rules and regulations which we ignored as well, all that attempt to professionalise and co-opt was so far down the line when stuff was already up and running, it was really easy to sweep aside ... it was just bizarre and made people really cross, the council were trying to take credit for things we were doing that they weren't even involved in.'[55]

Perhaps the most prominent form of recuperation is referred to within the movement as 'the local councillor issue'. An anarchist from Birmingham cites 'public shitty bad-mouthing' from a cohort of Labour Party members and representatives, including not only local councillors in official roles, but also well-meaning but ultimately reformist middle-class individuals whose sense of entitlement prompts them to attempt to lead working-class movements in pursuit of selfish careerist goals and self-promotion.[52] Many online articles by anarchist-inclined CMAG activists throughout the UK decry their experiences of state workers, professional bureau-crats and party politicians trying to co-opt and de-radicalise mutual aid efforts. One activist writes of their decision to disengage with the London

St Peter's Ward Covid-19 Mutual Aid group due to a takeover by 'councillors, ex-councillors, higher-ups in NGOs and Labour Party organisers'. The author did not believe their actions to be ill-intentioned, but argued they showed a 'deliberate and wilful disregard for the basic principles of mutual aid' by doing things like locking WhatsApp groups (excluding new members), dividing up coverage areas, establishing unelected formal leadership positions, holding up decisions, and shutting down conversations about organisational structure and radical tactics. There was a discussion of working with the council, including having requests for help administered through the council for 'safeguarding' reasons and insisting that volunteers are DBS checked. When the activist tried to remind the group of the principles of grassroots mutual aid, they were accused of 'politicising' the situation.[53]

Another activist raises similar concerns based on their experience of local councillors from the Labour Party trying to sabotage the mutual aid networks. The activist claims to have observed the same dynamics across many different groups throughout London and the UK more generally, and observed that the form of disruption is similar in each case: 'A local councillor joins a locally organised WhatsApp group and begins to post confusing or condescending messages, discouraging self-organised action and trying to assert council control.'[54] The criticisms and derailing of autonomous action usually revolve around issues of safeguarding, including publication of recipient addresses (on which many groups and the national website already provide information and training). Spender provides a screenshot of a conversation where the councillor attempts to talk from a position of authority about how the energy of the grassroots movement needs to be 'captured and managed in a responsible way'[55] illustrating explicitly and vividly the way in which the logic of the state inserts itself into the self-organised affairs of ordinary people and attempts to co-opt, mediate and alienate their energies.

Among other interviewees, there was a feeling that this was not deliberate. In one group, an original founder was a local councillor who ended up taking a back seat, after which the group transformed into one of the more radical groups: 'The kind of person who becomes a local councillor is often someone who has a civic mindset to get involved in mutual aid. She was actually quite useful as a link to local government, but she was smart enough to not get too involved.'[57] Michelle had a positive experience with a local councillor who was very active and helped the group to develop connections beyond the neighbourhood. Rich had developed a theory as to why councillors attempted to co-opt mutual aid: first of all, they were encouraged to do so by the Labour left; second, he thought that mutual aid was 'too busy for them', and they were unable to keep up with the level of activity, so they either 'backed down' as in his group, or 'in other groups they quashed it'. He drew on his knowledge of anarchist theory to understand this problem: 'to quote Malatesta, anarchism is not something that anarchists keep to themselves. Mutual aid is the answer, it's an obvious solution to a problem – in a time of anarchy, use anarchist methods – and most local councillors are civic-minded people who became councillors because they wanted to help the community. I think that's the same kind of people who would get into mutual aid even if they hadn't been councillors. I think they saw it just as the right thing to do at the time.'[57]

An interviewee from another group had a less positive experience, citing a Labour councillor who joined the group quite late, 'but there was still a bizarreness to it' – the councillor wanted to incorporate the mutual aid group with a residents' association which had previously declined cooperation. Later 'they [the Labour Party] realised they were completely out of step with their community and we were organising while they were on the back foot'.[55] She suggests the council sought to exploit the groups 'to do work that the council wasn't capable of doing, which was meeting needs in an emergency situation', and while she thought that the Conservative central government 'wasn't really paying attention' to mutual aid and 'don't care', she argued that 'the Labour Party always play some role in de-radicalising people, they want to contain any possible threat from the left so it doesn't get out of hand'.[55] Bobbie said they knew many other mutual aid groups had been 'taken over by councillors', citing knowledge of one ward where 'the Labour Party got involved and took over the whole infrastructure and turned it into a Labour-run charity'. Bobbie said they observed this almost happen in their own group, but it was averted by skilful facilitation: 'The facilitators/founders of my local group knew that other mutual aid groups had been taken over by councillors, and in the Zoom call right at the start of my local mutual aid group, which was attended by 50 or 60 people, 3 or 4 councillors were trying to get us to stop and slam [on] the brakes, but the main facilitator called them out on it and made sure their participation didn't shut the mutual aid efforts down.' Ronny also thought that the urge to regulate from the progressive left was not always deliberate, but that what happened in areas under progressive left jurisdiction like Islington (Jeremy Corbyn's ward) was 'even more insidious' because, while it is based in 'good intentions and try[ing] to help the mutual aid groups and allow them to organise', it is in the very nature of the council and the state that 'they cannot avoid trying to regulate the mutual aid groups into integrating them into the council and the state'. Ronny also argued that the advantages of mutual aid, in terms of the rapidity and effectiveness of its organising methods, ultimately lead 'the state and financial powers' to seek to recuperate it: 'For a period of time, the mutual aid groups were the main ones providing help for people in really difficult situations before the state or financial powers could help at all. They have been trying to incorporate and recuperate us ever since.'

Some interviewees mentioned the *emergence of hierarchies* within their group as a form of co-optation. For example, Amy said that although their group made a constitution as 'an unincorporated association', which instituted formal hierarchies in her particular group, she believes that there were hierarchies in place before that, 'it just went unnoticed that even without a structure some people have more power than others. This was a small group of people who were friends, who decided it would be better if there were a small group of people running things, and when it went to vote other people thought they didn't have the power to criticise or didn't feel comfortable to do so. The way it was sold to people was that it was necessary for legal liability reasons. That was a key thing in getting people to support it because they were scared.'[55]

Bobbie thought that their group was 'pretty good' in terms of avoiding or challenging hierarchies, but that they'd 'heard horror stories from other groups', particularly in terms of what has been articulated in other literatures as 'do-ocracy'.[56] In their group, this was avoided by having rotating roles. They said they had also 'heard some mention of patriarchal behaviour from men, and racist behaviour from white people. But in my own specific local group I haven't seen any of that, formally there is no hierarchy at all, the only informal hierarchy comes from the fact some people do much more work, which isn't necessary harmful.' They were more worried about exclusion than hierarchy and, in particular, that 'we probably don't reach certain people and do things in a way that isn't appealing to certain people, for example, the way our poster is designed I think would only appeal to certain groups and might not appeal to people from a certain cultural background, it might seem really middle class, or boujie, or white, or cutesy, or disconnected from reality, but I can't really know – I can make an effort to expand my imagination, but inherently I can't know fully.' They argued that while their group is predominantly white, middle class and privileged in some way, it was also a lot more diverse than is often assumed by people who stereotype the movement as being entirely this way: 'we have some nurses of all racialisations, a few younger people, early 20s, late teens, mostly people in their 30s, 40s and 50s, people from different countries, who speak different languages, different cultural backgrounds, first- and second-generation immigrants, I think it's quite diverse, people from my area are quite diverse. But nevertheless I think there are groups we can't reach out to, maybe that's inevitable. I think we do a reasonably good job of being inclusive.'[51] Rich recounted speaking to some people who attempted to set up a mutual aid group in Kent. It was based around local cooperatives, but fell apart immediately due to class tensions: 'farm workers and farm owners don't have much in common. It didn't need local government to get involved, that was just doomed', whereas mutual aid groups set up around existing anarchist groups, including Bristol and Newcastle, as well as the London group associated with the squatted social centre 'worked better'.

Another aspect of recuperation involved the *refusal to confront capital*. Anna Kleist argues that there were aspects of the movement that were recuperated from the start, for example the fact that much of the intention of the original groups was not radical or anti-capitalist, it was simply 'shopping on behalf of other people'.[57] Interviewees echoed this, with Bobbie questioning whether a lot of the 'mutual aid' groups were even doing mutual aid at all. 'For the majority of people, it's just, you need your shopping done, I'll do your shopping. They don't want to hear any more about it … they don't want political discussion or see it being linked to political questions.' But they also cited a visible presence of politicised anarchists attempting to intervene in this. Matt argued that although it may look as if CMAGs are simply doing the state's job by patching up capitalism where it fails – and there is a danger that this is the case – there is a greater danger in allowing people to suffer, and also said that, by offering help, you can highlight the failures of the state.[52]

Several interviewees cited the danger or actuality of *recuperation by accepting funding*. Nicole argued, 'I don't think you should receive funding as it will corrupt and compromise what is happening' by compromising prefiguration and splitting paid activists from other participants, although on the flipside it also gives groups more stability and permanence. Nicole's group had come against this issue directly when offered 'five grand' by the local councillor who was trying to co-opt them into the residents' association, but the group decided not to take it. One mutual aid group applied and got funding from a local council, making it clear that their solidarity fund would take some of that money but was not beholden to the council to do anything. 'Anything that doesn't make us reliant on some codified relationship or function is OK from my perspective – we wouldn't say no.'[S2] Rich echoed this, arguing that groups should not take state funding because 'there's a tendency for state agencies to want us to do their work, but they still want us to be accountable to them for their work, but of course we cannot accept that, we need to be clear that any work they get us to do is power they cede to us – it can seem a confrontational thing to say but it's necessary.' He was pleased that other people he organised with, 'even people from state socialist traditions were clear that we cannot accept state funding. We can ask them to fund the services, we can refer people to them … that's a moderate stance which others don't agree with but I believe a tool is a tool.'[S7] Ronny also argued that accepting state funding is 'ideally not desirable' as he believed that mutual aid is weakening and undermining the state: 'It has been unprepared and incapable of responding to the need of the people and if you are taking help from them or collaborating with them, you are just covering where they fall short. They will recover their power and try to raise their authority and you will just become another part of the institution, so you have to be aggressive towards them and take as much power and authority and legitimacy as you can from them.'[S4] However, he argued that 'sometimes you have to make concessions and work with them.'[S4] Amy argued that state funding is not desirable, but not essentially bad as compromises need to be made in the name of organisational sustainability. She continued that money from wealthy people with good politics would be preferable.[S6]

In the face of recuperation, how did groups endure or end? It seems that many of the mutual aid groups lost their energy and momentum after the first wave of the virus, and the movement was much less visible in the second wave. Interviewees cited several reasons for their groups' ending. Rich said: 'it ended because it wasn't needed any more. People found other things to do, other types of activism, the unions started to pick up, others got involved in anti-fascist organising. The way I think of it is not that the organisation ended, but it went dormant.'[57] He narrated that: 'We helped a lot of people and in the end what happened is civilisation didn't collapse and capitalism didn't end, it went back to the standard everyday crises.' But he argued that the exercise in infrastructure building was valuable and that the networks could still be drawn upon later. Michelle, who was relatively new to organising, argued that while she hoped it would continue, she thought 'it's likely we'll just go back to what was before.'[53] All but one interviewee took an antagonistic view of the relationship to the state and the social capital relationship. Matt said that: 'I don't think anyone now I work with will work with police or governmental bodies.'[52] Ronny argues that in other countries with stronger cultures of radical politics, such as Italy, 'there was a struggle by really ideologically minded people to make sure [recuperation] didn't happen.'[54] One argument that recurred throughout is that avoiding recuperation must prefigure something and/or involve creating or appropriating (commoning) infrastructure on a longer-term basis. How this is done is a topic for debate. Certainly, as the interviews illustrated, having a space (a squat or a social centre) was associated with groups who managed to ward off council/state power. Several of the interviewees, as well as online articles, argue that it is important to move beyond mere commodity exchange and helping activities, although it is not always clear what this might look like. If having a space is fundamental to maintaining the radicalism of mutual aid, one might imagine that actions such as squatting, eviction resistance and community self-defence ought to be built into any conception of mutual aid as radical. At the same time, there is a radical element to social reproduction, especially when linked to consciousness-raising around structural conditions. Many interviewees sought to avoid vanguardism and working exclusively with anarchists: 'even though they were from different groups – state socialist, communist, XR, anarchist, they were willing to work together and not to insist on being too dogmatic. I hope that I wasn't pushing the black flag when the red one might've worked.'[57]

Nevertheless, at least half of the interviewees argued for the importance of conscious politics. Nicole argued that although anarchy as an organising principle is effective, it is not sufficient: 'I think the natural spontaneous urge is good but the problem is that you can get takeovers, like we've been talking about; the explicit anarchist model is different in the sense that there are values and processes at the heart of it to ensure its integrity.' This might not be needed during the initial phases, 'when people band together and cooperate', but if you embed explicit anarchist principles during that process 'you can become consciously competent at it, which involves embedding values and processes within it to protect that model. Non-hierarchical models are often threatened because of the world that we live in that is all hierarchical, which is seen as default, so non-hierarchical models need protecting.'[S5]

Similarly, Matt argued that you need to go further than simply helping, towards actions like eviction support, until you may eventually 'start doing things that aren't necessarily legal'. He said all of the current activities are important, but easily recuperated, and drew an analogy with government ops against groups in the USA like the Black Panthers, saying: 'We've not been subject to COINTELPRO ops, but certainly people who work for the council, people who are involved in Labour Party activism, people in positions of power already saying you can do that, you can't do that.'[S2] Rich argued that the reason his group 'succeeded' whereas a lot of others 'failed' was that they 'worked collaboratively, because we had a few very active people who had worked in politics before and were smart enough to know that anarchist organising principles work better'. Having discussed this with radicals in other groups, he thought 'we were very lucky', and rather than being due to 'genius on our part', it was more to do with the timing and composition of group members: 'we had a core group of people willing to invest who were radicals', and 'I think our local councillor was smart enough to keep out the way.... I think we rolled the dice and won.'[S7]

In terms of how to politicise groups or embed anarchist principles, interviewees mentioned tactics like distributing literature as part of the standard welcome message,[58] interventions in group WhatsApp discussions,[59] and the idea of building an autonomous infrastructure, which some interviewees phrased in terms of the idea of 'dual power'.[S2, S7] This is a concept from class-struggle approaches in which a revolutionary situation can be created by building non-ruling-class institutions and power structures which gain sufficient strength to stop ruling-class institutions from being the only game in town. One interviewee stressed the importance of maintaining optimism and determination, citing an idea which he thought came from Žižek, that: 'every revolution fails except the last one, but the last one when it succeeds, redeems not only itself but all previous revolutions. I don't see any of this as a failure.' He argued that: 'Everyone who was involved in mutual aid is going to get involved again with a lot more experience and a lot more infrastructure and we will look back at this experience and say we didn't lose, we learnt.'[57] Currently writing in the spring of 2021, there is not a lot of evidence that the mutual aid movement did revive during the winter as this interviewee predicted; however there does appear to be a resurgence in radical protests and direct action[60] in the face of an incredibly repressive Police, Crime and Sentencing Bill.

Interestingly, even the least radical interviewee, who was completely new to activism, had perceived recuperation as an issue:

I think they are trying to utilise [CMAGs] using the discourse of the Second World War – trying to evade their own responsibility – you can see it in the glorification – glorifying the NHS worker and calling them heroes – slightly recycling 'aren't we a great nation all pulling together', but it's just about being human and doing what we do for each other, there's something very banal about it and the government is using that – I don't like that appropriation of it. I don't think they've discouraged it but I'm worried they're going to control it or turn it into a structure and try to make a new legal entity – I hope they don't. I wonder if they're scared. I think they're incredibly patronising – appropriating it like that.[53]

Ronny argued for the importance of staying radical by setting up more permanent infrastructures, like cooperatives, squats, permaculture, and 'a proper mutual aid network', and also re-emphasised the importance of having a space: 'having a physical space that you control is a really good way to work with people and provide something to people, it's a really important position of leverage'. He continued that, in his experience, people quickly and easily got 'used to you having very radical politics and having your anarchist flag, because they actually don't care that much if you're not pushing your ideology and you're just trying to help them – if you're willing to get your hands dirty, you'll find that people actually don't care if you're an anarchist or a squatter, even the people who may have had reticence, they get used to it and stop caring about it – it proves there's a lot of potential in reaching out to people.' He argued for the value of sticking to facts: 'I always go with the tangible facts first. I don't try to say we should do this because I'm an anarchist and this is the anarchist thing to do, I say – this is the most effective way, or I explain why I think it's

the most effective way.' He gave the example of CMAG involvement in a
rental strike: 'People got quite upset – and I had to say "this is just another
way for people to help each other out, and you don't have to get involved",
and not force them to agree.' He added that: 'I think mutual aid is also
about choosing the people you work with and if people cannot get their
head around it I think it's fine to say you'd get on better with a charity, we
don't need to be too obsessed with reaching out to every LibDem voter
out there.' The option to choose who you organise and have affinity with
is a fundamental aspect of anarchism, although its ease differs with the
composition of a group.

CONCLUSION

In this chapter, I have attempted to exemplify and build upon the anarchist
approach to disaster outlined in Chapters 4 and 5 by drawing on the case
of Covid-19 Mutual Aid Groups in the UK, with a focus on the perspective of the more radical and anarchist strands within the movement, using
interviews and published/online activist accounts. The movement did
not operate so much with an idea of capitalistic 'branding' as did OS, but
it appeared to be partially re-territorialised onto the state form. I argued
that, at some points, OS showed limits to networks and network tech,
showing the need to be grounded in space. Covid-19 Mutual Aid in some
ways showed the opposite, that is, the limits to a totally local movement
grounded only in experience, pragmatics, and chat groups. The anarchists
in the movement showed the need for links to wider politicised struggles,
and/or autonomous space.

Once again, the anarchist analysis of the incompatibility of the social
and political principles is borne out in the interviews. The social capital
approach, in which state power and citizen participation are complementary, is viable only for highly recuperated forms of activism, the
effectiveness of which tends to be undermined by slowness, power-politics,
and bureaucratic capture. Anarchist methods have advantages which
are recognisable to non-anarchists, in terms of speed, felt empowerment, flexibility in individual cases, ease of 'volunteering', and reduced
risk of exclusion and hierarchies. For this reason, grassroots disaster
organisations often default to anarchistic models even without anarchist
involvement or analysis. However, these kinds of tendentially anarchic
groups live constantly on the edge of recuperation by the powerful

discourses of social capital and resilience. My interviews suggested that autonomy and commoning are always on the verge of being lost, and also that disaster initiatives struggle to contribute to lasting networks. Nonetheless, anarchist methods are both effective and non-coextensive with state power, suggesting considerable potential for disaster responses as part of wider politically informed networking.

7
Conclusion

DISASTER ANARCHISM VERSUS CYBERNETIC RATIONALITY

In this book I have argued that the politics of how disasters are managed and resisted is one of the most important dynamics of the 21st century. Capitalism is becoming more and more crisis-prone, and we are currently at a critical moment of decomposition of capital. The decline of the oil economy and its associated structures alongside unprecedented and unpredictable climate change will either usher in a new Dark Age and collapse of civilisation, or else capitalism will undergo another of its epochal transformations.[1] Current discourse indicates that this will be through the introduction of new developments in artificial intelligence, automation and connectedness, new ways of disciplining workers' time, and digital forms of surveillance and social control.[2] This might lead to a hybrid scenario: an increase in authoritarian control through cybernetic management in resource-rich areas and a withdrawal of capital and state from peripheries. The new form of cybernetic authoritarianism may also co-opt ecological themes and mobilise people's fears about climate change and loss of access to resources through fascism, and there is indeed evidence that new forms of eco-fascism are rising. The anonymous author of an article 'Introduction to the Apocalypse'[3] argues that fascism copies and co-opts leftist revolutionary organising, and the new wave of social movement will be no exception: rather than taking communism as its model as in the earlier wave of mass fascism, the new model will take anarchism as its model. This would entail new forms of insidious totalitarian control, manipulation and surveillance through decentralised social technologies and policing.

Welcome to dystopia! This current conjuncture has a basis and a long precedent in a history that has often been ignored, and which I have attempted to outline in this book. This is the history of disaster studies and policy – currently termed Disaster Risk Reduction. In Chapter 2, I detailed the history of DRR, showing how the emergence of disaster studies follows the transformation of the relationship between state and capital and tends towards behaviourist and technocratic responses which emphasise social control and stability rather than humanitarian aspects, effectively carrying out counterinsurgency or public order policing against disasters and affected populations. The more integrated capitalism of the Fordist period responded more coherently to disasters, but today's approaches struggle to mitigate the effects of an increasingly crisis-prone capitalism. Capitalism is stabilised and protected by displacing shocks onto more peripheral territories. Labour becomes more precarious and mobile, and the state relinquishes its welfare functions in favour of New Public Management – a continuation of state and capitalist logics but with decentralised cybernetic components, which treat humans as interchangeable with machines in terms of their functions in meeting the needs of the totality. The emphasis is on indirect population control through technocratic environmental design rather than earlier top-down models of command and control. DRR has been highly imbricated in this transformation.

Early DRR scholars in some ways had the right idea. Their 'wisdom' continues to be echoed by contemporary theorists of social capital as well as Third Way social democrats and left-liberals. They laud the 'post-disaster utopias' where people 'put aside differences' to 'roll up their sleeves' and work together selflessly during the recovery effort, but their ingrained statist logic means they believe solidarity and mutual aid will only ever be temporary – differences and division 'inevitably' settle in and require a specialised bureaucracy to administrate. This mythology justifies the power- and resource-grabs associated with disaster capitalism, although it also reflects a Fordist capitalism/statism with some capacity to channel popular energies, thus to use 'post-disaster utopia' to the benefit of (for example) war efforts. As time goes on, this approach mutates into a post-Fordist disaster management model using cybernetic techniques.

Alongside the history of the transformation of capital, I also undertook a critical exegesis of some of the key assumptions of this ongoing mythology – which continues to dominate contemporary government and media discourse. The cybernetic rationality of DRR begins from the assumption that human subjects are rational, opportunity-seeking agents who can be manipulated through nudges, incentives, and coercion, enforced mainly through technocratic design. Alternatively, where this system fails, they become Hobbesian brutes who need to be repressed through top-down authoritarianism. This view ignores human diversity and complex human needs, desires, histories and cultures; it takes humans to function like cybernetic nodes plugged into and utterly malleable by an external system, who have neither their own ethics (the ethical function is taken on by the technocratic planners) nor their own desires, passions, sources of meaning, etc. (such variables are either treated as pathological or irrelevant, and are significant only indirectly, if they cause observable outcomes). With humans reduced in this way, subjective suffering has little significance, and established or intentional forms of life (whether traditional or emergent) also have no inherent value. 'Culture' is something to be modified and reprogrammed cybernetically, for optimal usefulness.

In this worldview, the stability and continuance of the existing system is paramount, and everything is subjugated to the need for 'control'. Politics in this model is competition for power among elites within a reality which never changes ontologically (the structures of social life remain the same whoever is in power). Thus, disasters are construed as beyond politics – they are predictable exceptions which can be dealt with technically, and 'efficiency' is defined in terms of a rapid return to 'normal', at the expense of democratic process, responsiveness to social movements and popular concerns. Implicit in discourses of 'risk reduction' and 'resilience' are market principles of efficiency and cost-effectiveness, which take precedence to the extent that loss of life, and swingeing attacks on human rights are accepted. This is the basis of securitised responses to disasters, such as the militarised policing of Hurricane Katrina and the reliance on police-enforced lockdown and media-induced moral panic during Covid-19, at the expense of medical and welfare goods such as testing and diagnosis, PPE and safe accommodation. Emergent groups and social movements are understood to be helpful only insofar as they can be co-opted as 'social capital', otherwise they are subsumed in a discourse of danger, disorder, violence, looting, rioting – a force of chaos to be repressed. DRR carves out a role for a specialised bureaucracy, which treats disasters as abstract and generic, empowering a subset of actors who 'own' the disaster policy/knowledge field in a way that gives the impression of expertise in responding to *any* given disaster, without specialist knowledge in specific 'disaster agents' or contexts of impact. The idea that all disasters and their impact on diverse people, groups and cultures can be managed in a similar way is an exercise in empire-building which justifies the need for central agencies like FEMA, SAGE and COBRA, whose implicit core purpose is ensuring a rapid return to capitalism-as-usual.

Chapter 3 covered critical theories and discourses around emergent dynamics in the world system and their relationship to disasters. The purpose of this chapter was twofold. First, I sought to contextualise the assumptions of the mainstream, neoliberal discourses outlined in the previous chapter, showing how they serve to legitimate the roles of capitalism and the state in the contemporary world system. This critique of mainstream paradigms was already covered to an extent in Chapter 2, and Chapter 3 expands on this by considering alternative frameworks in more detail, including left-liberal, neo-Marxist, world-systems and poststructuralist approaches. The chapter outlines how they theorise the roles played by the state, NGOs and the market in disaster preparedness, relief and recovery. These approaches provide important insights into the emerging dynamics of securitisation, politics of fear, moral panic, 'shock doctrine' and disaster capitalism. It was argued that these critiques are essential for understanding the current conjuncture, but that they do not offer much in the way of radical alternatives.

IN DEFENCE OF ANARCHISM

The main purpose of Chapter 3 was to lay the groundwork for setting out the specificity, original contribution, and *necessity* for an anarchist approach to understand and work within, against and beyond the disasters of capitalism. In this book, I aimed to advocate the importance of anarchism as an epistemological tool for understanding what movements are already doing, and also as a comprehensive ethical approach. I applied this approach to the case histories of two very visible social movements with strong anarchist elements in the current conjuncture. Anarchist theory works well to help understand movements' achievements and dilemmas, while Occupy Sandy, Covid-19 Mutual Aid and other disaster anarchist movements contribute much to our understanding of anarchism. The experience and analysis of such movements will become more useful and prevalent as capitalist shocks become more common and the state withdraws its resources even further from peripheral areas and economies. Disaster anarchist movements contribute to, and offer examples and inspiration to, a wider movement for anarchist utopias within, against and beyond the accelerating climate and resource catastrophes of capitalism.

Theory

In Chapter 4, I aimed to theoretically construct an anarchist theory of disaster. I drew on several texts and traditions within and adjacent to anarchism, including autonomist Marxism, feminism, post-development, and decolonial theory, (some) poststructuralists, theories of the commons and communisation, and ethnographic works on horizontalism and indigenous movements. Even though these theories are very diverse, they have in common a challenge to the assumption that everything is either part of the state or else is chaotic, violent or uncoordinated. They argue for the existence of an autonomous realm of social life that is organised according to a different principle and is structurally in conflict with the state. Anarchism, a specific political/ethical theory, is constructed in reference to anarchy, or horizontal power in everyday life, and seeks to expand anarchy. I argued that much of everyday life is already anarchy and explored anarchist theories of social organisation and mutual aid in the context of disasters. I also considered some possible objections to this view: (1) the post-anarchist objection to an essentialised human nature that is uncorrupted by power; (2) questions over why the social principle does not triumph; and (3) a question concerning whether an exclusive or elite group can still engage in mutual aid. I began to answer some of these objections, but they are elaborated further in the later case study chapters. I also developed some themes to lay the groundwork for the later chapters on social movement practices:

(1) The social principle as a logic of organisation is in conflict with, rather than complementary to the political principle and the state. The social principle reimagines the temporality and scale of radical social change. There is an emphasis on the small scale, on degrowth and social recomposition, on a society bubbling with transgressive life through overlapping societies, groups, and organisations whose affinities and relations are immeasurable and un-mappable. Social change is both immanent and prefigurative, and does not require scaling-up through unity or a vanguard in

order to be extended or politicised; such vanguardism tends to defer lived anarchy to the future. Transgression and insurrection are already a part of everyday life and are observable everywhere when everyday life is examined using an anarchist epistemology. Anarchist ethics argues that they need to be expanded.

(2) Mutual aid is a radical practice oriented by a set of ethical values that begins from a utopian reversal of perspective. Rather than merely a temporary suspension of division, disasters create the conditions for the reappearance of the social principle due to a weakening of the social order. Disaster utopias have the potential to change lives, shared beliefs and perspectives. They do not require state mediation, but must resist external power if they are to survive.

(3) Alternative economies and the commons refer to the idea that capitalism and its states are unlikely to surrender land and the means of production willingly. Communisation theory and insurrectionary anarchism provide a set of tactics for reappropriation of enclosed commons, including voluntaristic and insurrectionary approaches such as subsistence practices, economic localisation, and networking among different communes, as well as militant resistance to defend these autonomous/liberated spaces.

(4) Technology, infrastructure and resources is an area of debate which has important practical implications for the tactics adopted by movements in disasters. Anarchists take a very wide range of positions, ranging from optimistic, utopian projections for the use of technology to highly pessimistic fears and dystopian projections of the impact of unbridled technological progress. Anarchism also offers theories of tactical media and hacking, where technologies produced by and for capitalism can be reappropriated and repurposed.

(5) Repression and recuperation refer to the various ways in which the state acts to decompose and mediate immanent networked bonds and either commodify the creative energies of the grassroots or subordinate them to the political principle (or both). Repression is the action of attempting to subdue someone or something by force and usually aims to destroy, disrupt, disempower, or demoralise movements, whereas co-optation, used synonymously with recuperation, means subsuming outsiders into the elite/mainstream/

state in order to manage opposition and maintain stability. Co-optation can occur via the state, often via the formal charity sector and discourses of social capital, or by capitalism through commodification. Co-opted initiatives lose much of the vital force of the social principle, becoming primarily political-principle or instrumental entities.

These five themes were followed and developed in the structure of the subsequent empirical chapters, which provide the case studies of Occupy Sandy (OS) and Covid-19 Mutual Aid Groups (CMAGs). The core argument throughout has been that the state needs the grassroots to survive, but the opposite is not the case: There is a radical difference between social and political principles, not the complementary overlap assumed in social capital theory. Although spontaneous order can be momentarily helpful for the system by filling in gaps left by state and capital during disasters, thus reducing some kinds of disorder and danger to the system, ultimately the state and capital will seek to exploit and reappropriate unmediated relationships by re-coding and re-ordering mutual aid relationships and peripheral economies into new political allegiances that can be subordinated and exploited by disaster capitalists.

Mutual aid: case studies

In Chapter 5, I drew on the case of Occupy Sandy, which mobilised relief after Hurricane Sandy in the northeast USA in 2012. I undertook interviews in New York on the third anniversary of the hurricane in 2015. In Chapter 6, I drew on the case of Covid-19 Mutual Aid Groups, which mobilised during the coronavirus pandemic of 2020. This mobilisation was international, but in my fieldwork I focused on groups in London during the first lockdown in the spring and summer of 2020. Both movements referred to their practices using the terminology of 'mutual aid' and both organised using decentralised and horizontalist, notionally non-hierarchical principles, that can be understood in epistemological terms as instances of the social principle, or anarchy in action. Politically, both had significant anarchist elements, although they also encompassed a range of other ideological positions. The contexts of these movements, as well as their political content, also exhibited many differences.

Organisationally both movements illustrated how anarchist organising models are highly effective in disaster situations, ironically even in the terms of the state. Anarchist movements are able to mobilise rapidly and exhibit a flexibility and adaptability that bureaucratised institutions often lack. For this reason, anarchist movements, when viewed from a transcendental state's-eye view, can often be misrecognised as exhibiting neoliberal virtues of 'resilience' and 'social capital'. OS illustrated in practice that self-organised networks with little bureaucracy create faster and easier connections than bureaucratic organisations, giving them greater speed, flexibility and connectedness. While communities were organising mutual aid spontaneously and independently of any social movement, OS offered activists and volunteers disillusioned with the traditional agencies an opportunity to 'plug in' to existing efforts. CMAGs also organised along anarchist principles to an extent, although this was somewhat complicated by a nested structure, parts of which replicated the territorial categories of the state (e.g. national, and borough/council ward). Again, anarchist organising principles were felt to be more flexible and adaptable than hierarchical approaches, capable of fast and efficient organising, and also better able to understand and meet participants' needs. They were also seen to have affective/emotional advantages, such as making participants feel empowered and providing a sense of connectedness nurtured through consensus processes (although this was not always the case, especially when particular perspectives were sidelined or silenced).

Mutual aid can be understood as a space for the development of radical ethics, which expands as the state recedes. The relationship between mutual aid, radical values and prefigurative politics was shown to be rich and deeply imbricated, yet also messy and complex. Interviewees in both OS and CMAGs expressed strong concerns that mutual aid might simply paper over the cracks left by the receding state in order to ensure the return of the smooth running of capitalism. Since nearly everyone I spoke to was broadly radical, most of them tended to favour accounts of mutual aid which viewed it as a form of direct action that prefigures a stateless society and as raising awareness of structural conditions. Some argued that this meant that the 'helping' aspects of mutual aid should be linked to more radical actions, such as occupations, eviction resistance, community self-defence, protests, and being explicit and vocal about radical politics. It is important not to underplay the very real divisions in both of the movements between these more radical perspectives and those who wished to keep 'politics' separate from mutual aid, nor to suggest these are two mutually exclusive 'camps'. Some radicals used 'politics' to mean representative politics and thus saw their radical work as apolitical, while others were in favour of downplaying radical claims for tactical reasons, such as not alienating potential recipients. This book has argued that apolitical mutual aid is not possible and that seemingly 'apolitical' perspectives serve to reinforce the status quo. Sometimes, the political/apolitical struggle maps broadly onto the related dichotomy of the social versus the political principle: the 'apolitical' is the politically recuperated variant, involving an undeclared 'common sense' politics which recuperates social principle movements under political hegemony. At other times, the perceived fetishising of political slogans or words, or of 'politics' as sectarian or party identities, get in the way of the operation of the social principle.

It was argued that even where explicit politics is avoided, mutual aid may have political effects through the recomposition of the social principle (or social recomposition), through prefiguring a more equal and stateless society and gift economies, through structural critique and consciousness-raising, and through direct action. It was argued that the general critique of anarchist movements – that non-hierarchy is impossible – is deeply flawed. Mutual aid is easier to practise in relatively homogeneous and equal groups, but where there is intent it is not impossible to harmonise across differences. In the context of capitalist inequalities, differences manifest in both values and in socio-economic status of participants, both within and between activist groups and communities.

Both OS and CMAG movements experienced issues around defining the boundaries of inclusion, for example, the extent to which shared values and principles should be a prerequisite for mutual aid. Usually, movements veer towards inclusion, which means limiting exclusion to those who themselves hold exclusive or oppressive values (e.g. fascists). The orientation to action and relationships rather than ideology leads to inclusiveness, but is easily mistaken as apolitical and recuperated by middle-class values associated with NGO activities. Furthermore, inclusiveness in a highly unequal society tends to reinforce hierarchies between helpers and helped. Undermining this distinction is fundamental to the principle of mutuality in mutual aid.

Alienation between helpers and helped leads to a further difficulty linked to the voluntaristic nature of groups. Voluntarism is essential to anarchist organising (people cannot be forced, coerced or incentivised to stay).[4] This means that activists who come from outside a community may drop useful projects that communities may have come to rely on.[5] Even those working within their own community may find that their time is overstretched, for example if they need to return to work. While consistency and commitment are important, they are not always possible in the absence of external resources or longer-term infrastructure as activists are prone to burnout and also need resources to survive. This is not a serious conceptual problem for the organisation of entire anarchist societies or in certain other contexts, such as those with a universal income. It is, however, a problem in contexts of neoliberalism and precarity, where participation in dominant systems is both difficult to avoid and tends to sap energy and motivation. This difficulty seems to have increased over time, as earlier activists (e.g. 1970s–80s) could 'drop out' more easily and with fewer costs, and this coincided with more vibrant, sustainable movements. There may be much to learn from global Southern social movements about sustaining commitment in precarious conditions. Southern movements among the poor are nearly always dealing with extremely precarious situations, such as insecure, informal or squatted housing, lack of basic services and shortage of income, yet often exhibit remarkable continuity and longevity. What this looks like is incredibly diverse, but examples of autonomous solutions include squatting or occupying entire areas (barrios or land projects) with organised community structure, self-provision of services like schooling, community health and water, autonomous food growing, and militant campaigns demanding various kinds of provision and sanctions against repression.[6]

One mitigation against replicating neoliberal precarity comes from anarchist organising principles themselves, which is to encourage the proliferation of smaller alternative projects rather than a single large group or united front. In this way, the impact of a single group dissolving is less likely to be experienced as collapse. Instituting alternative economies and commons is an essential response to issues of alienation and inequality. One example of commoning is the occupation of public space – a tactic notoriously used by OWS, which tends to bring movements into conflict with state agencies. OS used a more dispersed spatial strategy that was also more localised, and, through cooperation with churches and community centres used as distribution hubs, led to a less conflictual situation. CMAGs tended to organise online, creating common virtual spaces for communication, information and knowledge, with physical aid being undertaken by individuals under conditions of social distancing. This was a less conflictual strategy than the occupation of physical space.

The idea of logics of aggregation – which can occur online and through the repeated use of slogans – was particularly important for both OWS and OS. This was considered a form of the commons and a claim to space which is gaining increasing purchase in the internet age, but which is limited in certain ways. The ongoing importance of being grounded in space and territoriality was illustrated through the CMAGs, where those associated with a social centre or squat were often better able to maintain their radicalism while reaching out to wider communities than those which only operated through WhatsApp groups. Some interviewees viewed the NGO sector, local and national state agencies, existing technological infrastructures, and the architectural infrastructures of cities as potential terrains of struggle for commoning, while others stressed the importance of new local projects such as cooperatives and community gardens.

The issue of money and use of funds was an area of both tension and possibility. OS used funds from its broad network to set up grassroots participatory budgeting projects, while CMAGs set up solidarity funds, although it was argued that there are dangers associated with the commodification and outsourcing of mutual aid when the role of richer/ privileged participants is reduced to mere donors. One big difference between Occupy Sandy and Covid-19 Mutual Aid is that donations for the former seemed to be channelled towards the commons (setting up housing cooperatives, community gardens, sustainable projects) whereas donations in the latter were often aimed at individuals via solidarity funds. I think this is problematic and probably emblematic of the general context of individualisation. The use of state or NGO money was also controversial as a potential channel of recuperation, particularly when conditions were attached.

I also considered activists' attitudes towards and uses of technology and infrastructure. I argued that, traditionally, anarchists are wary of modernity, progressivism, extractivism and techno-fixes. Nevertheless, there are strands of techno-utopianism within anarchism, particularly associated with the open-source movement and hacker culture, which focus on dispersed, uncontrollable networks. There is a latent conflict between this strand and eco-anarchist and primitivist views, which reject technology as part of civilisation and thus alienation from nature. Many anarchists prefer to use technologies which prefigure smaller-scale socio-technical infrastructure and meet certain ethical criteria, technologies for decentralised living, and the situated and ethical ('tactical') use of technology. In the case studies, OS's use of technology for mobilisation was unprecedented, and the first of its kind and scale in mutual aid disaster relief. There was a strong strand of tech-optimism in the Occupy movement, drawing on the history in OWS where internet technology linked localised occupations to a global movement. However, the tactical use of exploitative profit-making company Amazon, was not unproblematic. With the CMAGs, technology was used in ways which mirrored and intensified established uses in society, with all the groups working mainly virtually. Technologies were used to substitute for face-to-face interaction. There were also links to an international movement through publishing on anarchist websites. Both movements used a multiplicity of technologies to mobilise donations and mutual aid, sometimes 'hacking' mainstream technologies created for commercial means, and sometimes creating their own open-source alternatives.

Recuperation and repression were argued to be two sides of the same coin of social control, with repression referring to the action of subduing someone or something by force, and recuperation/co-optation meaning a process of subsuming outsiders into the elite/mainstream in order to manage opposition and maintain stability. For OS and the CMAGs, there were similarities in the contexts within which both movements were operating, particularly in terms of the ways in which the states securitised disaster conditions and attempted to recuperate movement energies to mobilise them in the interests of stabilising capital. The state and media tended to downplay the radical aspects of both movements and misrecognised their criticisms or unwillingness to work with traditional state and NGO agencies as apolitical, or as justifying the rollback of the state, rather than as prefiguring something new.

While previous movements like Common Ground after Katrina and OWS had been violently repressed by the state, OS and CMAGs were more prone to de-radicalisation through recuperation in neoliberal discourse and policy or NGO-isation through bureaucratisation and funding. OS was a disaster for the reputation of the state, putting established disaster relief efforts to shame and showing that horizontal movements are effective even within the terms of the state. It was almost impossible for the state to stay silent on the issue, and the DHS document, *The Resilient Social Network* was analysed as an emblematic exercise in the attempted co-optation of the creative energies of the grassroots into a de-radicalised associationalist discourse of 'social capital', creating conditions for re-coding and re-ordering mutual aid relationships, infrastructure and peripheral economies into political allegiances that can be subordinated to the logic of the state and exploited by disaster capitalists.

The recuperative strategies of the state appeared more well-honed during the coronavirus pandemic. Although my interviewees were anarchists, the wider movement was less politically coherent than OS and partly incorporated in the resilience agenda from the start. It was argued that a large part of the movement was non-radical or at least less radical than anarchists, some responding to government and media signalling in favour of community support, others emerging from a disillusioned left-wing reformist movement following the electoral defeat of Jeremy Corbyn. This large contingent of non/less-radicals created a dynamic which further recuperated or repressed radical or potentially radical factions by silencing political discussions, reducing mutual aid to mere 'helping' functions and preventing more radical direct actions like resisting evictions and police brutality. There was also a dynamic involving the adoption of rule-based discourses and organisational structures deriving from bureaucratised NGOs; the emergence of unchallenged hierarchies and closed core groups; the refusal to confront capital; and recuperation through the acceptance of funding with conditions attached. Nevertheless, anarchist members of the CMAGs persisted, and their experiences have much to tell us about dynamics of recuperation, as did the experiences of OS.

Utopia

What is the utopianism of disaster anarchism? This has remained implicit throughout this book, but I would like to contend that all critique and prefigurative practice has a utopian vision, even if this is partial, imperfect, impossible, and a product of its times. Utopias do not have to be blueprints, and they do not have to be closed, but they can offer practical ethical guidance and inspiration in the present and can help shape desires for a future beyond capitalist disasters. In this book, I argued that anarchists need a new theory and practice of mutual aid in, against and beyond disasters to address the post-Fordist context. Often anarchists have responded as if they are still fighting the older Fordist context, thinking that simply decentralising is enough, and that defending anarchism in cybernetic terms as 'efficient' and 'flexible' will win people over to the new society. The analysis of changed context and its recuperation of decentralising approaches and of disaster utopias has shown that this is not sufficient. However, as the state withdraws, spaces are created for experimenting with new values, economic models, forms of life, etc. Utopias help us to transgress hegemonic 'common sense', pointing towards what is desired and valued rather than what is commonplace. I have argued elsewhere that prefiguration is a form of utopia, because it produces utopian affects such as *hope* which can help us believe that another world is possible.[7] People in a 'culture of silence'[8] may go through life not thinking about what they desire because they do not think it is possible or they are focused on surviving; the dominant system is treated as an outer envelope identical with 'reality' or 'what is possible'. Utopias indicate, stimulate, point to, ask questions about what people desire, which can be transformative. Affected communities can suddenly experience an 'outside' in the aftermath of a disaster, a possibility of organising through the social principle without top-down control, and this experience makes the present order seem both intolerable and changeable. Sometimes it is only with experience of the constituent power of the social principle that the question of the desirability of the present is even asked.

Drawing on my theoretical analysis and the interviews with activists and their experiences of prefigurative alternatives, but also on conjecture and extrapolation, I would like to propose some utopian counter-principles for anarchist disaster response and relief. My hope is for these to form a starting point, rather than an end point, for discussions, political imagination, radical pedagogy and consciousness-raising.

(1) Cybernetic responses start from impacts on systems, ignore affects, and think from the perspective of power. It is crucial to reverse this perspective and instead start from impacts on concrete humans and other living beings and the meaningful structures of life which are embedded in objects, habitats, etc. When we look at them from the perspective of people and communities rather than the stability of the state/capitalism,

disasters are often experienced not so much as manageable emergencies but instead as a kind of collapse of the order of the world assumed in their 'common sense', a collapse of cosmic order (for instance, the world as a safe and predictable place), an unthinkable event or a nightmare come true with deep emotional impacts, such as trauma and grief. Disasters are not normal. This experiential aspect is a huge hurdle to approaches which seek to normalise and manage disaster: such affects have to be denied, disavowed, channelled, or tamed. From a reversed perspective, the very fact that disasters are normalised indicts the system of social life. Those who trust authorities, trust them to protect people from such cosmic ruptures; those who distrust authorities, often distrust them precisely because they are unable or unwilling to do this. In most cases, disasters should not be happening, and they definitely should not be *routinely* happening. This blows the lid off the claims of disaster technocrats to useful expertise. It does not necessarily discredit disaster management as such; the exceptional harms caused by disasters justify a lot of effort to foresee and avoid them. Yet if one gets to the point of disaster management (the main focus of DRR), one has in a sense *already failed*. Avoidable or not, a disaster is always a partial collapse in the ability of a social world to meet needs and provide stable sources of meaning; it cannot be 'managed' without belittling the suffering involved.

(2) People are not just nodes. Anarchist views of human nature or personality vary greatly, from theories which emphasise external relations and determinants (class, civilisation, positionality ...) to those positing pre-personal vital forces, to those drawing on existentialist views of responsibility or Stirnerian uniqueness. Without getting into the debates among these positions, they all reverse perspective in the sense of starting from the position of each person. In contrast, cybernetic terms such as 'control' and 'coordination', even when they appear decentralised, assume a god's-eye/state's-eye, functionalist view, in which people are moulded or nudged to perform extrinsic tasks in the interests of the system. This is compatible with a certain degree of relative autonomy of individual actors to respond rationally or irrationally to incentives and deterrents, but it is ultimately a top-down approach, considering disasters in terms of how they affect the powerful or the system. A truly horizontalist utopianism would facilitate people to 'plug in' to tasks – and create new tasks – based on their preferences and capabilities. It should be easy to just turn up, or contact a group organising aid, and quickly find one's way to an activity

CONCLUSION

suited to one's abilities and principles. (This is historically how anarchists have organised large-scale events such as summit protests, with different 'affinity groups' or 'spokes' taking on different tasks). This approach would encourage multiple small groups and a proliferation of projects with different emphases, methods, and some overlap and redundancy, rather than either centrally managed disaster efforts under a FEMA-like lead body, or 'left-unity' initiatives focusing all energies on a single campaign. The latter approach often risks activists burning out and raises the danger of communities with persistent needs being abandoned when another issue becomes the fashion of the moment.

(3) People are neither behaviourist rational subjects nor Hobbesian brutes. They are complex and diverse bundles of forces held together by meanings and desire-structures deriving from historical, social, political and personal circumstances, as well as individual differences. State simplifications, and those of money as universal equivalent (for instance, abstract labour-power), are necessarily reductive and exclusionary. If a simple, invariant human nature existed (whether it be that of a computer node, a stockbroker, a blank slate, a Hobbesian aggressivity, or anything else), it would allow the construction of systems designed around this core nature, which thus function smoothly, fairly and without remainder. In fact, people vary greatly, in ways which are barely understood. Any utopian model must take account of this: a blueprint or model perfect for some people will usually be inappropriate for others. This recognition also precludes the idea that any person, model or system should 'control' a group or population through authority or design, as there will always be constitutive exclusions and forces of excess in such cases.

(4) Disasters are not 'risks' or 'security threats'. This seems a paradoxical thing to say: in an everyday sense, disasters are clearly both risks and threats to human security. What is meant here, however, is that the application of risk and security frames to disasters are functionally inappropriate. Disasters cannot be shot or tased or thrown in jail; Mother Nature cannot be given an ASBO.[9] The state may think it can use network disruption against pandemics, but it is hardly applicable to other disaster agents. Even moral panics are powerless against disasters: it is easy enough to panic about (say) looters, 'covidiots' or evacuation refusers, but this likely has little effect on natural or systemic sources of disasters. Such panics tend in fact to increase the harm caused by disasters by adding an additional level of trauma for survivors, some of whom may even be

179

incapable of complying with top-down disaster responses which fail to take account of personal capabilities and circumstances (a 'stay at home' order, for instance, assumes that everyone has a secure place to live). Therefore, securitisation and moral panics around disasters should be avoided. Rather, compassionate, humanitarian responses to people traumatised or devastated by disasters should be encouraged. This is perfectly realistic; most people's first impulse is already to help, not to repress. However, this does not seem to override responsiveness to moral panics and shaming. Compassionately, it is important to recognise that disaster circumstances leave survivors more stressed and distressed than normal circumstances, and also that some of their normal coping strategies will be unavailable. As a result, norms should be loosened, not tightened, during disasters. Disasters are human disasters and not crises of order. Tolerance for deviance must be greater, not less. This does not preclude communities deciding to institute their own rules or protection measures, but these should be democratic, ideally decided by consensus, and part of a structure of voluntaristic groups and communities. Emphasis should be placed on ensuring access to the goods necessary for survival, rather than securitising or moralising them. Criminalisation and condemnation of atypical or incomprehensible reactions must stop. People should have a right to respond autonomously to disasters, with an assumption that most people, most of the time, will respond cooperatively through mutual aid.

(5) Encourage and trust mutual aid. During disasters, normal organisations and procedures often stop working. Bureaucracies become too slow, fight among themselves, or fixate on maintaining control. Approaches based on the social principle are more fluid and cannot be recuperated into social capital discourse without losing much of this fluidity. Mutual aid responses should therefore be in the lead of disaster response. The criterion for effective response is not a technical efficiency criterion or a model, but the creation of relations which generate flows to affected communities. Mutual aid practices are first of all grassroots and participatory. People coming into the situation have a right to participate on their own terms, but the community affected is always the first responder. Diversity of tactics is important, both to include a wider range of difference, and to allow the testing of different responses.

(6) People providing mutual aid should seek to respond to the real needs and desires of affected people or communities. They should also take into account human needs and capabilities – both those which are

standard to most humans, and those which vary individually or across groups. External actors – including mutual aid groups, state agencies and NGOs – should focus on meeting specific, concrete needs as requested by survivors. A worthwhile response is defined by its relationship to concrete survivor needs, not the overall social impact of the response. Practical tasks, such as delivering food or providing first aid, should not be tied to wider systems of control. Spatial control measures which interfere with volunteer practices should be avoided. Public and commercial spaces and resources which are inactive due to a disaster should usually be made available for survivors and volunteers.

(7) Market rationality, cost-effectiveness and efficiency are *not* desirable aspects of disaster responses. Efficiency is generally a way of achieving marginal improvements in standard processes taking place in predictable settings. The main gains are economic, not human, and the human cost of disasters renders such concerns irrelevant. The best responses to disasters are not efficient but have sufficient slack and redundancy to handle outlying cases and unforeseen circumstances (which are likely to arise frequently, due to the limits of state simplification). Standardised, McDonaldised packaged commodities are a staple of neoliberalism – whether in cost-effective health services, standardised best practice, or Competence Based Education and Training.[10] These methods are generally ineffective in meeting *diverse* needs or dealing with emergent situations or complex problems. They are contrary to the humanising treatment of each unique individual.

(8) Disaster preparation should be inclusive and, instead of monological 'education' or 'training', should encourage awareness of different views and angles on disasters, as well as the critical capacity and autonomy to assess and choose among these, in response to human-scale suffering and scarcity. Teaching people 'the one way' to optimally stay safe or deliver services during an unpredictable emergency is at once exclusionary, politically dangerous, and misleading. It is exclusionary because those unable or unwilling to follow the one specified method are excluded, or even (in contexts of moral panics) shamed and demonised. It is politically dangerous, because it encourages uncritical belief in rote-learnt scripts and uncritical trust in authority. It is misleading because it creates an exaggerated sense that the answers are 'already known' and fails to develop critical capacities regarding uncertain information and unknown or rapidly changing situations. Development of basic survival/prepping,

self-help and mutual aid skills through skill-shares can also help prepare people to play an active role during disasters.

(9) Post-disaster repair/rebuilding is just as important as the immediate response to the disaster itself. The political/economic misuse of disasters to socially cleanse or gentrify areas, transform cities in line with top-down agendas, or profiteer on rebuilding are callous and politically reactionary. There is no 'return to normal' without restoration of sources of survival and of the sense of cosmic order. Survivors have a right to the expect restoration of pre-survival levels of prosperity, if necessary by redistribution. Plans for rebuilding and post-disaster changes are choices for the affected community, not the central state or other external actors. Where possible, cooperative measures put in place during disasters should be retained and expanded within affected communities. Individualising support should be avoided in favour of creating sustainable commons – for example through forming cooperatives and longer-term projects for decentralised food and energy production.

BROADER RELEVANCE AND LIMITATIONS

International relevance

I do not claim to be formulating a global theory of disasters or a globally applicable formula for disaster relief. Indeed, core to my argument has been a critique of the dominant paradigm which *does* treat disasters as 'generic' and disaster management as a standardised package. One enormous limit to this book is that both of the examples hail from rich, developed nations and that I do not cover any examples from the global South, which is much more prone to disasters and the effects of disasters and experiences issues such as famine and food and water insecurity that are not covered in these pages. This is not only an issue which limits the global applicability of the theory, but also its comprehensiveness – 'Third World issues' like food and water insecurity are likely to be issues of increasing import even in seemingly rich countries like America in the very near future (food banks have already proliferated in both the UK and USA), and interviews with activists and communities experienced in dealing with these issues would have much to offer. Further research is clearly needed here.

While this work focuses on the UK and USA (in fact, on two of the three major global cities),[11] my contention is that the approach taken in this book does have wider relevance for international movements, though I wish to be careful not to overstate this. Disasters are becoming more frequent due to climate change, with impending climate catastrophe. Finding ways to recompose communities while also dismantling the structures which got us into this mess is increasingly a question of survival as well as emancipation. Anarchism offers an excellent way to do this, because its emphasis is on decentralised community response; it is also particularly adaptable to situational variations because it favours local action. In addition, state responses to disasters take place within similar parameters, and neoliberalism is a background problem in most of the world. Anarchist responses are thus available to handle a wide variety of disasters in different social conditions involving different disaster agents. There is a danger that mutual aid could be used to justify the further withdrawal of funds and de-linking of peripheries on global as well as national and city-scales, but these are problems of capitalism rather than problems of anarchism. It seems dubious at this stage to refrain from directly meeting needs in the (probably vain) hope that the resultant gaps will be filled by the state. The danger of recuperation has already been discussed extensively, and this book depends on an important distinction between autonomous and recuperated types of self-organisation. When states are absent for reasons of disaster, austerity or depletion, mutual aid responses will tend to be autonomous as a matter of course. If capitalism recomposes, likely it will seek to recuperate horizontalist practices, but it is by no means guaranteed that it will succeed. If it does not, autonomous movements need to be ready to substitute for a decaying state and build a new society.

Anti-capitalist, horizontalist, and often explicitly anarchist movements are currently organising in/against/beyond natural disasters around the globe. In the context of Covid-19, mutual aid groups of various kinds are prevalent worldwide. Examples include mutual aid groups in Poland[12] and grassroots organisations in Spain, supported by the networks, knowledge and infrastructure of previous movements, including 15M, anti-racist, feminist and migrant movements.[13] Movements have arisen in Brazil to support precarious cultural workers.[14] In Delhi, India, civil society actors, including NGO and social workers, engaged in extra-institutional direct action to resist state violence against oppressed

Muslim minorities, and to coordinate the supply of food and medicine to communities in need.[15] In China, examples include an online support group for women affected by domestic violence; there was also a spontaneous response, the Red Helmets, when Covid-19 first broke out in Wuhan.[16] A movement in Singapore, PinkDot, which is usually associated with protest, has directed its community work inward for Covid-19, delivering care packages to LGBT activists in need.[17] There are also significant anarchist movements in Indonesia[18] and the Philippines,[19] which have long histories in anti-colonial struggles. Cuba is an oft-cited example of a highly effective disaster mitigation and management system, and while this is facilitated by legislation and strong national leadership it also relies on strong community-based knowledge and networked organisation.[20] Similarly in Venezuela, there was strong community group involvement in the Covid-19 response; Venezuelan community groups have been organising to counteract the impacts of inflation and economic collapse for a long time.[21] In South Africa, the informal settlement movement Abahlali base'Mjondolo initially took to the streets, protesting the emphasis on Covid-19 over routine health/hygiene problems of the poor before reorganising for mutual aid. The group appears to have continued anti-eviction direct action even during the country's particularly draconian lockdown.[22]

Beyond the context of Covid-19, one could consider a wide range of cases, from disaster relief in Puerto Rico to global health movements like ACT-UP.[23] In the global South, self-organisation to meet urgent community needs in areas like clean water, sewage, basic healthcare, eviction resistance and firefighting is often an integral part of political organising; these same networks will also usually be the first responders in the more exceptional kind of disasters. Struggles for 'service delivery', such as those in South Africa and the Argentine *piqueteros*, also respond to everyday disaster. These types of activism are distinct from but nonetheless affinal to the self-help, DIY approaches taken by autonomous social movements in the North, which often encompass lower-tech ways of life such as eco-communes and squatting. One might also look at the massive upsurge in community self-help projects following economic crashes – such as those in Argentina in 2001 and Greece after 2008 – as examples of disaster anarchism. In Argentina, the responses to the sudden loss of survival sources ranged from worker occupations of factories, and their management as cooperatives, to community assemblies and militant street protests.[24] In Greece, initiatives ranged from striking doctors providing free healthcare, to protesters disrupting eviction-related auctions.[25] Campaigns such as those relating to the Bhopal disaster and movements related to extractivist pollution and resultant accidents/ disasters in the Niger Delta put disasters in more of a structural context.[26] There are probably many more examples I am unaware of. Anarchists in Europe have also been active in struggles around precarity, including anti-austerity protests, base-union organising, and support for refugees following the 2015 crisis. Sites like Lesbos and Calais often have the feel of permanent disasters, which are constantly worsened by statist depletion and repression, so the issue of disaster anarchism is certainly relevant to refugee solidarity organising.

My hope is that the theory and examples developed in this book will act as inspiration for movements elsewhere. Nonetheless, the very brief overview above shows there are many other movements I could have drawn on (and would very much like to in further studies, given the opportunity), and drawing on different examples may well have induced me to tell a very different story. Different areas and communities are facing very different threats; climate change, pandemics, and the collapse or reconfiguration of capital/state relations will not affect everyone equally nor in the same way, and different areas also have different social movement compositions and histories, as well as different underlying problems. In this book I have argued that anarchism is a particularly adaptable ideology because it favours local knowledge and action, but other approaches such as degrowth and the cooperative movement, decolonial struggles and indigenous movements also have much to offer.

Precarity, stress and everyday disaster

The book may also have a contribution to make to our understanding of precarity, stress and everyday disaster. Although I have argued that disasters should not be treated as 'generic', neither are they inherently different from smaller emergencies and accidents or from larger-scale catastrophes. The complexity of human and ecological impact is the same, and differs mainly quantitatively or in scale. Disasters differ from one another, first in terms of disaster type, and second in terms of the situation of the people affected (e.g. North vs South). The only thing generic to disasters is that normal means of meeting needs have broken down, threatening the integrity of everyday life (seen as a system of meanings, desires, relations and actions). Rupture in the structure of everyday life is something that happens to many people struggling to make ends meet in precarious economies, outside of 'exceptional' situations. There may be a difference in the 'disaster agent' when homes are destroyed by flooding or earthquakes and when police demolish a migrant camp or evict a squat, or when Syrians flee the country after their homes are bombed, but the human impact on an experiential level may be similar. In Chapter 3, I critiqued mainstream approaches which portray the networked, high-speed structure of the neoliberal economy in a positive light. The neoliberal economic system fails to offer economic security and has corroded social 'safety nets' – both those of welfare states and those arising informally in communities. Mainstream approaches to disaster ignore the way in which everyday life under capitalism for many people is already a disaster and an existential threat. Even in the North, issues like homelessness and food insecurity are severe enough for anarchist responses to arise (Food Not Bombs, squatters' movements, etc.). The critique and alternatives put forward in this book therefore have relevance beyond the boundaries of 'exceptional' disasters.

Indeed, neoliberal capitalism *relies on* a state of permanent or imminent disaster for a large swathe of the human population. Precarity creates a new subset of workers who are actually core or central to production within the new economy, yet who are at the same time peripheral because they are denied social rights.[27] Under precarity, systems of work are rationalised and standardised in a manner that strips people of their humanity, perceiving value only in terms of homogenised and quantifiable outputs in a process that has been termed McDonaldisation.[28] This process is taking place not only within the world of work, but also in the field of education and learning,[29] and it penetrates wider society as people seek to quantify ever more aspects of their own lives using self-tracking devices such as Fitbits.[30] These processes have been interpreted by John Preston as an 'existential threat' because they completely negate the need to theorise the internal life of the subject, reducing people to their digital and measurable outputs, and reducing human activity to mechanical action.[31] Workers are treated as 'components of a machine',[32] or a system of cybernetic nodes with fragmented working hours. There is no clear distinction between working and leisure time, yet time is measured as homogeneous units, subordinating people's experience of temporality to clocks and machines.[33] Workers/consumers are also increasingly channelled into 'prosumption' activities (such as social media use) which produce value for capital without remuneration. In addition, many are unable to find employment at all, and the threat of being thrown on the scrap-heap or into the insecure, semi-criminalised informal sector is used to instil fear in those workers who are employed. Over time, capitalism seems to destroy more jobs than it creates, and its ability to provide incomes or subsistence in the event of massive robotisation must at least be questioned. Even if it manages to do so, the new jobs will likely be quantified, surveillance-intensive nightmares which leave much to be desired at a qualitative level.

Precarity leads to feelings of insecurity and anxiety that constitute an existential threat in a variety of ways. Temporary and zero-hour contracts cause feelings of uncertainty about access to resources needed for a stable life and personal development. Endless cycles of debt trap people in perpetual toil and deferred pleasure. Casualised contracts, unpaid internships, intermittent work and labour migration impact on sociality as maintaining close friendships and starting a family become increasingly difficult.[34] People are expected to be always on-call and communicable by employers, family, friends and lovers through mobile phones and the internet without physical social contact, while working from home dissolves the boundaries between work, family and leisure.

This book also contributes to ways to theorise psychological responses to disaster beyond the idea of resilience. Tied to its history in psychology, the concept of 'resilience' is often heralded as a panacea for mental health as well as social ills, placing responsibility for dealing with social and ecological stresses on individuals.[35] People under conditions of intense stress are told to deal with this by attending wellbeing and mindfulness classes and developing a positive mental attitude.[36] This has become particularly significant under the austerity politics being imposed on many Western nations after the sub-prime mortgage crisis of 2008, as well as in the transition from a Fordist to a post-Fordist, precarious economy.[37] This book has shown that dynamics of empowerment and disempowerment are more complex than this. For many people, exercising agency through mutual aid is empowering, whereas top-down approaches increase trauma. Yet this empowerment also takes place in a field with affective risks, so to speak, such as traumatic repression and burnout. The critique of resilience and the recomposition of social reproduction resonates far more widely than in the disaster field. There is a need for further work on the links between climate change, mental health and resistance, and on mutual aid as a means of developing holistic approaches to individual, community and ecological health.

RECONSIDERING DISASTER:
DOES 'UTOPIAN' MEAN 'IMPOSSIBLE'?

Anarchism is not exactly the humanitarian optimism alleged by critics, but my account also suggests that it is both utopian and ethically oriented. I mean 'utopian' in the broad sense, as the expression and actualisation of hopes and desires and as an attempt to build a better world. Yet those convinced that people are *really* atomised utility-maximisers, Hobbesian brutes or cybernetic nodes are likely to see such approaches as wishful thinking, romanticising survival, and 'irrelevant' to the historical situation. The main objection that I anticipate to this work is the Hobbesian argument that humans in a state of anarchy cannot organise themselves appropriately to deal with global issues like climate change. I hope to have refuted this already in the foregoing chapters: There is plenty of evidence that mutual aid works surprisingly well. There are other possible objections from the left that deserve to be engaged with. British journalist and political commentator George Monbiot, who has become emblematic of the environmental left, sums up the statist critique of anarchist approaches to climate change and disaster in an article 'Climate change is not anarchy's football'.[38] In this, he argues that 'stopping runaway climate change must take precedence over every other aim', necessitating alliances with states and capitalism. He sees anarchists as exploiting climate change for ideological ends. He also argues that anarchism confuses ends and means – climate change is a reality and should not be used to engineer an idealistic 'anarchist utopia'. In a similar vein, David Harvey[39] argues that social movements can only be a supplement to state-centred power. They might be better at local action, but cannot address larger-scale issues like climate change as they are inherently particularistic.

My response to this is to emphasise that prefiguration is a creative process. Both Monbiot and Harvey accuse anarchists of confusing ends and means as they reject prefiguration and instead seek instrumental approaches. These approaches misunderstand the nature of prefiguration and the problems with using statist means, which all too easily mutate into ends (or at least into unchangeable 'necessities'). Anarchist utopianism does not seek to 'engineer' an ideologically preconceived alternative in a distant future. Rather, anarchists try to build a new society in the here-and-now, while also rethinking issues of scale and the world system. A focus on particular issues does not preclude awareness of structural problems; rather, downscaling and localisation are often effective responses to structural asymmetries. They are also generally simple to implement once barriers are removed. It is *ceteris paribus* much easier to proliferate self-sufficient eco-villages or localise food production than it is (for example) to power Northern cities with solar plants in the Sahara or capture carbon at the bottom of the ocean. The main barriers to the former, other than voluntary take-up, are state repression and recuperation. Had it not been for the waves of repression and the more subtle commodification of countercultural movements from the 1960s to the present, it is conceivable that climate change would already have been 'solved'.

These arguments have been dealt with elsewhere in depth, by theorists of degrowth, which are complementary to anarchism. Degrowthers tend to be critical of eco-modernist approaches like recent social democratic discourse around the idea of a 'Green New Deal', which tend to displace rather than solve environmental problems, promise 'to change everything while keeping everything the same', while doing nothing to tackle current levels of production, consumption and expectations of economic growth.[40] The resultant technocratic control-fantasies and intrusive behavioural nudging interventions (from congestion charges, bin inspections and bird feeding bans, to calls for 'climate change lockdowns', one-child policies, dog turd DNA testing or bans on pets)[41] provide constant fuel for sensationalist hysteria against environmentalism while failing to dint governments' focus on economics or the constant increase in resource consumption due to GDP growth. Gains from green technology or efficiency gains tend to be rapidly cancelled out by economic growth. Technological fixes designed to improve efficiency risk a 'rebound effect'. For example, when a less resource-exhaustive technology is used, people's behaviour around that technology may change as costs may go down and people may use it more;[42] or the resource costs may be displaced elsewhere, as for example when replacing fossil fuels with sustainable technology that requires the exploitative mining of rare minerals.[43] Remaining within a growth economy means that 'efficiency and conservation simply mean capital accumulation plowed back to further growth'.[44]

Degrowth would require a wholesale societal change of culture, values and (crucially) socio-technical infrastructure, a move towards qualitative rather than quantitative value, away from monolithic assessments based on efficiency or profit, and towards more localised forms of living. It is not necessarily an austere vision; people have much to gain from decreased work stress, greater autonomy, community, the revival of crafts, etc. Many anarchists already live aspects of their lives in ways compatible with degrowth, with lower resource consumption but not necessarily any decrease in wellbeing. At times, anarchist activism is a joyful pursuit. The limit to degrowth within a statist mould is that the state may be unable to achieve the social transformations involved, as well as having disincentives to do so (particularly reduced control and tax income). Today, projects of culture/value change are often unsuccessful or counterproductive, because they rely on the moulding of individuals conceived as cybernetic nodes or rational subjects. Change in what people actually value is only possible at the affective/psychological level. While technocrats can thereby fantasise about realising impossible combinations of amoral accumulation with ethics, in practice the basically capitalist and manipulative nature of the enterprise contradicts and undermines its goals: it cannot prefigure non-capitalist futures because its means are so thoroughly capitalist.

While few dare say it, effective degrowth requires at least anti-capitalism, if not anarchism. Achieving a qualitatively improved or at least tolerable life without maintaining massive resource consumption is likely possible, but it is not something a capitalist society or a technocratic state can provide. Qualitative improvements in human security, meeting basic needs, providing meaning and satisfying desires are all possible without quantitative growth if there are moves towards economic and political dispersal (transferring resources 'downwards') and/or towards less alienated, more fulfilling ways of life. Scarcity is created by enclosures and precarity; consumption can be reduced by a proliferation of squats, communes, DIY solutions, cooperatives, allotments, and so on, and the state, instead of trying to repress or recuperate these, needs simply to get out of the way and let it happen. Lower- or intermediate-technology living, or high-tech living with open-source, decentralised technologies also entails increased empowerment for individuals and communities.

The state's and capital's choices among green technologies are driven by a wish to keep their profits and centralised power intact. Less radical sustainable-technology models that rest on ideas of 'green growth' produce a form of authoritarian technocracy, which divides society into experts and users, whereby the former 'become the bureaucrats or the bosses who control and appropriate the surplus of the system'.[45] On the other hand, certain technologies are impossible in an anarchist set-up. A society powered by nuclear energy requires centralised authority to run and administer nuclear power plants, and therefore 'cannot be a society of equals or mutual aid'.[46] The vision I hope to put forward is not of one single 'anarchist utopia' as Monbiot projects, nor as Harvey understands it, a fetishisation of organisation that leads to dangerously ineffective chaos. Rather, there would be a proliferation of small-scale alternatives: housing and worker cooperatives, community and permaculture gardens, localised food and energy production collectives, engaging in various overlapping solidarities and mutual aid.

States and capital are today playing catch-up. Social movements, especially anarchists, have been alert to environmental collapse, social precarity and capitalist system instability for a very long time. Indeed, movements have been *finding solutions* to these problems long before states or capital recognised that they even exist. States spent decades suppressing radical ecological movements before finally accepting that climate change is a real danger, since when they have thoroughly failed even to reach global agreements on the way forward. Even today, with crisis widely recognised, states are still evicting protest camps from forests to mine coal and build oil pipelines and roads, as well as squats and eco-projects to make room for profit-seeking operations. Yet states and capitalists do not seem to recognise the incongruity. Put simply, states are now trying to solve in ways unthreatening to capital, things which anarchic social movements have already solved in ways threatening to both capital and the state. This is not without precedent. When revolutions are defeated, states often end up taking on the tasks of the revolutionaries, performing what Gramsci terms a 'passive revolution'.[47] For example, it took decades from the Russian Revolution and the failed revolutions in Europe for states/capital to recognise the need for universal welfare provision (a concession they conceded at the first sign of crisis); it took 70 years from the 1848 revolutions for the reforms sought by radicals, such as national self-determination, universal suffrage and the removal of absolute monarchs, to be implemented after the First World War. The same is today the case for disasters and ecological crisis. If we could travel in time to a squatted district in Europe in the 1970s or 1980s, or an even earlier hippie commune or festival, we would already find people who are asking – and answering – the question of how to have enjoyable, meaningful lives without engaging in a 'rat race' of endless production and consumption. This was also tied, of course, to questions of alienation, to whether consumer society is fulfilling, to incapacities to meet work demands, and a reconsideration of whether abstract money and power, or rather pleasure, the body and relations to others and nature, are the sources of value. Radical theorists of the time such as Ivan Illich were already talking about the propensity of humans to destroy their environment and the irreversible change that would occur if lifestyles based on mass consumption continued.[48] If the same questions are now being asked in the halls of power – in the World Economic Forum (WEF), for example – this indicates how slow the powerful have been to catch up. Worse: they have spent the intervening decades denying the problems and trying to suppress or commodify (and thus bring back *into* the structure of endless ecocidal growth) the very movements which were, at a local level, already answering their questions. What is more, they now raise disaster and climate change minus the libidinal, existential, relational and anti-authoritarian elements of the first wave of political ecologists. They raise them as if they were technical problems to be met using rational egos, regulation and nudging, thus denying the very systemic aspects of the problem which were so clear to their forebears. If it takes another 50 years for the elite to realise that technocracy is insufficient to the task, it may well be too late. Those placing faith in state/capitalist solutions might do well to consider the similarities between the climate issue today and earlier fears of nuclear war, which similarly concerned an earlier wave of activists. States have so far failed to eliminate the threat of nuclear war, and indeed, it has arguably increased since then, despite the end of the Cold War – previously the main *raison d'être* for nuclear stockpiles. It seems unlikely they will succeed with climate change where they failed to handle this superficially far more manageable problem.

The easiest way to make a dint in climate change would be the proliferation of localised communities and networks with extensive commoning and/or mutual aid, with communities providing most of what they consume, qualitative values surpassing quantitative, and reducing connection to global value chains. States, if they wished to, could encourage this by providing resources without strings, implementing land reform, or simply by removing legal barriers to such projects. The trouble is, of course, that states and capital would have to concede some of their power to make a dint in ecological crisis – and this is something they are systematically unprepared to do. The powerful today only accept solutions which keep their own position untouched. Both the state and capitalism (universal equivalence through money) are simplifying systems. As long as they hold power, solutions will be similarly standardised. They can dream all they like about integrating 'social capital' into their systems, but their very system relies on disempowering or sucking energy from the sources of social life. Social capital is to the social principle, one might say, as capital is to labour: the state seeks a political equivalent to the M–C–M' cycle through a similar exploitation of social energy, with a constant tendency to kill the goose that lays the golden eggs.[49] This is why the anarchist distinction between social and political principles is more appropriate for understanding disaster responses than the associationalist theory of social capital and resilience. The paradox of telling people to stay at home and at the same time to get out and help others, to organise as a community while the very fabric of community life is criminalised, is the latest manifestation of the absurdity of the Third Way dream of having one's cake and eating it: maintaining neoliberal capitalism (and its behaviourist correlates) untouched, while also attaining a range of social, egalitarian, ecological, and other goals at least to a social democratic extent. It is self-contradictory and self-defeating to try to use the social and political principles at the same time.

It is not the anarchist vision (or visions) which is irrelevant to disasters in post-Fordism. Rather, the state and capital are making themselves increasingly irrelevant to the survival of vast swathes of humanity, both during disasters and in normal times of 'everyday disaster'. By treating disasters as exercises in social control, cybernetic manipulation, and accumulative opportunism, states and capitalists make themselves irrelevant to the needs of disaster survivors and of networks seeking to respond to suffering, just as capital's flight into finance and virtuality has made it increasingly irrelevant to the lives and subsistence of most of the world's population (and relevant only as threats or adversaries). Today, the powerful are not only failing to find solutions; in many cases, they are getting in the way or making things worse. This book has charted an emergent alternative: mutual aid networks using anarchist organising models to respond at a grassroots level. While there are many practical difficulties, this model is already showing its usefulness as an alternative to hierarchical models in situations where capital and the state are paralysed. It provides, at the very least, a way to mitigate humanitarian catastrophes, and at its best, it also prefigures a better society.

Notes

1. INTRODUCTION

1. The cost of Sandy has since been superseded by Hurricane Harvey. For up-to-date statistics see: National Climatic Data Centre, National Oceanic and Atmospheric Administration (2020) 'Billion dollar weather and climate disasters: Table of events', www.ncdc.noaa.gov/billions/events (accessed January 2020).
2. Cornish, Flora; Montenegro, Cristian; van Reisen, Kirsten; Zaka, Flavia and Sevitt, James, 'Trust the process: Community health psychology after Occupy', *Journal of Health Psychology* 19(1), 2014, pp. 60–71. See also Marom, Yotam, 'Occupy Sandy: From relief to resistance', Waging Nonviolence, 13 November 2012, http://wagingnonviolence.org/feature/occupy-sandy-from-relief-to-resistance/ (accessed January 2020).
3. Goldstein, Katherine, 'Is Occupy Wall Street outperforming the Red Cross in hurricane relief?', *Slate*, 4 November 2012.
4. Bachom, Sandi, '"Got mold? Cold? FEMA?" Hurricane Sandy nightmare continues in Rockaway', *Huffington Post*, 26 March 2013. Halbfinger, David M., 'Anger grows at response by Red Cross', *The New York Times*, 2 November 2012.
5. Ambinder, Eric; Jennings, David M.; Blachman-Biatch, Isadora; Edgemon, Keith; Hull, Peter and Taylor, Anna, *The Resilient Social Network*, Department of Homeland Security Science and Technology Directorate (DHS) Publication Number: RP12-01.04.11-01, 30 September 2013, pp. 24–25.
6. 'OS income and expenditures: Public summary', Google Documents, https://docs.google.com/spreadsheets/d/1deBIKIJsuYCmtyONLonHmG6PKiuAG4qSZeLFR4UASNY/pub?single=true&gid=14&output=html&widget=true (accessed January 2020).
7. Garber, Megan, 'Occupy Sandy hacks Amazon's wedding registry (in a good way)', *The Atlantic*, 5 November 2012.
8. crow, scott, *Black Flags and Windmills: Hope, Anarchy and the Common Ground Collective* (Oakland, CA: PM Press, 2014).
9. Ambinder et al., *The Resilient Social Network*.
10. World Health Organization, *Coronavirus (COVID-19) Dashboard*, https://covid19.who.int/ (accessed 1 May 2021).
11. Robinson, Andrew, 'Avoiding recuperation: Thinking from the outside', *Anarchy: A journal of desire armed* 64(Fall–Winter), 2007, pp. 37–49.
12. Preston, John, *Grenfell Tower: Preparedness, Race and Disaster Capitalism* (Cham: Palgrave, 2018). O'Connell, Mark, 'Why Silicon Valley billionaires

are preparing for the apocalypse in New Zealand', *Guardian*, 15 February 2018.

13. Crabapple, Molly, 'Puerto Rico sketchbook: The anarchist bikers who came to help', *Paris Review*, 11 December 2017.

14. Anonymous, 'Autonomous disaster relief', *It's Going Down*, no date, https://itsgoingdown.org/autonomous-disaster-relief/ (accessed January 2020).

15. Anonymous, 'When flood waters run dry: Hurricane Harvey, climate change and social reproduction', *It's Going Down*, 21 January 2020, https://itsgoingdown.org/when-flood-waters-run-dry-hurricane-harvey-climate-change-social-reproduction/ (accessed 8 April 2021).

16. Mutual Aid Disaster Relief, https://mutualaiddisasterrelief.org/ (accessed 8 April 2021).

17. Anonymous, 'Mexico: Political statement from the Autonomous Brigades after the earthquakes', *It's Going Down*, 21 September 2017, https://itsgoingdown.org/mexico-autonomous-brigades-earthquakes/ (accessed January 2020).

18. Jon, Ihnji and Purcell, Mark, 'Radical resilience: Autonomous self-management in post-disaster recovery planning and practice', *Planning Theory & Practice* 19(2), 2018, pp. 235–251.

19. 325, 'Appeal from anarchist comrades concerning Typhoon Yolanda (Philippines)', 14 November 2013, https://325.nostate.net/2013/11/14/appeal-from-anarchist-comrades-concerning-typhoon-yolanda-philippines/ and 'Report about continuing autonomous Typhoon Yolanda disaster relief initiatives by anarchists (Philippines)', 3 January 2014, https://325.nostate.net/2014/01/03/report-about-continuing-autonomous-typhoon-yolanda-disaster-relief-initiatives-by-anarchists-philippines/(accessed January 2020).

20. Act for Freedom, 'Trieste, Italy: On the devastation of the Rosandra valley', 12 May 2012, https://actforfree.nostate.net/?p=9177 and 'Earthquake in Emilia Romagna (Italy): Drones, surveillance and social control', https://actforfree.nostate.net/?p=10073 (accessed January 2020).

21. Lawrence, Felicity, 'First goal of David Cameron's "nudge unit" is to encourage healthy living', *Guardian*, 12 November 2010. Preston, John, 'Classed practices: Pandemic preparedness in the UK', pp. 29–58 in Preston, John and Firth, Rhiannon, *Coronavirus, Class and Mutual Aid in the UK* (Cham: Palgrave, 2020), p. 35.

22. Hannigan, John, *Disasters without Borders: The International Politics of Natural Disasters* (Cambridge: Polity Press, 2012), p. 13.

23. Ibid., p. 27.

24. Ibid., pp 13–14.

25. Marshall, Peter, *Demanding the Impossible: A History of Anarchism* (Oakland: PM Press, 2009).

26. Clastres, Pierre, *Society Against the State* (Oxford: Blackwell, 1977).

27. Morland, Dave, *Demanding the Impossible? Human Nature and Politics in 19th-century Social Anarchism* (London: Cassell, 1998).

28. Franks, Benjamin, *Anarchisms, Postanarchisms and Ethics* (London: Rowman and Littlefield, 2019).
29. Gordon, Uri, *Anarchy Alive! Anti-Authoritarian Politics from Practice to Theory* (London: Pluto, 2008).
30. Delmotte, Fabien, 'A return to Occupy Wall Street: What lessons can we learn?', autrefutur.net, 5 April 2016, www.autrefutur.net/A-Return-to-Occupy-Wall-Street-what-lessons-can-we-learn (accessed 23 November 2018).
31. Three of seven OS activists I interviewed explicitly mentioned an affinity with anarchism.
32. Stirner, Max, *The Ego and Its Own*, trans. Steven Byington (London: Rebel Press, 1993 [1844]).
33. See Chapter 4 for further discussion on Kropotkin and Stirner. Bakunin, Mikhail, *God and the State* (New York: Dover Books, 1970 [1882]).
34. Preston and Firth, *Coronavirus, Class and Mutual Aid*.
35. Warwick, John, 'Market vs state vs commons: Which future are we heading towards?', *Organise!* 93, 2020, https://organisemagazine.org.uk/2020/11/17/organise-93/ (accessed 18 May 2021).
36. Fisher, Mark, *Capitalist Realism: Is There No Alternative?* (Winchester, Hants: John Hunt Publishing, 2009).
37. The website is no longer active, but was previously located at http://interoccupy.net/
38. Bondesson, Sara, *Vulnerability and Power: Social Justice Organizing in Rockaway, New York City, after Hurricane Sandy* (Uppsala: Department of Government, Upsala University, 2017), p. 42.
39. Gordon, *Anarchy Alive!*, pp. 18–20.
40. Bevington, Douglas and Dixon, Chris, 'Movement-relevant theory: Rethinking social movement scholarship and activism', *Social Movement Studies* 4(3), 2005, pp. 185–208.

2. BACKDROP: MAINSTREAM DISASTER STUDIES

1. These clusters are similar to those identified by Hannigan, *Disasters without Borders*. Bondesson, *Vulnerability and Power*, divides them more broadly into the top-down managerialist and technocratic approaches of DRR (corresponding to i and iii of my categories) and social justice approaches that emphasise inclusion, participation, and empowerment (overlapping with ii and implicitly assuming iv). Sementelli subdivides the literature into 'decision theories' focused on policies and procedures, 'administrative theories' focused on managerial leadership, 'economic theories' focused on resource allocation and 'social theories' focused on critical theory and inequalities. Sementelli, Arthur, 'Toward a taxonomy of disaster and crisis theories', *Administrative Theory & Praxis* 29(4), 2007, pp. 497–512.

2. Lash, Scott and Urry, John, *The End of Organised Capitalism* (Cambridge: Polity, 1987).

3. Boltanski, Luc and Chiapello, Ève, 'The new spirit of capitalism', *International Journal of Politics, Culture, and Society* 18(3–4), 2005, pp. 161–188.

4. Galison, Peter, 'The ontology of the enemy: Norbert Wiener and the cybernetic vision', *Critical Inquiry* 21(1), 1994, pp. 228–266 is the seminal text here. However, the origin story of cybernetics is disputed (see note 7 this chapter), and Norbert Wiener himself did not adopt the term until after the war, when he had disavowed his military work. The lines of influence between cybernetics and disaster studies are also ambiguous – however there is no doubt that the cybernetic paradigm had enormous influence and resources attached during the Cold War. See also Wiener, Norbert, *Cybernetics: or Control and Communication in the Animal and Machine* (Cambridge, MA: MIT Press, 1965 [1948]).

5. Pickering, Andrew, *The Cybernetic Brain* (Chicago: University of Chicago Press, 2010).

6. Kline, Ronald, 'How disunity matters to the history of cybernetics in the human sciences in the United States, 1940–1980', *History of the Human Sciences* 33(1), 2020, pp. 12–35.

7. Kline in 'How disunity matters' and Pickering in *The Cybernetic Brain* both argue that cybernetics is so broad and diverse that it is impossible to narrate a single history or theoretical basis, and this is probably true of disaster studies as well. In this context, it is worth noting that there are some excellent anti-authoritarian and anarchist theorists and researchers working on cybernetics, in particular: Swann, Thomas, *Anarchist Cybernetics: Control and Communication in Radical Politics* (Bristol: Bristol University Press, 2021). See also Swann, Thomas, 'Anarchist cybernetics', Institute for Anarchist Studies, 13 May 2021, https://anarchiststudies.org/acybernetics/ (accessed 14 May 2021); Duda, John, 'Cybernetics, anarchism and self-organisation', *Anarchist Studies* 21(1), 2013, pp. 52–72; and Tektological Serendipity, 'One captain or many rowers? A cybernetic metaphor', *Tektological's Newsletter*, 21 February 2021, https://tektology.substack.com/p/one-captain-or-many-rowers (accessed 14 May 2021). I have yet to engage with anarchist cybernetics in depth, and there are questions to be grappled with over whether it is inherently functionalist and authoritarian or contains liberatory potential. This an ongoing project that I am working on separately; however, when I refer to cybernetics in this book it is to the dominant paradigm, particularly its intersection with structural functionalism and behaviourism.

8. Heyck, Hunter, *Age of System: Understanding the Development of Modern Social Science* (Baltimore, MD: Johns Hopkins University Press, 2015).

9. Wolfenstein, Martha, *Disaster: A Psychological Essay* (New York: Routledge, 1957).

10. Fritz, Charles E., *Disasters and Mental Health: Therapeutic Principles Drawn from Disaster Studies* (Newark, DE: University of Delaware Disaster Research Center, 1996), p. 6.
11. Ibid., p. 25.
12. Barton, Allen H., *Communities in Disaster: A Sociological Analysis of Collective Stress Situations* (New York: Doubleday, 1969).
13. Erikson, Kai, 'Notes on trauma and community', *American Imago* 48(4), 1991, pp. 455–472.
14. Miller, Clark, 'Scientific internationalism in American foreign policy: The case of meteorology, 1947–1958', pp. 167–218 in C. Miller and P.N. Edwards (eds), *Changing the Atmosphere: Expert Knowledge and Environmental Governance* (Cambridge, MA: MIT Press, 2001).
15. Quarantelli, Enrico Louis, 'Introduction: The basic question, its importance, and how it is addressed in this volume', pp. 1–8 in E.L. Quarantelli (ed.), *What Is a Disaster? A Dozen Perspectives on the Question* (London: Routledge, 1998).
16. Quarantelli, Enrico Louis, *Major Criteria for Judging Disaster Planning and Managing their Applicability in Developing Countries* (Newark, DE: University of Delaware Disaster Research Center, 1998).
17. Ibid., pp. 9–12.
18. Solnit, Rebecca, *A Paradise Built in Hell: The Extraordinary Communities that Arise in Disaster* (New York: Penguin, 2010), p. 123.
19. Quarantelli, *Major Criteria*, pp. 12–14.
20. Sementelli, 'Toward a taxonomy of disaster and crisis theories', p. 508.
21. Bolin, Robert and Stanford, Lois, *The Northridge Earthquake: Vulnerability and Disaster* (New York: Routledge, 1998).
22. Oliver-Smith, Anthony and Hoffman, Susanna M., 'Introduction: Why anthropologists should study disasters', pp. 3–22 in S.M. Hoffman and A. Oliver-Smith (eds), *Catastrophe and Culture: The Anthropology of Disaster* (Santa Fe, TX: School of American Research Press, 2002).
23. Oliver-Smith, Anthony, 'The brotherhood of pain: Theoretical and applied perspectives on post-disaster solidarity', pp.156–172 in A. Oliver-Smith and S.M. Hoffman, *The Angry Earth: Disaster in Anthropological Perspective* (London: Routledge, 1999).
24. It is not clear that there is a direct line of influence from structuralism proper to structural approaches in disaster studies, as often the term 'structure' is used without reference to critical literatures. Nevertheless, the use of structure in disaster studies picks up on similar concerns, for example the unequal impact of disasters on groups structurally disadvantaged by race, gender, class, etc. This is not to say that structuralism and poststructuralism proper have not intervened in and critiqued disaster studies (which is the subject of the following chapter) but the influence of these more critical perspectives in the mainstream policy field has been minimal.
25. Hannigan, *Disasters without Borders*, p. 60.

26. Ibid., p. 60.
27. Ibid., p. 61.
28. Miller, 'Scientific internationalism'.
29. Beck, Ulrich, *Risk Society: Towards a New Modernity* (London: Sage, 1992).
30. Hannigan, *Disasters without Borders*, p. 67.
31. Ibid., p. 67.
32. E.g. Drury, John; Cocking, Chris and Reicher, Steve, 'The nature of collective resilience: Survivor reactions to the 2005 London bombings', *International Journal of Mass Emergencies and Disasters* 27(1), 2009, pp. 66–95.
33. Tierney, Kathleen, *The Social Roots of Risk: Producing Disasters, Promoting Resilience* (Stanford, CA: Stanford University Press, 2014).
34. Mileti, Dennis S., *Disasters by Design: A Reassessment of Natural Hazards in the United States* (Washington, DC: Joseph Henry Press, 1999).
35. Enarson, Elaine Pitt, *Women Confronting Natural Disaster: From Vulnerability to Resilience* (Boulder, CO: Lynne Rienner Publishers, 2012).
36. Barusch, Amanda S., 'Disaster, vulnerability, and older adults: Toward a social work response', *Journal of Gerontological Social Work* 54(4), 2011, pp. 347–350.
37. Fothergill, A.; Maestas, E.G.M. and Darlington, J.D., 'Race, ethnicity and disasters in the United States: A review of the literature', *Disasters* 23(2), 1999, pp. 156–173.
38. Hartman, Chester and Squires, Gregory D. (eds), *There is No Such Thing as a Natural Disaster: Race, Class and Hurricane Katrina* (Abingdon: Routledge, 2006).
39. Bankoff, Greg and Hilhorst, Dorothea, 'Introduction: Mapping vulnerability', pp. 1–10 in G. Bankoff, G. Frerks and D. Hilhorst (eds), *Mapping Vulnerability: Disasters, Development, and People* (London: Earthscan Publications, 2004). See also Jones, Eric C. and Murphy, Arthur D., *The Political Economy of Hazards and Disasters* (New York: AltaMira Press, 2009).
40. Bondesson, *Vulnerability and Power*.
41. Berkes, Fikret and Colding, Johan, *Navigating Social-ecological Systems: Building Resilience for Complexity and Change* (New York: Cambridge University Press, 2003). Goldstein, Bruce Evan, 'Resilience to surprises through communicative planning', *Ecology and Society* 14(2), 2009, p. 33. Walker, Brian and Westley, Frances, 'Perspectives on resilience to disasters across sectors and cultures', *Ecology and Society* 16(2), 2011, p. 4.
42. For critique, see Neocleous, Mark, 'Resisting resilience', *Radical Philosophy* 178, 2013, pp. 2–7.
43. Lim, Wee Kiat, 'Understanding risk governance: Introducing sociological neoinstitutionalism and Foucauldian governmentality for further theorizing', *International Journal of Disaster Risk Science* 2, 2011, pp. 11–20.
44. Preston, John; Chadderton, Charlotte; Kitigawa, Kaori and Edmonds, Casey, 'Community response in disasters: An ecological learning framework', *International Journal of Lifelong Education* 34(6), 2015, pp. 727–753.

45. Stallings, Robert A. and Quarantelli, Enrico L., 'Emergent citizen groups and emergency management', *Public Administration Review* 45, 1985, pp. 93–100.

46. Simo, Gloria and Bies, Angela, 'The role of nonprofits in disaster response: An expanded model of cross-sector collaboration', *Public Administration Review* 67(1), 2007, pp. 125–142.

47. Barenstein, Jennifer E. Duyne and Leeman, Esther, *Post-Disaster Reconstruction and Change: Communities' Perspectives* (London: CRC Press, 2013). Mathbor, Golam M., 'Enhancement of community preparedness for natural disasters: The role of social work in building social capital for sustainable disaster relief and management', *International Social Work* 50(3), 2007, pp. 357–369.

48. Berkes and Colding, *Navigating Social-ecological Systems*.

49. Eakin, Hallie; Eriksen, Siri; Eikeland, Per-Ove and Øyen, Cecile, 'Public sector reform and governance for adaptation: Implications of New Public Management for adaptive capacity in Mexico and Norway', *Environmental Management* 47, 2011, pp. 338–351.

50. Majchrzak, Ann; Jarvenpaa, Sirkka L. and Hollingshead, Andrea. 'Coordinating expertise among emergent groups responding to disasters', *Organization Science* 18(1), 2007, pp. 147–161.

51. Hannigan, *Disasters without Borders*.

52. Goody, Jack, 'Civil society in an extra-European perspective', pp. 149–164 in S. Kaviraj and S. Khilnani (eds), *Civil Society: History and Possibilities* (Cambridge: Cambridge University Press, 2001).

53. Putnam, Robert, *Making Democracy Work: Civic Traditions in Modern Italy* (Princeton, NJ: Princeton University Press, 1993).

54. Leadbeater, Charles, 'Opportunities for social enterprise growth from changes to world and local economies', pp. 24–27 in *Social Enterprise World Forum: Conference Report* (Edinburgh: CEIS, 2008).

55. Powell, John A.; Jeffries, Hasan Kwame; Newhart, Daniel W. and Steins, Eric, 'Towards a transformative view of race', pp. 59–84 in C. Hartman and G.D. Squires (eds), *There is No Such Thing as a Natural Disaster: Race, Class and Hurricane Katrina* (Abingdon: Routledge, 2006).

56. Mathbor, 'Enhancement of community preparedness'. See also Nakagawa, Yuko and Shaw, Rajib, 'Social capital: A missing link to disaster recovery', *International Journal of Mass Emergencies and Disasters* 22(1), 2004, pp. 5–34; Pelling, Mark, 'Participation, social capital and vulnerability to urban flooding in Guyana', *Journal of International Development* 4, 1998, pp. 469–486; Aldrich, Daniel P., *Building Resilience: Social Capital in Post-disaster Recovery* (Chicago: University of Chicago Press, 2012).

57. The Invisible Committee, 'Fuck off, Google', pp. 99–129 in *To Our Friends* (South Pasadena, CA: Semiotext(e), 2014).

58. Appadurai, Arjun, 'Disjuncture and difference in the global cultural economy', *Public Culture* 2(2), 1990, pp. 1–23.

59. Hardt, Michael and Negri, Antonio, *Empire* (Cambridge, MA: Harvard University Press, 2000).

60. Held, David, *Democracy and the Global Order: From the Modern State to Cosmopolitan Governance* (Cambridge: Polity Press, 1995).

61. Van Dijk, Jan, *The Network Society* (London: Sage, 2012 [1991]).

62. Castells, Manuel, *The Rise of the Network Society* (Oxford: Blackwell, 1996).

63. Arquilla, John and Ronfeldt, David, 'The advent of netwar (revisited)', pp. 1–28 in J. Arquilla and D. Ronfeldt (eds), *Networks and Netwars: The Future of Terror, Crime, and Militancy* (Santa Monica, CA: RAND Corporation, 2001).

64. Castells, *The Rise of the Network Society*, p. 469.

65. Ibid., p. 349.

66. Van Dijk, *The Network Society*, p. 129; Barassi, Veronica, 'Ethnographic cartographies: Social movements, alternative media and the spaces of networks', *Social Movement Studies* 12(1), 2013, pp. 48–62.

67. Van Dijk, *The Network Society*, pp. 136–137.

68. Arquilla and Ronfeldt, 'The advent of netwar (revisited)', p. 20.

69. Ibid., p. ix.

70. Karatzogianni, Athina and Robinson, Andrew, *Power, Resistance and Conflict in the Contemporary World: Social Movements, Networks and Hierarchies* (London: Routledge, 2009), p. 127.

71. Hann, Christopher Michael and Elizabeth Dunn (eds), *Civil Society: Challenging Western Models* (London: Routledge, 1996).

72. Hannigan, *Disasters without Borders*, p. 10.

73. Halpin, Stephanie Hoopes, *Non-profit Groups in Superstorm Sandy: Local Surge Capacity or Long Term Recovery?* (New Brunswick, NJ: Rutgers University, School of Public Affairs and Administration, 2013).

74. Preston et al., 'Community response in disasters'.

75. Smith, Easton, 'The state, Occupy and disaster: What radical movement builders can learn from the case of Occupy Sandy', 2014, https://thetempworker. wordpress.com/2014/08/29/the-state-occupy-and-disaster-what-radical-movement-builders-can-learn-from-the-case-of-occupy-sandy/ (accessed 16 January 2020).

76. Fisher, William F., 'Doing good? The politics and antipolitics of NGO practices', *Annual Review of Anthropology* 26(1), 1997, pp. 439–464.

77. Wolch, Jennifer, 'The shadow state: Transformations in the voluntary sector', pp. 197–221 in J. Wolch and M. Dear (eds), *The Power of Geography* (London: Routledge, 2015 [1989]).

78. Townsend, Janet G.; Porter, Gina and Mawdsley, Emma, 'The role of the transnational community of non-government organizations: Governance or poverty reduction?', *Journal of International Development* 14(6), 2002, pp. 829–839.

79. Williams, Andrew; Cloke, Paul and Thomas, Samuel, 'Co-constituting neoliberalism: Faith-based organisations, co-option, and resistance in the

UK', *Environment and Planning A* 44(6), 2012, pp. 1479–1501. Fyfe, Nicholas R., 'Making space for "neo-communitarianism"? The third sector, state and civil society in the UK', *Antipode* 37(3), 2005, pp. 536–557.

80. Watkins, Heather, *The Potential and Constraints of Local Participation and the Concept of Social Capital,* PhD Thesis, University of Nottingham, 2013, p. 85.

81. Malsin, Jared, 'Best of enemies: Why Occupy activists are working with New York City's government', *Time,* 13 November 2012.

82. Clark, John P., 'Disaster anarchism: Hurricane Katrina and the shock of recognition', pp. 193–216 in J.P. Clark, *The Impossible Community: Realizing Communitarian Anarchism* (New York: Bloomsbury, 2013).

83. Cohen, Charles and Werker, Eric D., 'The political economy of "natural" disasters', *Journal of Conflict Resolution* 52(6), 2008, pp. 795–819.

84. Barnes, Marian and Prior, David (eds), *Subversive Citizens: Power, Agency and Resistance in Public Services* (Bristol: Policy Press, 2009).

85. Hannigan, *Disasters without Borders,* p. 134. Bankoff, G., 'Rendering the world unsafe: "Vulnerability" as Western discourse', *Disasters* 25, 2001, pp. 19–35.

86. Dolhinow, Rebecca, 'Caught in the middle: The state, NGOs, and the limits to grassroots organizing along the US–Mexico border', *Antipode,* 37(3), 2005, pp. 558–580.

87. Ambinder et al., *The Resilient Social Network,* p. A-1.

88. Smith, 'The state, Occupy and disaster'.

89. Ambinder et al., *The Resilient Social Network,* p. A-1.

90. Ibid., p. D-1.

91. Ibid., pp. 12–14.

92. Ibid., p. D-1.

93. Ibid., pp. 12–14.

94. Wolf, Naomi, 'Revealed: How the FBI coordinated the crackdown on Occupy', *Guardian,* 29 December 2012. Schjonberg, Mary Frances, 'Federal government studies Occupy Sandy movement', *Anglican Communion News Service,* 19 March 2014, www.anglicannews.org/news/2014/03/federal-government-studies-occupy-sandy-movement.aspx (accessed 16 January 2020). Hintze, Thomas, 'Homeland Security study praises Occupy Sandy, with murky intentions', *Truthout,* 2 April 2014, www.truth-out.org/news/item/22837-dhs-study-praises-occupy-sandy-with-murky-intentions (accessed 16 January 2020).

95. Ambinder et al., *The Resilient Social Network,* p. A-3.

96. Clark, 'Disaster anarchism', p. 206.

97. Public Health England, 'Guidance on shielding and protecting people who are clinically extremely vulnerable from COVID-19', 21 March 2020, www.gov.uk/government/publications/guidance-on-shielding-and-protecting-extremely-vulnerable-persons-from-covid-19 (accessed 18 May 2021).

98. Alexander, Jon, 'Johnson's message is very deliberate and very dangerous: Here's how to combat it', *Medium*, 10 May 2020, https://medium.com/@jonjalex/johnsons-message-is-very-deliberate-and-very-dangerous-here-s-how-to-combat-it-d336cae96348 (accessed 15 July 2020).
99. Danius, Sara; Jonsson, Stephan and Spivak, Gayatri Chakravorty. 'An interview with Gayatri Chakravorty Spivak', *boundary 2* 20(2), 1993, pp. 24–50.
100. Quarantelli, *Major Criteria*, pp. 8–10.
101. Ibid., p. 8.
102. Ibid., p. 18
103. Ibid., p. 12.
104. Ambinder et al., *The Resilient Social Network*, p. 11.
105. For a brief history of 'stay put' policies, and a critique of how they have been used as a generic strategy in all kinds of disasters, see Preston, John, 'The Grenfell Tower fire: "Stay put" and eliminationism', pp. 31–54 in Preston, *Grenfell Tower*. Preston argues that 'stay put' policy and securitised lockdown serves a social purpose of containment and control of populations rather than being a technically optimal strategy for saving lives. In fact, these policies often force people to remain in the path of danger. Preston argues that this strategy has always tended to tacitly prioritise the survival of the white middle classes and has acted as a form of eliminationism against the urban, racialised poor. For a discussion of how this dynamic played out during the Covid-19 pandemic, see Preston and Firth, *Coronavirus, Class and Mutual Aid in the UK*, especially Chapter 3, 'Classed practices: Pandemic preparedness in the UK', pp. 29–56. While limiting social contacts makes epidemiological sense during a pandemic like Covid-19, there is a range of other ways this could have been done, even from a state-centric perspective, which would have avoided a securitised lockdown and classed moral discourse: for example widespread and rapid no-questions-asked testing, community engagement and education, and financial support for positive cases to isolate.
106. Klein, Naomi, *The Shock Doctrine: The Rise of Disaster Capitalism* (London: Penguin, 2007).

3. CRITICAL APPROACHES: PRECARITY, SECURITISATION AND DISASTER CAPITALISM

1. Hannigan, *Disasters without Borders*.
2. CASE Collective, 'Critical approaches to security in Europe: A networked manifesto', *Security Dialogue* 37(4), 2006, p. 445.
3. Agamben, Giorgio, *State of Exception* (Chicago: University of Chicago Press, 2005).
4. Buzan, Barry; Wæver, Ole and De Wilde, Jaap, *Security: A New Framework for Analysis* (Boulder, CO: Lynne Rienner Publishers, 1998), p. 23.

5. Bigo, Didier and Tsoukala, Anastassia, 'Understanding (in)security', pp. 1–9 in D. Bigo and A. Tsoukala (eds), *Terror, Insecurity and Liberty: Illiberal Practices of Liberal Regimes after 9/11* (London: Routledge, 2008), p. 1.

6. Ashley, Richard K. and Walker, R.B.J., 'Conclusion: Reading dissidence/writing the discipline: Crisis and the question of sovereignty in international studies', *International Studies Quarterly* 34(3), 1990, p. 369.

7. Bigo and Tsoukala, 'Understanding (in)security'.

8. Buzan, Barry and Wæver, Ole, *Regions and Powers: The Structure of International Security* (Cambridge: Cambridge University Press, 2003).

9. Hall, Stuart; Critcher, Chas; Jefferson, Tony; Clarke, John and Roberts, Brian, *Policing the Crisis: Mugging, the State and Law and Order* (London: Macmillan, 1978). Cohen, Stanley, *Folk Devils and Moral Panics: The Creation of the Mods and Rockers*, 3rd edn (London: Routledge, 2002 [1972]).

10. Butler, Judith, *Precarious Life: The Powers of Mourning and Violence* (London: Verso, 2006). Mbembé, Achille, *Necropolitics* (Durham, NC: Duke University Press, 2003).

11. Bigo and Tsoukala, 'Understanding (in)security'.

12. Hussain, Yasmin and Bagguley, Paul, 'Securitized citizens: Islamophobia, racism and the 7/7 London bombings', *Sociological Review* 60(4), 2012, pp. 715–734.

13. Neal, Andrew W., *Exceptionalism and the Politics of Counter-terrorism: Liberty, Security and the War on Terror* (London: Routledge, 2009).

14. Yancy, George and Butler, Judith, 'What's wrong with All Lives Matter?', *The New York Times*, 12 January 2015.

15. Chadderton, Charlotte, 'The militarisation of English schools: Troops to Teaching and the implications for Initial Teacher Education and race equality', *Race Ethnicity and Education* 17(3), 2014, pp. 407–428. Neocleous, Mark, *Critique of Security* (Edinburgh: Edinburgh University Press, 2008).

16. Wæver, Ole, 'Securitization and desecuritization', pp. 39–69 in R.D. Lipschutz (ed.), *On Security* (New York: Columbia University Press, 1995).

17. Campbell, David, *Writing Security* (Minneapolis, MN: University of Minnesota Press, 1998). Neocleous, *Critique of Security*.

18. Agamben, *State of Exception*.

19. Luchies, Timothy, 'Towards an insurrectionary power/knowledge: Movement-relevance, anti-oppression, prefiguration', *Social Movement Studies* 14(5), 2015, pp. 523–538. Massumi, Brian (ed.), *The Politics of Everyday Fear* (Minneapolis, MN: University of Minnesota Press, 1993). Wæver, 'Securitization and desecuritization'.

20. Bauman, Zygmunt, *Liquid Modernity* (Cambridge: Polity Press, 2000). Berardi, Franco 'Bifo', *Precarious Rhapsody: Semiocapitalism and the Pathologies of the Post-alpha Generation* (Colchester: Minor Compositions, 2009). Harvey, Charles, 'Sex robots and solipsism: Towards a culture of empty contact', *Philosophy in the Contemporary World* 22(2), 2015, pp. 80–93.

Brown, Wendy, 'American nightmare: Neoliberalism, neoconservatism, and de-democratization', *Political Theory* 34(6), 2006, pp. 690–714.

21. Frank, Robert H.; Gilovich, Thomas and Regan, Dennis T., 'Does studying economics inhibit cooperation?', *Journal of Economic Perspectives* 7(2), 1993, pp. 159–171.

22. Massumi, *The Politics of Everyday Fear.*

23. Minton, Anna, *Ground Control: Fear and Happiness in the Twenty-first-century City* (London: Penguin, 2012).

24. Pyles, Loretta; Svistova, Juliana and Ahn, Suran, 'Securitization, racial cleansing, and disaster capitalism: Neoliberal disaster governance in the US Gulf Coast and Haiti', *Critical Social Policy* 37(4), 2017, pp. 582–603.

25. Chandler, Jahaan, 'Social theory and the Occupy movement: An exploration into the relationship between social thought and political practice', MA thesis, University of New Orleans, 2014.

26. Solnit, Rebecca, 'The name of the hurricane is climate change', *The Nation*, 6 November 2012.

27. Davis, Mike, *Ecology of Fear: Los Angeles and the Imagination of Disaster* (New York: Vintage Books, 1998).

28. Klein, *The Shock Doctrine*, p. 17.

29. Marom, 'Occupy Sandy: From relief to resistance'.

30. Pyles et al., 'Securitization, racial cleansing, and disaster capitalism', p. 585.

31. Klein, *The Shock Doctrine*.

32. Marx, Karl. *Capital*, 2 vols, ed. Tom Griffith (Ware, Herts: Wordsworth, 2003), vol. 1, p. 502.

33. Berardi, Franco 'Bifo', *After the Future* (Edinburgh: AK Press, 2011).

34. Van Gelder, Sarah, 'Introduction: How Occupy Wall Street changes everything', in S. Van Gelder (ed.), *This Changes Everything: Occupy Wall Street and the 99% Movement* (San Francisco: Berrett-Koehler Publishers, 2011), p. 3.

35. Harvey, David, 'The right to the city: From capital surplus to accumulation by dispossession', pp. 17–32 in S. Banerjee-Guha (ed.), *Accumulation by Dispossession: Transformative Cities in the New Global Order* (New Delhi: Sage, 2010). See also his *Justice, Nature, and the Geography of Difference* (Oxford: Blackwell, 1996), *Spaces of Hope* (Berkeley: University of California Press, 2000) and *The New Imperialism* (Oxford: Oxford University Press, 2003).

36. Klein, *The Shock Doctrine*, p. 15.

37. Friedman, Milton, *Capitalism and Freedom* (Chicago: University of Chicago Press, 1982 [1962]), p. ix.

38. Greenberg, Miriam, 'The disaster inside the disaster: Hurricane Sandy and post-crisis redevelopment', *New Labor Forum* 23(1), 2014, p. 48.

39. Hannigan, *Disasters without Borders*, p. 156.

40. Jones, Imara, 'What Hurricane Sandy should teach us about climate justice', *Colorlines*, 15 Nov. 2012.

41. Pyles et al., 'Securitization, racial cleansing, and disaster capitalism', p. 585.
42. Ibid., p. 582.
43. Ibid., p. 586.
44. Greenberg, 'The disaster inside the disaster', p. 48.
45. Postone, Moishe, *Time, Labor and Social Domination* (Cambridge: Cambridge University Press, 1993).
46. Preston, John and Firth, Rhiannon, 'The Viracene and capitalism', pp. 11–28 in Preston and Firth (eds), *Coronavirus, Class and Mutual Aid in the UK*.
47. Midnight Notes Collective, *Midnight Oil: Work, Energy, War, 1973–92* (New York: Semiotext(e), 1992). DeAngelis, Massimo, *The Beginning of History: Value Struggles and Global Capital* (London: Pluto Press, 2006).
48. Midnight Notes Collective, 'The new enclosures', *Midnight Notes* #10, 1990, p. 1.
49. Ibid., p. 2.
50. Chang, Ha-Joon and Grabel, Ilene, *Reclaiming Development* (London: Zed, 2004). Soederberg, Susanne, *The Politics of the New International Financial Architecture: Reimposing Neoliberal Domination in the Global South* (London: Zed, 2004).
51. Harvey, *The New Imperialism*, p. 122.
52. Gore, Charles, 'The rise and fall of the Washington Consensus as a paradigm for developing countries', *World Development* 28(95), 2000, pp. 789–804.
53. Wade, Robert, 'Financial regime change', *New Left Review* 53, 2008, pp. 5–21.
54. Chang and Grabel, *Reclaiming Development*, p. 2.
55. Farmer, Paul, 'Social scientists and the new tuberculosis', *Social Science & Medicine* 44(3), 1997, pp. 347–358.
56. Chang and Grabel, *Reclaiming Development*, pp. 231–4.
57. Harvey, *The New Imperialism*, p. 133; DeMartino, George, 'Global neoliberalism, policy autonomy, and international competitive dynamics', *Journal of Economic Issues* 33(2), 1999, pp. 343–349. Mkandawire, Thandika, *Crisis Management and the Making of 'Choiceless Democracies': State, Conflict and Democracy in Africa* (Boulder, CO: Lynne Rienner, 1999).
58. Robinson, William I., *Global Capitalism and the Crisis of Humanity* (Cambridge: Cambridge University Press, 2014).
59. Bauman, Zygmunt, *Collateral Damage: Social Inequalities in a Global Age* (Cambridge: Polity, 2011).
60. Greenberg, 'The disaster inside the disaster'. Welty, Emily E., 'Occupy Wall Street as "American Spring"?', *Peace Review* 26(1), 2014, pp. 38–45.
61. Hartman, Chester and Squires, Gregory D., 'Editors' introduction: Pre-Katrina, post-Katrina', pp. 3–6 in C. Hartman and G.D. Squires (eds), *There Is No Such Thing as a Natural Disaster: Race, Class and Hurricane Katrina* (New York: Routledge, 2006).
62. Taylor, Paul C., *Race: A Philosophical Introduction* (Cambridge: Polity, 2013), pp. viii–ix.

63. E.g. Foti, Alex, 'Mayday Mayday! Euro flex workers time to get a move on', *transversal texts*, April 2005, https://transversal.at/transversal/0704/foti/en (accessed 21 May 2021); Precarias a la deriva, 'Adrift through the circuits of feminized precarious work', *transversal texts*, April 2004, https://transversal.at/transversal/0704/precarias-a-la-deriva/en (accessed 21 May 2021).

64. Federici, Silvia, 'Precarious labour: A feminist perspective', *Journal of Aesthetics and Protest* 1(9), 2008, pp. 123–140.

65. Castillo, Mariano, 'Peru seemed to do everything right. So how did it become a Covid-19 hotspot?' *CNN World*, 25 May 2020. McCoy, Terence and Traiano, Heliosa, '"It will kill a lot of people": Brazil's overcrowded favelas brace for coronavirus', *Independent*, 22 March 2020. TNN, 'Senseless in Chenai: How we violated the curfew in place', *The Times of India*, 26 March 2020. Preston and Firth, *Coronavirus, Class and Mutual Aid in the UK*.

66. Moore, Jason W., 'The Capitalocene, part II: Accumulation by appropriation and the centrality of unpaid work/energy', *Journal of Peasant Studies* 45(2), 2018, pp. 237–279.

67. Moore, Jason W., 'World accumulation and planetary life, or, Why capitalism will not survive until the "last tree is cut"', *IPPR Progressive Review* 24(3), 2017, pp. 175–202.

68. Ibeanu, Okechukwu, 'Oiling the friction: Environmental conflict management in the Niger Delta, Nigeria', *Environmental Change and Security Project Report* 6, 2000, pp. 19–32.

69. Amin, Samir, *Delinking: Towards a Polycentric World* (London: Zed Books, 1990).

70. Ferguson, James, 'Seeing like an oil company: Space, security, and global capital in neoliberal Africa', *American Anthropologist* 107(3), 2005, pp. 377–382.

71. Karatasli, Sahan Savas; Kumral, Sefika; Scully, Ben and Upadhyay, Smriti, 'Class, crisis and the 2011 protest wave: Cyclical and secular trends in global labor unrest', pp. 184–200 in I. Wallerstein, C. Chase-Dunn and C. Suter (eds), *Overcoming Global Inequalities* (London: Paradigm, 2015).

72. Amin, Samir, *The Liberal Virus* (London: Pluto, 2004).

73. Robinson, Andrew, 'The oppressive discourse of global exclusion: The "war on terror" as a war on difference and freedom', pp. 253–274 in M. Mullard and B.A. Cole (eds), *Globalization, Citizenship and the War on Terror* (Cheltenham: Edward Elgar, 2007).

74. Wallerstein, Immanuel, *World Systems Analysis: An Introduction* (Durham, NC: Duke University Press, 2004).

75. Akuno, Kali, 'Until we win: Black labor and liberation in the disposable era', pp. 61–73 in M. Truscello and A. Nangwaya (eds), *Why Don't the Poor Rise Up? Organizing the Twenty-first Century Resistance* (Oakland, CA: AK Press, 2017).

76. Sassen, Saskia, *Expulsions: Brutality and Complexity in the Global Economy* (Cambridge, MA: Belknap Press, 2014), p. 10.

77. Karatasli et al., 'Class, crisis and the 2011 protest wave', p. 185.
78. Scott, James C., *Weapons of the Weak: Everyday Forms of Peasant Resistance* (New Haven, CT: Yale University Press, 1985), pp. 76–77.
79. Virilio, Paul, *Popular Defence and Ecological Struggles* (New York: Semiotext(e), 1990).
80. Banerjee, Subhabrata Bobby, 'Voices of the governed: Towards a theory of the translocal', *Organization* 18, 2011, pp. 323–344.
81. Virno, Paolo, *A Grammar of the Multitude* (Cambridge, MA: MIT Press, 2004).
82. Grubačić, Andrej and O'Hearn, Denis, *Living at the Edges of Capitalism: Adventures in Exile and Mutual Aid* (Berkeley: University of California Press, 2016).
83. Clover, Joshua, *Riot, Strike, Riot: The New Era of Uprisings* (London: Verso, 2016), p. 28.
84. See Chapter 4 for Kropotkin; see also Grubačić and O'Hearn, *Living at the Edges of Capitalism*, pp. 110–176; and Khasnabish, Alex, 'Cultivating the radical imagination in the North of the Americas', pp. 119–132 in Truscello and Nangwaya (eds), *Why Don't the Poor Rise Up?*
85. Tsilimpounidi, Myrto and Walsh, Aylwyn, *Remapping 'Crisis': A Guide to Athens* (Alresford: Zero Books, 2014).
86. Grubačić and O'Hearn, *Living at the Edges of Capitalism*, pp. 104–109.
87. Gramsci, Antonio, *Selections from Prison Notebooks* (London: Lawrence and Wishart, 1971).
88. Scott, James C., *Domination and the Arts of Resistance: Hidden Transcripts* (New Haven, CT: Yale University Press, 1990).
89. Foucault, Michel, *Society Must be Defended* (Harmondsworth: Penguin, 1988).
90. Gramsci, *Prison Notebooks*, p. 327.
91. Amoore, Louise (ed.), *The Global Resistance Reader* (New York: Routledge, 2005).
92. Foucault, Michel, 'The ethic of care for the self as a practice of freedom', in J. Bernauer and D. Rasmussen (eds), *The Final Foucault* (Cambridge, MA: MIT Press, 1988), pp. 1–20.
93. Scott, *Domination and the Arts of Resistance*, pp. 74–75.
94. Ibid., p. 89.
95. Ibid., p. 282.
96. Hickey, Samuel and Mohan, Giles, *Participation: From Tyranny to Transformation* (London: Zed Books, 2004).
97. Roy, Arundhati, 'The NGO-ization of resistance', *Massalijn*, 4 September 2014, http://massalijn.nl/new/the-ngo-ization-of-resistance/ (accessed 19 May 2021).
98. Fisher, 'Doing good? The politics and antipolitics of NGO practices'.
99. Esteves, Ana Margarida; Motta, Sara C. and Cox, Laurence, '"Civil society" versus social movements', *Interface: A journal for and about social movements* 1(2), 2009, pp. 1–21.

100. Petras, James and Veltmeyer, Henry, *Globalization Unmasked: Imperialism in the 21st Century* (London: Zed Books, 2001).

101. 'Coronavirus: A call for solidarity in a time of crisis', Abahlali base'Mjondolo, 22 March 2020, http://abahlali.org/node/17029/ (accessed 21 August 2020).

102. Croatoan, *Who Is Oakland: Anti-oppression Activism, the Politics of Safety, and State Co-optation*, April 2012, https://escalatingidentity.wordpress.com/2012/04/30/who-is-oakland-anti-oppression-politics-decolonization-and-the-state/ (accessed 19 May 2021).

103. Fowler, Alan, 'Non-governmental organizations as agents of democratization: An African perspective', *Journal of International Development* 5(3), 1993, p. 335.

104. Williams, Andrew; Cloke, Paul and Thomas, Samuel, 'Co-constituting neoliberalism: Faith-based organisations, co-option, and resistance in the UK', *Environment and Planning A* 44(6), 2012, pp. 1479–1501. Però, Davide, 'Migrants' practices of citizenship and policy change', pp. 244–264 in C. Shore, S. Wright and D. Però (eds), *Policy Worlds: Anthropology and the Analysis of Contemporary Power* (Oxford: Berghahn Books, 2011).

105. Croatoan, *Who Is Oakland*.

106. Hannigan, *Disasters without Borders*, p. 9.

107. Benjamin, Walter, 'Thesis IX', in *On the Concept of History*, trans. D. Redmond (1974 [1942]), from www.marxists.org/reference/archive/benjamin/1940/history.htm (accessed 22 August 2020).

108. McLaverty-Robinson, Andrew, 'Walter Benjamin: Messianism and revolution – Theses on history', *Ceasefire*, 5 November 2013, https://ceasefiremagazine.co.uk/walter-benjamin-messianism-revolution-theses-history/ (accessed 19 May 2021).

109. Virilio, *Popular Defence and Ecological Struggles*.

110. Quarantelli, Enrico L., *Catastrophes Are Different from Disasters: Some Implications for Crisis Planning and Managing Drawn from Katrina* (Newark, DE: University of Delaware Disaster Research Center, 2005).

111. Gordon, Uri, 'Dark tidings: Anarchist politics in the age of collapse', pp. 249–258 in R. Amster, A. DeLeon, L. Fernandez, A.J. Nocella II and D. Shannon (eds), *Contemporary Anarchist Studies* (London: Routledge, 2009).

112. Jasanoff, Sheila (ed.), *Learning from Disaster: Risk Management after Bhopal* (Philadelphia, PA: University of Pennsylvania Press). Jasanoff, Sheila (ed.), *States of Knowledge: The Co-production of Science and the Social Order* (London: Routledge, 2004).

4. TOWARDS AN ANARCHIST APPROACH TO DISASTER

1. Kropotkin, Peter, *The State: Its Historic Role*, trans. Vernon Richards (London: Freedom Press, 1997 [1897]).

2. Ibid., p. 10.

3. Marshall, *Demanding the Impossible*, p. 324.

4. Kropotkin, *The State*, p. 31.
5. Ibid., p. 24.
6. Ibid., p. 11.
7. Ibid., p. 25.
8. Ibid., p. 33.
9. Ibid., p. 31.
10. Ibid., p. 48.
11. Ibid., p. 49.
12. Ibid., p. 49.
13. Ibid., p. 59.
14. Ehrenreich, Barbara and English, Deirdre, *Witches, Midwives and Nurses: A History of Women Healers* (New York: The Feminist Press, 2010 [1973]), p. 45.
15. Federici, Silvia, *Caliban and the Witch: Women, the Body and Primitive Accumulation* (New York: Autonomedia, 2004).
16. Mies, Maria, *Patriarchy and Accumulation on a World Scale: Women in the International Division of Labour* (London: Zed Books, 2014 [1986]).
17. Merchant, Carolyn, *The Death of Nature: Women, Ecology and the Scientific Revolution* (New York: Harper and Row, 1980).
18. Escobar, Arturo, *Encountering Development: The Making and Unmaking of the Third World* (Princeton, NJ: Princeton University Press, 1995). Shiva, Vandana, *Staying Alive: Women, Ecology and Development* (London: Zed Books, 1989).
19. Mignolo, Walter D., *Local Histories/Global Designs* (Princeton, NJ: Princeton University Press, 2012). Lugones, Maria, 'Coloniality and gender', *Tabula Rasa* 9, 2008, pp. 73–102.
20. Kinna, Ruth, 'Fields of vision: Kropotkin and revolutionary change', *SubStance* 36(2), 2007, pp. 67–86.
21. Stirner, *The Ego and Its Own*. The reader may also wish to compare the newest edition, which translates Stirner's terminology very differently: Stirner, Max, *The Unique and Its Property*, trans. Wolfi Landstreicher (Baltimore, MD: Underworld Amusements, 2017 [1844]).
22. Landauer, Gustav, *For Socialism*, trans. D.J. Parent (St Louis: Telos Press, 1983 [1911]).
23. Buber, Martin, *I and Thou* (London: Continuum, 2004 [1923]).
24. Reich, Wilhelm, *The Mass Psychology of Fascism* (London: Souvenir Press, 1997 [1933]).
25. Kropotkin, Peter, *Mutual Aid: A Factor of Evolution*, ed. Will Jonson (Scotts Valley, CA: CreateSpace Independent Publishing Platform, 2014 [1902]), *passim* but see especially pp. 13–21.
26. Buber, *I and Thou*.
27. Stirner, *The Ego and Its Own*, p. 179.
28. Kropotkin, *Mutual Aid*, p. 14.

29. Ward, Colin, 'Anarchy in Milton Keynes', *The Raven* 18(5), 1992, http://theanarchistlibrary.org/library/colin-ward-anarchy-in-milton-keynes.pdf (accessed November 2021).

30. Kropotkin, *Mutual Aid*, pp. 145–6.

31. Ward, 'Anarchy in Milton Keynes', p. 4.

32. Ward, Colin, *Anarchy in Action* (London: Aldgate Press, 1973).

33. Negri, Antonio, *Insurgencies: Constituent Power and the Modern State* (Minneapolis, MN: University of Minnesota Press, 1999) p. 324.

34. Holloway, John, *Change the World without Taking Power* (London: Pluto, 2005).

35. Castoriadis, Cornelius, *The Imaginary Institution of Society* (Cambridge, MA: MIT Press, 1988).

36. Virno, *A Grammar of the Multitude*.

37. Agamben, Giorgio, *The Coming Community* (Minneapolis, MN: University of Minnesota Press, 1990).

38. Deleuze, Gilles, *Nietzsche and Philosophy* (London: Continuum, 2006 [1983]).

39. Zerzan, John, 'The mass psychology of misery', in *Future Primitive Revisited* (Post Townsend, WA: Feral House, 2012).

40. Kropotkin, *Mutual Aid*, pp. 145–191.

41. Clastres, Pierre, *Society Against the State*, trans. Robert Hurley (Oxford: Blackwell for Mole Editions, 1977).

42. Bird-David, Nurit, 'Sociality and immediacy: or, Past and present conversations on bands', *Man* 29(3), 1994, pp. 583–603.

43. Ibid., p. 597.

44. Katsiaficas, Georgy, *The Subversion of Politics: European Autonomous Social Movements and the Decolonization of Everyday Life* (Oakland, CA: AK Press, 2006 [1997]), p. 5.

45. Laclau, Ernesto and Mouffe, Chantal, *Hegemony and Socialist Strategy: Towards a Radical Democratic Politics* (London: Verso, 1985).

46. Day, Richard J.F., *Gramsci is Dead: Anarchist Currents in the Newest Social Movements* (London: Pluto, 2005).

47. Sitrin, Marina, *Horizontalism: Voices of Popular Power in Argentina* (Edinburgh: AK Press, 2007).

48. Graeber, David, *Direct Action: An Ethnography* (Oakland, CA: AK Press, 2009).

49. Zibechi, Raúl, *Dispersing Power: Social Movements as Anti-State Forces* (Edinburgh: AK Press, 2010).

50. Marshall, *Demanding the Impossible*, p. 324.

51. Newman, Saul, *From Bakunin to Lacan: Anti-authoritarianism and the Dislocation of Power* (Lanham, MD: Lexington Books, 2001), pp. 117–121. For variations on this critique, see also May, Todd, *The Political Philosophy of Poststructuralist Anarchism* (University Park, PA: Pennsylvania State

University Press, 1994) and Call, Lewis, *Postmodern Anarchism* (Lanham, MD: Lexington Books, 2002).

52. Ferretti, Federico, 'Evolution and revolution: Anarchist geographies, modernity and poststructuralism', *Environment and Planning D: Society and Space* 35(5), 2017, p. 894.
53. Morris, Brian, *Kropotkin: The Politics of Community* (Oakland, CA: PM Press, 2018), p. 178.
54. Turcato, Davide, *Making Sense of Anarchism: Errico Malatesta's Experiments with Revolution 1889–1900* (London: AK Press, 2015).
55. Ferretti, 'Evolution and revolution', pp. 905–906.
56. Peterson, Abby, *Contemporary Political Protest* (Aldershot: Ashgate, 2001).
57. Robinson, Andrew, 'Life is magical: Affect and empowerment in Autonomous Social Movements', pp. 33–55 in A. Starodub and A. Robinson (eds), *Riots and Militant Occupations: Smashing a System, Building a World – A Critical Introduction* (London: Rowman and Littlefield, 2018), pp. 46–47.
58. Kropotkin, *The State*, p. 40.
59. False consciousness is usually associated with Marxist theory and refers to the inability of the proletariat to perceive the true nature of their exploitation, particularly from within dominant paradigms of thought, due to the socio-discursive power of the bourgeoisie (often glossed as its control of 'ideological apparatuses' such as the media and the Church). The idea of false consciousness is often rejected, particularly by liberals and poststructuralists but also by anarchists, because it relies on a split between a theorist who is a 'knowing subject' and a majority deemed ignorant and hoodwinked. This view may encourage vanguardism and hierarchical politics. However, many anarchist and anarchistic practices, such as feminist consciousness-raising, anarchist free schools and forms of propaganda, have operated with some assumptions that people might not always be aware of their own interests, and there are links between ideas of false consciousness and anarchist ideas of psychological alienation, for example Stirner's 'spooks' or Reich's 'character armour'.
60. Negri, *Insurgencies*, p. 327.
61. Deleuze, Gilles and Guattari, Félix, *Anti-Oedipus* (London: Continuum, 2004 [1972]); see also Reich, *The Mass Psychology of Fascism*.
62. Clastres, *Society Against the State*.
63. Lagalisse, Erica Michelle, '"Marginalizing Magdalena": Intersections of gender and the secular in anarchoindigenist solidarity activism', *Signs: Journal of Women in Culture and Society* 36(3), 2011, pp. 653–678.
64. Lagalisse, Erica, *Occult Features of Anarchism: With Attention to the Conspiracy of Kings and the Conspiracy of the Peoples* (Oakland, CA: PM Press, 2019), pp. 51–52.
65. Chatterton, Paul, 'So what does it mean to be anti-capitalist? Conversations with activists from urban social centres', *Urban Studies* 47(6), 2010: 1205–1224.

66. For the argument that it is harder to sustain non-hierarchical structures with more diverse and heterogeneous groups, see Rothschild, Joyce and Whitt, J. Allen, *The Cooperative Workplace: Potentials and Dilemmas of Organizational Democracy and Participation* (New York: Cambridge University Press, 1986).

67. Leach, Darcy K., 'Culture and the structure of tyrannylessness', *Sociological Quarterly* 54, 2013, pp. 181–191. Leach, Darcy K., 'An elusive "we": Antidogmatism, democratic practice, and the contradictory identity of the German Autonomen', *American Behavioral Scientist*, 52(7), 2009, pp. 1042–1068.

68. Buber, *I and Thou*.

69. Levinas, Emmanuel, *Humanism of the Other* (Urbana, IL: University of Illinois Press, 2006 [1972]).

70. Stirner, *The Ego and Its Own*, p. 179.

71. Hannigan, *Disasters without Borders*.

72. Ibid., p. 8.

73. Solnit, *A Paradise Built in Hell*, pp. 8–9.

74. Ibid., p. 5.

75. Ibid., pp. 6–7.

76. Ibid., p. 2.

77. Bowles, Samuel, 'Policies designed for self-interested citizens may undermine "the moral sentiments": Evidence from economic experiments', *Science* 320, 2008, pp. 1605–1609.

78. Preston et al., 'Community response in disasters'.

79. Robinson, 'The oppressive discourse of global exclusion', p. 261.

80. Robinson, 'Life is magical', pp. 41–45.

81. Day, *Gramsci Is Dead*.

82. Katsiaficas, *The Subversion of Politics*.

83. Welty, 'Occupy Wall Street as "American Spring"?'

84. Smith, R.C.; Gunn, Richard and Wilding, Adrian, 'Alternative horizons: Understanding Occupy's politics', Open Democracy, 6 December 2013, www.opendemocracy.net/en/participation-now/alternative-horizons-understanding-occupys-po/ (accessed 19 May 2021).

85. Hardt, Emily, *In Transition: The Politics of Place-based, Prefigurative Social Movements*, PhD thesis, University of Massachusetts, 2013, Open access dissertations 744, p. 133.

86. Clark, 'Disaster anarchism'.

87. John, Beatrice and Kagan, Sacha, 'Extreme climate events as opportunities for radical open citizenship', *Open Citizenship* 5(1), 2014, pp. 60–75.

88. Millner-Larsen, Nadja, 'Demandless times', *WSQ: Women's Studies Quarterly* 41 (3), 2013, pp. 113–130.

89. Raekstad, Paul and Gradin, Sofa Saio, *Prefigurative Politics: Building Tomorrow Today* (Cambridge: Polity, 2020).

90. Boggs, Carl, 'Marxism, prefigurative communism and the problem of workers' control', *Radical America* 11(6) and 12(1) (special double issue): 99–122.
91. Gordon, Uri, 'Prefigurative politics between ethical practice and absent promise', *Political Studies* 66(2), 2018, p. 530.
92. Raekstad and Gradin, *Prefigurative Politics*, p. 15.
93. Garforth, Lisa, 'No intentions? Utopian theory after the future', *Journal for Cultural Research* 13(1), 2009, pp. 5–27.
94. The idea of 'plugging in' was used by interviewees and is discussed in Chapter 5.
95. The term 'lifeboat communism' was coined as a critical account by Lear, Ben, 'Lifeboat communism: A review of Franco 'Bifo' Berardi's *After the Future*', *Viewpoint Magazine*, 18 May 2012, www.viewpointmag.com/2012/05/18/lifeboat-communism-a-review-of-franco-bifo-berardis-after-the-future/ (accessed May 2019).
96. Cohn, Norman, *The Pursuit of the Millennium: Revolutionary Millenarians and Mystical Anarchists of the Middle Ages* (Oxford: Oxford University Press, 1970).
97. The Invisible Committee, *The Coming Insurrection* (Los Angeles, CA: Semiotext(e), 2009), pp. 80–81.
98. Noys, Benjamin, 'The fabric of struggles', pp. 7–22 in Benjamin Noys (ed.), *Communization and Its Discontents* (Colchester: Minor Compositions, 2012), p. 10.
99. The Invisible Committee, *The Coming Insurrection*, p. 35.
100. Out of the Woods, 'Disaster communism, part 1: Disaster communities', *libcom.org*, 2014, http://libcom.org/blog/disaster-communism-part-1-disaster-communities-08052014 (accessed 19 May 2021).
101. Out of the Woods, 'Disaster communism, part 2: Communisation and concrete utopia', *libcom.org*, 2014, https://libcom.org/blog/disaster-communism-part-2-communisation-concrete-utopia-14052014 (accessed 18 May 2021).
102. Virno, Paolo, 'Virtuosity and revolution: The political theory of exodus', pp. 132–46 in M. Hardt and P. Virno (eds), *Radical Thought in Italy* (Minneapolis, MN: University of Minnesota Press, 1996).
103. The Invisible Committee, *The Coming Insurrection*, p. 34.
104. Berardi, *After the Future*, p. 177.
105. Endnotes, 'What are we to do?', *libcom.org*, 2 January 2012, http://libcom.org/library/what-are-we-do-endnotes (accessed 18 May 2019).
106. Lear, 'Lifeboat communism'.
107. Berardi, *After the Future*, p. 153.
108. Tiqqun, *Introduction to Civil War* (Los Angeles: Semiotext(e), 2010).
109. The Invisible Committee, *The Coming Insurrection*, p. 97.
110. Ibid., p. 119.
111. Gordon, 'Dark tidings'.

112. Ibid.

113. Gordon, 'Prefigurative politics between ethical practice and absent promise', drawing on Bürge, Abiral, *Catastrophic Futures, Anxious Presents: Lifestyle Activism and Hope in the Permaculture Movement in Turkey*, Master's dissertation, Sabancı University, Istanbul, 2018.

114. Ibid., p. 534.

115. Mauss, Marcel, *The Gift: Forms and Functions of Exchange in Archaic Societies* (London: Cohen & West, 1970).

116. Bollier, David, 'The stubborn vitality of the gift economy', in *Silent Theft: The Private Plunder of Our Common Wealth* (New York: Routledge, 2002), pp. 38–39.

117. Anonymous, *Desert*, The Anarchist Library, 2011, http://theanarchistlibrary. org/library/anonymous-desert (accessed 1 August 2019).

118. Ibid.

119. Ibid.

120. Ibid.

121. The Invisible Committee, *To Our Friends*, pp. 120–129.

122. Mcm_cmc, 'Fully Automated Luxury Communism: A utopian critique', *libcom.org*, 14 June 2015, https://libcom.org/blog/fully-automated-luxury-communism-utopian-critique-14062015 (accessed 20 May 2021).

123. Bastani, Aaron, *Fully Automated Luxury Communism* (London: Verso Books, 2019).

124. Williams, Alex and Srnicek, Nick, '#Accelerate: Manifesto for an accelerationist politics', pp. 347–362 in R. Mackay and A. Avanessian (eds), *#ACCELERATE: The Accelerationist Reader* (Falmouth: Urbanomic, 2014).

125. Noys, Benjamin, *Malign Velocities: Accelerationism and Capitalism* (Winchester: Zero Books 2014), p. 7.

126. Proudhon, Pierre Joseph, *The Philosophy of Poverty* (New York: Arno Press, 1972 [1896]), p. 179.

127. Bookchin, Murray, *Post-scarcity Anarchism* (San Francisco: Ramparts, 1971).

128. Aday, Sean; Farrell, Henry; Lynch, Marc; Sides, John; Kelly, John and Zuckerman, Ethan, 'Blogs and bullets: New media in contentious politics', *United States Institute of Peace* 65, 2010, p. 18.

129. Lovejoy, Kristen and Saxton, Gregory D., 'Information, community, and action: How nonprofit organizations use social media', *Journal of Computer-Mediated Communication* 17(3), 2012, pp. 337–353.

130. Curran, Giorel and Gibson, Morgan. 'WikiLeaks, anarchism and technologies of dissent', *Antipode* 45(2), 2013, pp. 294–314.

131. Kostakis, Vasilis; Latoufis, Kostas; Liarokapis, Minas and Bauwens, Michel, 'The convergence of digital commons with local manufacturing from a degrowth perspective: Two illustrative cases', *Journal of Cleaner Production* 197, 2018, pp. 1684–1693.

132. Moore, John, 'A primitivist primer', The Anarchist Library, 2009, http:// theanarchistlibrary.org/library/john-moore-a-primitivist-primer (accessed 20 May 2021).

133. Zerzan, *Future Primitive Revisited*.
134. Perlman, Fredy, *Against His-Story, Against Leviathan!* (Detroit: Black and Red, 1983).
135. Merchant, *The Death of Nature*.
136. Gardiner, Michael E., 'Critique of accelerationism', *Theory, Culture & Society* 43(1), 2017, pp. 29–52.
137. Winner, Langdon, *The Whale and the Reactor: A Search for Limits in an Age of High Technology* (Chicago: University of Chicago Press, 1985) pp. 29–37.
138. Illich, Ivan, *Tools for Conviviality* (New York: Marion Boyars, 2001 [1973]).
139. Morozov, Evgeny, *The Net Delusion: The Dark Side of Internet Freedom* (New York: Public Affairs, 2011).
140. Berardi, *Precarious Rhapsody*, p. 42.
141. Lazzarato, Maurizio, 'Immaterial labour', pp. 132–146 in M. Hardt and P. Virno (eds), *Radical Thought in Italy* (Minneapolis, MN: University of Minnesota Press).
142. Benson, Rodney, 'Shaping the public sphere: Habermas and beyond', *American Sociologist* 40(3), 2009, pp. 175–197.
143. Van Dijck, José, *The Culture of Connectivity: A Critical History of Social Media* (Oxford: Oxford University Press, 2013).
144. Illich, *Tools for Conviviality*, pp. 80–81.
145. Prieur, Ran, 'TechJudge', *Ran Prieur's Website*, 2011, www.ranprieur.com/tech.html (accessed 25 June 2019).
146. Capra, Fritjof, *The Turning Point: Science, Society, and the Rising Culture* (New York: Bantam, 1983). Derrik Jensen, *A Language Older than Words* (Hartford, VT: Chelsea Green Publishing, 2004).
147. Cudworth, Erika and Hobden, Steve, *Posthuman International Relations: Complexity, Ecologism and Global Politics* (London: Zed Books, 2011).
148. Ibid., pp. 184–186.
149. Bernes, Jasper, 'Between the devil and the Green New Deal', *Commune Mag* 2, 2019, https://communemag.com/between-the-devil-and-the-green-new-deal/ (accessed 21 May 2021).
150. Moore, Jason W., *Capitalism in the Web of Life: Ecology and the Accumulation of Capital* (London: Verso Books, 2015).
151. Bondesson, *Vulnerability and Power*.
152. Gordon, Uri, 'Anarchism and the politics of technology', *Working USA* 12(3), 2009, p. 499.
153. Pickard, Victor W., 'Cooptation and cooperation: Institutional exemplars of democratic internet technology', *New Media & Society* 10(4), 2008, pp. 625–645.
154. Himanen, Pekka, *The Hacker Ethic and the Spirit of the Information Age* (New York: Random House, 2001). See also Wark, McKenzie, *A Hacker Manifesto* (Cambridge, MA: Harvard University Press 2004).
155. Truscello, Michael, 'The architecture of information: Open source software and tactical poststructuralist anarchism', *Postmodern Culture* 13(3), 2003.

156. Davis, Sarah R., *Hackerspaces: Making the Maker Movement* (Cambridge: Polity Press, 2017).
157. Firth, Rhiannon, *Utopian Politics: Citizenship and Practice* (London: Routledge, 2012).
158. Serge, Victor, *What Every Radical Should Know about State Repression: A Guide for Activists* (Melbourne: Ocean Press, 2005).
159. Arendt, Hannah, *The Origins of Totalitarianism* (New York: The World Publishing, 1962 [1951]).
160. Dunlap, Alexander, 'Permanent war: Grids, boomerangs and counter-insurgency', *Anarchist Studies* 22(2), 2014, pp. 55–79.
161. Virilio, Paolo, *Pure War* (Los Angeles: Semiotext(e), 2008 [1983]).
162. Kittrie, Nicholas N., *The War Against Authority: From the Crisis of Legitimacy to a New Social Contract* (Baltimore, MD: Johns Hopkins University Press, 1995).
163. Dragonowl, Lupus, 'The future of insurrection', *Anarchy: A journal of desire armed* 70/71 and 72/73, 2011, http://anarchymag.org/2016/06/the-future-of-insurrection/ (accessed 16 July 2019).
164. Ibid.
165. Clark, 'Disaster anarchism', pp. 193–192.
166. Robinson, 'Thinking from the outside: Avoiding recuperation'.
167. Vaneigem, Raoul, *The Revolution of Everyday Life*, trans. D. Nicholson-Smith (London: Rebel Press (2006 [1967]).
168. Law, Larry, 'The spectacle: A skeleton key', *Spectacular Times* 08 (London: Pocketbook Series, no date), p. 13, https://libcom.org/files/Spectacular%20Times%20the%20Skeleton%20Key.pdf (accessed 3 November 2021).
169. Hardt and Negri, *Empire*.
170. Deleuze, Gilles and Guattari, Félix, *A Thousand Plateaus: Capitalism and Schizophrenia* (London: Bloomsbury, 1988).
171. Robinson. 'Thinking from the outside: Avoiding recuperation'.
172. Fisher, *Capitalist Realism*.
173. Scott, *Domination and the Arts of Resistance*.
174. Ward, *Anarchy in Action*.
175. Dragonowl, 'The future of insurrection'.
176. Ibid.
177. Ibid.
178. Day, *Gramsci Is Dead*, pp. 14–15.
179. Kropotkin, *The State*, p. 45.
180. Deleuze and Guattari, *A Thousand Plateaus*, pp. 501–522.
181. Esteves, Motta and Cox, Lawrence, '"Civil society" versus social movements', *Interface: A journal for and about social movements* 1(2), 2009, pp. 1–21.
182. Crn Blok, 'The NGO sector: The Trojan horse of capitalism', The Anarchist Library, 2014, https://theanarchistlibrary.org/library/crn-blok-the-ngo-sector-the-trojan-horse-of-capitalism (accessed 19 July 2019).

5. OCCUPY SANDY MUTUAL AID, NEW YORK, 2012

1. Welty, 'Occupy Wall Street as "American Spring"?'
2. Unpublished article by journalist Bill Weinberg (personal communication, 12 May 2016).
3. Shepard, Ben, 'From flooded neighborhoods to sustainable urbanism: A New York diary', *Socialism and Democracy* 27(2), 2013, pp. 42–64.
4. Manski, Rebecca, 'Beyond the box: The Occupy movement's new vision for disaster relief', *The Humanist* 73(1), 2013, https://thehumanist.com/magazine/january-february-2013/up-front/beyond-the-box (accessed 21 May 2021).
5. Ambinder et al., *The Resilient Social Network*.
6. Milburn, Eleanor, 'Occupy Sandy: A 21st century platform organization', 17 December 2012, www.academia.edu/6314032/Occupy_Sandy_A_21st_Century_Platform_Organization (accessed 21 May 2021).
7. Quote from Occupy volunteer in unpublished article by journalist Bill Weinberg (personal communication, 12 May 2016).
8. Goldstein, 'Is Occupy Wall Street outperforming the Red Cross in hurricane relief?'
9. Cornish et al., 'Trust the process'; Halbfinger, 'Anger grows at response by Red Cross'.
10. Bachom, '"Got mold? Cold? FEMA?"'
11. Malsin, 'Best of enemies'.
12. crow, *Black Flags and Windmills*, pp. 128–129.
13. Ambinder et al., *The Resilient Social Network*.
14. Ibid., p. 3.
15. Ibid., pp. 19, 41.
16. Hickey, Ryan, 'To destroy is to build: Occupy Sandy and mutual aid', *Occupied Times*, December 2012, http://theoccupiedtimes.org/?p=7656; Shepard, 'From flooded neighbourhoods to sustainable urbanism'.
17. Ambinder et al., *The Resilient Social Network*.
18. Conroy, William, 'The (im)mobilities of mutual aid: Occupy Sandy, racial liberalism, insurgent infrastructure', *ACME: An International e-Journal for Critical Geographies* 18(4), 2019.
19. Mutual Aid Disaster Relief, https://mutualaiddisasterrelief.org/ (accessed 21 May 2021).
20. Sitrin, Marina, 'Horizontalism: From Argentina to Wall Street', *NACLA Report on the Americas* 44(6), 2011, p. 8.
21. Hardt, Michael and Negri, Antonio, 'The fight for "real democracy" at the heart of Occupy Wall Street', *Foreign Affairs*, 11 October 2011.
22. There are many sources that interpret Occupy Wall Street's values as anarchist, or trace their lineage to anarchism. For a handful of examples, see: Graeber, David, 'Occupy Wall Street's anarchist roots', *Al Jazeera*, 20 November 2011; Hall, Budd L., '"A giant human hashtag": Learning and the

#Occupy movement', pp. 127–140 in B.L. Hall; D. Clover; J. Crowther and E. Scandrett, (eds), *Learning and Education for a Better World: The Role of Social Movements* (Rotterdam: Sense publishers, 2012), p. 130; Hammond, John L., 'The anarchism of Occupy Wall Street', *Science & Society* 79(2), 2015, pp. 288–313; Bray, Mark, *Translating Anarchy: The Anarchism of Occupy Wall Street* (Winchester: John Hunt Publishing, 2013); Pickerill, Jenny and Krinsky, John, 'Why does Occupy matter?', *Social Movement Studies* 11(3–4), 2012, pp. 279–287.

23. This draws on my own experience of involvement with Occupy! Nottingham, where conspiracy theorists had a vocal presence. See also: Burns, Jennifer, 'Ron Paul and the new libertarianism', *Dissent* 59(3), 2012, pp. 46–50. The hijacking of left-wing movements by the right, or the infiltration of social movements with conspiracy theories is of course nothing new, nor specific to Occupy Wall Street. See also Lagalisse, *Occult Features of Anarchism*.

24. New York City General Assembly, *Principles of Solidarity*, 17 September 2011, https://web.archive.org/web/20120915065231/http:/www.nycga.net/resources/documents/principles-of-solidarity/ (accessed 21 May 2021). See also Welty, Emily; Bolton, Matthew; Nayak, Meghana and Malone, Christopher (eds), *Occupying Political Science: The Occupy Wall Street Movement from New York to the World* (New York: Springer, 2012).

25. crow, *Black Flags and Windmills*, pp. 114–116.

26. Deleuze and Guattari contrast arborescent thought, characterised by insistence on totalising principles and binary thought, with rhizomic thought or nomad sciences, which emphasise heterogeneous links between concepts. See Deleuze and Guattari, *A Thousand Plateaus*, pp. 3–28.

27. Ambinder et al., *The Resilient Social Network*, p. 52.

28. Beito, David T., 'Mutual aid, state welfare, and organized charity: Fraternal societies and the "deserving" and "undeserving" poor, 1900–1930', *Journal of Policy History* 5(4), 1993, pp. 419–434. It may also be worth noting that a lot of the early anarchists were also work-cultists who thought everyone has to work and people who don't work should either be forced to work or starve (particularly evident in Proudhon and Bakunin and some of the syndicalists). 'Abolition of work' and related ideas of autonomy come fairly late – after the rise of mass production, consumer society and near-full employment. For an anarchist perspective critical of work, see Black, Bob, *The Abolition of Work and Other Essays* (Port Townsend, WA: Loompanics Unlimited, 1986).

29. Smith, 'The state, Occupy and disaster'.

30. Ibid.

31. Shepard, 'From flooded neighbourhoods to sustainable urbanism'.

32. Hickey, 'To destroy is to build'.

33. Vasudevan, Alexander, 'The autonomous city: Towards a critical geography of occupation', *Progress in Human Geography* 39(3), 2015, pp. 316–337.

34. Solnit, *A Paradise Built in Hell*, p. 5.

35. Gordon, 'Dark tidings'.

36. Hickey, 'To destroy is to build'.
37. Shepard, 'From flooded neighbourhoods to sustainable urbanism'.
38. Gordon, 'Dark tidings', p. 225.
39. Millner-Larsen, 'Demandless times'.
40. Manski, 'Beyond the box', p. 6.
41. Pickerill and Krinsky, 'Why does Occupy matter?', p. 283.
42. Manski 'Beyond the box', p. 6.
43. Moffitt, Benjamin, *The Global Rise of Populism: Performance, Political Style and Representation* (Stanford, CA: Stanford University Press, 2016), p. 25. See also Tormey, Simon, *Populism: A Beginner's Guide* (London: OneWorld Publications, 2019).
44. Preston et al., 'Community response in disasters', p. 748.
45. Time's Up!, https://times-up.org/ (accessed 21 May 2021).
46. Shepard, Benjamin, 'DIY urbanism as an environmental justice strategy: The case study of Time's Up! 1987–2012', *Theory in Action* 7(2), 2014, p. 67.
47. Shepard, 'From flooded neighbourhoods to sustainable urbanism'.
48. Bondesson, *Vulnerability and Power*, p. 42.
49. Cornwall, Andrea, 'Whose voices? Whose choices? Reflections on gender and participatory development', *World Development* 31(8), 2003, pp. 1325–1342.
50. For the classical statement of this viewpoint, see Freeman, Jo, 'The tyranny of structurelessness', pp. 1–5 in *Untying the Knot* (London: Anarchist Federation, 2005 [1972]). In my view, Freeman has been comprehensively rebutted from an anarchist viewpoint by Cathy Levine in her response. See Levine, Cathy, 'The tyranny of tyranny', pp. 5–7 in *Untying the Knot* (London: The Anarchist Federation, 2005 [original publication date unknown]). Freeman's arguments are continuously re-hashed in radical movements, however.
51. Phoenix Insurgent, 'Occupied with class: The middle class in the Occupy movement', pp. 66–74 in Aragorn! (ed.) *Occupy Everything: Anarchists in the Occupy Movement 2009-2011* (Berkeley, CA: LBC Books, 2012).
52. On the diversity of social movements, see Leach, Darcy K., 'Culture and the structure of tyrannylessness', *Sociological Quarterly* 54, 2013, pp. 181–191; Leach, Darcy K. 'An elusive "we": Antidogmatism, democratic practice, and the contradictory identity of the German autonomen', *American Behavioral Scientist* 52(7), 2009, pp. 1042–1068. On the demographic composition of the Occupy movement, see Castells, Manuel, *Networks of Outrage and Hope: Social Movements in the Internet Age* (Cambridge: Polity, 2015), pp. 166–168.
53. Maeckelbergh, Marianne, 'Horizontal democracy now: From alterglobalization to occupation', *Interface: A journal for and about social movements* 4, 2012, pp. 207–234.
54. Unpublished article by journalist Bill Weinberg (personal communication, 12 May 2016).
55. Conroy, 'The (im)mobilities of mutual aid'.

56. Pilisuk, Marc; McAllister, JoAnn and Rothman, Jack, 'Coming together for action: The challenge of contemporary grassroots community organizing', *Journal of Social Issues* 52(1), 1996, pp. 15–37.

57. crow, *Black Flags and Windmills*, pp. 209–211.

58. Halvorsen, Sam, 'Beyond the network? Occupy London and the global movement', *Social Movement Studies* 11(3–4), 2012, p. 431.

59. Foran, John, 'Beyond insurgency to radical social change: The new situation', *Studies in Social Justice* 8(1), 2014, p. 19.

60. Juris, Jeffrey S., 'Reflections on #Occupy Everywhere: Social media, public space, and emerging logics of aggregation', *American Ethnologist* 39(2), 2012, pp. 259–279.

61. Pickerill and Krinsky, 'Why does Occupy matter?'

62. Goyens, Tom, 'Social space and the practice of anarchist history', *Rethinking History* 13(4), 2009, pp. 439–457.

63. Halvorsen 'Beyond the network?'

64. Swann, Thomas and Husted, Emil, 'Undermining anarchy: Facebook's influence on anarchist principles of organisation in Occupy Wall Street', *The Information Society* 33(4), 2017, pp. 192–204.

65. Nir, Sarah Maslin, 'Storm effort causes a rift in a shifting Occupy movement', *The New York Times*, 30 April 2013, www.nytimes.com/2013/05/01/nyregion/occupy-movements-changing-focus-causes-rift.html?_r=0 (accessed 7 January 2020); John, Beatrice and Kagan, Sacha, 'Extreme climate events as opportunities for radical open citizenship', *Open Citizenship* 5(1), 2014, pp. 60–75.

66. Staten Island Tool Library, https://toollibrary.tumblr.com/ (accessed 21 May 2021).

67. Respond & Rebuild, www.respondandrebuild.org/resources/ (accessed 21 May 2021).

68. Strike Debt, 'Shouldering the costs: Who pays in the aftermath of Hurricane Sandy?', 10 December 2012, http://strikedebt.org/sandyreport/ (accessed 13 December 2018).

69. Neuhauser, Alan, 'Occupy Sandy lost track of where donors intended cash to go, critics say', *DNA Info New York*, 11 February 2013, www.dnainfo.com/new-york/20130211/red-hook/confusion-surrounds-occupy-sandys-880k-hurricane-relief-money (accessed 7 January 2019); West, James, 'What happened to the money that Occupy Sandy raised?', *Mother Jones*, 18 June 2013, www.motherjones.com/environment/2013/06/occupy-sandy-once-welcomed-now-questioned/ (accessed 21 May 2021).

70. Ambinder et al., *The Resilient Social Network*, p. 36.

71. Hammond, John L., 'The anarchism of Occupy Wall Street', *Science & Society* 79(2), 2015, pp. 288–313.

72. Malsin, 'Best of enemies'.

73. Nir, 'Storm effort causes a rift in a shifting Occupy movement'.

74. Smith, 'The state, Occupy and disaster'.

75. Karpf, David, 'Comment on "Organization in the crowd: Peer production in large-scale networked protests"', *Information, Communication & Society* 17(2), 2014, pp. 261–263.

76. Bennett, W. Lance; Segerberg Alexandra and Walker, Shawn, 'Organization in the crowd: Peer production in large-scale networked protests', *Information, Communication & Society* 17(2), 2014, pp. 232–260; Agarwal, S.D.; Bennett, W. Lance; Johnson, C.N. and Walker, Shawn, 'A model of crowd enabled organization: Theory and methods for understanding the role of Twitter in the Occupy protests', *International Journal of Communication* 9 (2014), p. 27.

77. Linnell, Mikael, 'Citizens response in crisis: Individual and collective efforts to enhance community resilience', *Human Technology* 10(2), 2014, pp. 68–94.

78. Karpf, 'Comment on "Organization in the crowd"', p. 262.

79. Husted, Emil, 'From creation to amplification: Occupy Wall Street's transition into an online populist movement', *Civic Engagement and Social Media: Political Participation Beyond the Protest*, 2015, pp. 153–173.

80. Preston et al., 'Community response in disasters', p. 728.

81. Bratich, Jack, 'Occupy all the dispositifs: Memes, media ecologies, and emergent bodies politic', *Communication and Critical/Cultural Studies* 11(1), 2014, pp. 64–73.

82. Karatzogianni, Athina and Schandorf, Michael, 'Surfing the revolutionary wave 2010–12: A technosocial theory of agency, resistance and orders of dissent in contemporary social movements', pp. 43–74 in A.D. Ornella (ed.), *Making Humans: Religious, Technological and Aesthetic Perspectives* (Freeland, Oxon: Interdisciplinary Press, 2015); see also Barassi, 'Ethnographic cartographies'.

83. Karatzogianni, Athina, *Firebrand Waves of Digital Activism 1994–2014: The Rise and Spread of Hacktivism and Cyberconflict* (Basingstoke: Palgrave Macmillan, 2015), p. 3.

84. Garber, 'Occupy Sandy hacks Amazon's wedding registry (in a good way)'.

85. Ambinder et al., *The Resilient Social Network*. See Chapter 2 this volume for discussion.

86. Videos of these events are available on YouTube: www.youtube.com/ watch?v=C5lkrMQzfo8

87. Mutual Aid Disaster Relief, https://mutualaiddisasterrelief.org/about/ (accessed 14 January 2020).

88. Smith, 'The state, Occupy and disaster'.

89. Ambinder et al., *The Resilient Social Network*, pp. 12–14.

90. Ibid., p. 25.

91. My own experience was that three of seven interviewees, along with several others I met but did not interview, would not usually be described as 'young', while Castells in *Networks of Outrage and Hope* draws on survey data to declare that the majority, but not all, participants of OWS who camped in Zuccotti Park were 'relatively young' between 20 and 40, but that the wider movement included a substantial presence of 'middle age union members, as

well as working class people in their fifties' and 'numerous veterans' (p. 167). Figures for OS are not available, but the movement's background in OWS seems a reasonable basis to doubt the unfounded claims that they came from nowhere and were exclusively young.

92. Ambinder et al., *The Resilient Social Network*, p. 46.
93. Smith, 'The state, Occupy and disaster'.
94. Gosztola, Kevin, 'Occupy Sandy does not signify that Occupy Wall Street has found "new purpose"', *ShadowProof*, 12 November 2012, http://shadowproof.com/2012/11/12/occupy-sandy-does-not-signify-occupy-wall-street-has-found-new-purpose/ (accessed 21 May 2021).
95. Dean, Jodi, 'Occupy and UK Uncut: The evolution of activism', *Guardian*, 27 December 2012, p. 34; and Malsin, 'Best of enemies'.
96. Ambinder et al., *The Resilient Social Network*, p. A-3.
97. Smith, 'The state, Occupy and disaster'.
98. Out of the Woods, 'Disaster communism, part 1'.
99. Clark, *The Impossible Community*, pp. 193–215; Solnit, *A Paradise Built in Hell*, pp. 231–313; crow, *Back Flags and Windmills*, passim.
100. Mutual Aid Disaster Relief, 'Repression vs. resilience', https://mutualaiddisasterrelief.org/repression/ (accessed 17 January 2020).
101. Hartman and Squires, *There Is No Such Thing as a Natural Disaster*.
102. These points were given as a potential explanation for the state's relative tolerance of the grassroots compared to the aftermath of Katrina by interviewee Emily.
103. Bondesson, *Vulnerability and Power*, p. 56.

6. COVID-19 MUTUAL AID, LONDON, 2020

1. Preston and Firth, *Coronavirus, Class and Mutual Aid in the UK*.
2. Perraudin, Frances and Weaver, Matthew, 'Could COVID-19 have entered the UK earlier than thought?', *The Guardian*, 1 June 2020.
3. The differential effects of the policies on specific groups, particularly the working class, are examined in Preston and Firth, *Coronavirus, Class and Mutual Aid in the UK*.
4. Preston, J., 'Classed practices', pp. 29–55 in Preston and Firth, *Coronavirus, Class and Mutual Aid in the UK*.
5. I was personally involved in a group myself, delivering meals to vulnerable people by bicycle. It was very hard to think or write about anything else during this time, and I began writing a book on the UK government response with my colleague and comrade John Preston, and I realised it would be remiss not to include a chapter on CMAGs in this book.
6. See for example, Drury, John; Carter, Holly; Ntontis, Evangelos and Guven, Selin Tekin, 'Public behaviour in response to the COVID-19 pandemic: Understanding the role of group processes', *BJPsych Open* 7(1), 2021. See also the work of the Community Support and Mutual Aid group at the University

of Sussex: www.sussex.ac.uk/research/projects/groups-and-covid/ (accessed 26 March 2021).

7. In conversation with Emma O'Dwyer, I was informed that, in a large-scale study of 854 CMAGs, barely any respondents were anarchists. The full research has yet to be published, but a preliminary blog shows that participants were disproportionately members of political parties, and most often left-wing. This may be due to selection bias (anarchists may be less likely to take part in a survey if it is perceived to be from a non-anarchist perspective, or the option simply may not have been available). Nevertheless, in the context of a very large movement of mostly left-liberals, anarchist activists are potentially hard to access and I was only able to do so through my existing networks. More on Emma O'Dwyer's research can be found on the *LSE Blog*, at https://blogs.lse.ac.uk/politicsandpolicy/covid19-mutual-aid-solidarity/ (accessed 21 May 2021).

8. For an example of the former, see Dinosaur, Laura, 'Stay at fucking home', *Freedom News*, 23 March 2020, https://freedomnews.org.uk/2020/03/23/stay-at-fucking-home/ (accessed 12 May 2021). For an example of the latter, see Enough 14, 'Prison-state #UK comes into law : #coronavirus', https://enoughisenough14.org/2020/04/02/prison-state-uk-comes-into-law-coronavirus/ (accessed 12 May 2021).

9. Donaghey, J., '"It's going to be anarchy" (fingers crossed): Anarchist analyses of the Coronavirus/COVID-19 pandemic crisis', *Anarchist Studies Blog*, 13 April 2020, https://anarchiststudies.noblogs.org/article-its-going-to-be-anarchy-fingers-crossed-anarchist-analyses-of-the-coronavirus-covid-19-pandemic-crisis/#_ednref1 (accessed 21 May 2021).

10. Covid-19 Mutual Aid UK, https://covidmutualaid.org/ (accessed 21 May 2021).

11. Ibid.

12. Ibid.

13. Ibid.

14. Ibid.

15. Ibid.

16. Ibid.

17. Louise from the National Food Service, 'Safeguarding training for Mutual Aid networks', delivered via Zoom, no date, https://docs.google.com/document/d/1VcZGiNo2c-dTyblJBQVojS3y-jKPjIXLn8_ECoEPczo/edit (accessed 21 May 2021).

18. It is somewhat disputable that Nicole's position was apolitical as she had been involved in animal rights and environmental activism in the past, but may have been operating with a narrow definition of politics that did not include direct action or prefigurative politics.

19. This refers to 'Michelle' who was a member of the Liberal Democrat Party, although her views were somewhat more complex than simply 'liberal mainstream'; she expressed a long-running desire to get involved in more

grassroots activism, particularly feminist activism, and she was very sympathetic to anarchist organising and was involved in radical networks, although she seemed to conflate this with participation in representative politics and party political organising, taking something of an associationalist/ social capital view that the two were compatible.

20. This included Nicole, who had a background in Extinction Rebellion and animal rights activism, which she stated was 'not that political', as well as Ronny, who was a highly politicised and educated anarchist, yet who sought to influence through example, inclusion and outreach rather than an explicit political agenda; and Rich, who was somewhat between this category and the next insofar as he was also highly politicised as an anarchist but was very happy to be involved with anyone so long as they were willing to work with radical ideas, and not insist on being too dogmatic – he only sought to exclude fascists and conservatives who sought to silence rather than engage with anarchist ideas.

21. This category included interviewees with the pseudonyms Bobbie, Matt and Amy (the latter of whom described becoming politicised as an anarchist during Mutual Aid organising).

22. For a critique of this position, see, e.g. the South Essex Heckler, 'An explainer on our (changing) position on the COVID-19 crisis', *Anarchist News*, https:// anarchistnews.org/content/uk-anarchist-collective-explains-anti-new- normal-position (accessed 26 March 2021).

23. Return Fire, 'The difference between "just coping" & "not coping at all": Social reproduction, COVID-19, cybernetics', *Return Fire* 6(2), Winter 2020–2021, https://returnfire.noblogs.org/files/2021/03/Return-Fire-vol.6- chap.2-pg71-pg150.pdf (accessed 13 May 2021).

24. F., G., 'To the MAN: Zero evictions call-out', *Freedom News*, 17 March 2020, https://freedomnews.org.uk/to-the-man-zero-evictions-call-out/ (accessed 28 October 2020).

25. London Renters Union, 'Join us', https://londonrentersunion.org/join/ (accessed 18 March 2020).

26. The Resi-Rectors, 'UK: Evictions make us sick!', *squat.net*, 2 May 2020, https://en.squat.net/2020/05/02/uk-evictions-make-us-sick/ (accessed 20 May 2020).

27. Anon., '"Tear gas can't stop us": Police fire projectiles at Ohio students after school moves to close due to Coronavirus', 11 March 2020, https:// itsgoingdown.org/tear-gas-cant-stop-us-dayton/ (accessed 20 May 2020). Anon., '"Warzone": MIT students enraged by Coronavirus banishment', *The Daily Beast*, 12 March 2020, www.thedailybeast.com/warzone-mit-students- enraged-by-coronavirus-banishment (accessed 20 May 2020).

28. Anon., 'Workers launch wave of wildcat strikes as Trump pushes for "return to work" amidst exploding Coronavirus', *It's Going Down*, 12 March 2020, https://itsgoingdown.org/workers-walk-off-job-coronavirus/ (accessed 20 May 2020).

29. Anon., via Nantes Indymedia, France, 'The worst virus ever ... authority', trans. Anarchists Worldwide, The Anarchist Library, https://325.nostate. net/2020/03/16/france-the-worst-virus-ever-authority (accessed 14 December 2021).

30. Round Robin, 'Insurrection in times of #Coronavirus', *Enough* 14, 18 March 2020, https://enoughisenough14.org/2020/03/18/insurrection-in-times-of-thecoronavirus/ (accessed 19 March 2020).

31. O'Dwyer, Emma, 'COVID-19 mutual aid groups have the potential to increase intergroup solidarity – but can they actually do so?', *LSE Blog*, 23 June 2020, https://blogs.lse.ac.uk/politicsandpolicy/covid19-mutual-aid-solidarity/ (accessed 17 February 2021).

32. Ibid.

33. De Angelis, Massimo, *Omnia sunt communia: On the Commons and the Transformation to Postcapitalism* (London, Zed Books, 2017).

34. *Freedom News*, 'London activists occupy Paddington Green Police Station', 9 February 2020, https://freedomnews.org.uk/london-activists-occupy-paddington-green-police-station/ (accessed 21 May 2021).

35. A few spaces in Europe did try to keep operating as normal, notably the Rigaer94 squat in Berlin. However, this was unsuccessful due to repression: police surrounded the building at times when events were planned, and made legal threats. Rigaer94, 'Berlin: On the closure of Kadterschmiede and our handling of open spaces', *squat.net*, 8 May 2020, https://en.squat. net/2020/05/08/berlin-on-the-closure-of-kadterschmiede/ (accessed 21 May 2021). European anarchists are not used to working in contexts where it is easier to organise a protest than a get-together.

36. GRASS, 'Green Radical Anticapitalist Social Space', *Network 23*, 30 May 2020, https://network23.org/grass/ (accessed 21 May 2021).

37. DBS (Disclosure and Barring Service) checks were a controversial issue that were imbricated in the attempted recuperation of mutual aid into depoliticised forms of social capital, which will be discussed in more detail below.

38. Anarchist websites with good UK and international coverage of Covid-19 include: 325.nostate.net; itsgoingdown.org; freedomnews.org.uk; crimethinc. com; anarchistagency.com; enoughisenough14.org

39. Zuri, Eshe Kiama, '"We've been organising like this since day" – why we must remember the Black roots of mutual aid groups', *Gal-Dem*, 5 June 2020, https://gal-dem.com/weve-been-organising-like-this-since-day-why-we-must-remember-the-black-roots-of-mutual-aid-groups/ (accessed 17 February 2021).

40. Lagalisse, Erica, *'Good Politics': Property, Intersectionality and the Making of the Anarchist Self*, PhD dissertation, Department of Anthropology, McGill University, Montreal, 2016.

41. Preston, John and Firth, Rhiannon, 'The pandemic is the new front line in the war on the working classes', *The Big Issue*, 2 March 2021, www.bigissue.

com/opinion/the-pandemic-is-the-new-front-line-in-the-war-on-the-working-class/ (accessed 3 March 2021).

42. Dickey, Megan Rose, 'Gig workers have created a tool to offer mutual aid during COVID-19 pandemic', *Tech Crunch*, 18 March 2020, https://techcrunch.com/2020/03/18/gig-workers-collective-covid-19/ (accessed 3 March 2021).

43. *Freedom News*, 'Overkill on Gloucester Road: Bristol occupation evicted', 11 March 2021, https://freedomnews.org.uk/2021/03/11/overkill-on-gloucester-road-bristol-occupation-evicted/; *Freedom News*, 'Northumberland: Alnwick Community Larder forced to close following "vandalism" allegation', 21 February 2021, https://freedomnews.org.uk/2021/02/21/northumberland-alnwick-community-larder-forced-to-close-following-vandalism-allegation/ (both accessed 21 May 2021).

44. *Freedom News*, 'London: Eviction of the Pie 'n' Mash squat café – We must push for no evictions in this crisis!', 18 March 2020, https://freedomnews.org.uk/london-eviction-of-the-pie-n-mash-squat-cafe-we-must-push-for-no-evictions-in-this-crisis/ (accessed 22 March 2020).

45. Lent, Adam and Studdert, Jessica, *The Community Paradigm*, New Local Report, 2020, www.newlocal.org.uk/wp-content/uploads/2019/03/The-Community-Paradigm_New-Local-2.pdf (accessed 21 May 2020).

46. Public Health England, 'Guidance on social distancing for everyone in the UK', 21 March 2020, https://www.gov.uk/government/publications/covid-19-guidance-on-social-distancing-and-for-vulnerable-people/guidance-on-social-distancing-for-everyone-in-the-uk-and-protecting-older-people-and-vulnerable-adults (accessed 14 December 2021). This guidance has now been withdrawn and was superseded. The quoted passage was previously available via a different link with the title 'Guidance on shielding and protecting people defined on medical grounds as extremely vulnerable from COVID-19'. It is worth noting that government advice and web pages change frequently so this link may not be available in the longer term. The quoted passage also appears frequently on local government sites that refer back to the gov.uk website.

47. Grayson, Deborah, 'Mutual aid and radical neighbourliness', *Lawrence and Wishart Blog*, 28 April 2020, https://lwbooks.co.uk/mutual-aid-and-radical-neighbourliness (accessed 21 May 2021).

48. Ibid.

49. Rogers, J., 'Mutual aid in London: A cautionary tale', *Freedom News*, 21 March 2021, https://freedomnews.org.uk/mutual-aid-in-london-a-cautionary-tale/ (accessed 13 May 2021).

50. Louise from the National Food Service, 'Safeguarding training'.

51. Grayson, 'Mutual aid and radical neighbourliness'.

52. *Freedom News*, 'Mutual aid: It's a class sabotage!', 5 May 2020, https://freedomnews.org.uk/mutual-aid-its-a-class-sabotage/ (accessed 20 May 2020).

53. Rogers, 'Mutual aid in London'.
54. Spender, C., 'Local councils are already trying to sabotage the mutual aid networks', *Freedom News*, 16 March 2021, https://freedomnews.org.uk/local-councils-are-already-trying-to-sabotage-the-mutual-aid-networks/ (accessed 22 March 2021).
55. Ibid.
56. Firth, *Utopian Politics*, p. 139.
57. Kleist, Anna, 'Five quick thoughts on the limits of Covid-19 mutual aid groups and how they might be overcome', *Freedom News*, 5 April 2020, https://freedomnews.org.uk/five-quick-thoughts-on-the-limits-of-covid-19-mutual-aid-groups-how-they-might-be-overcome/ (accessed 21 May 2021).
58. A pamphlet containing a series of essays by Big Door Brigade was mentioned more than once. Big Door Brigade. *What Is Mutual Aid?*, no date, https://bigdoorbrigade.com/what-is-mutual-aid/ (accessed 21 May 2021).
59. All interviewees mentioned this dynamic – the extent to which this was taken on board by groups is variable, as discussed in the previous section on political silencing as form of recuperation.
60. For more context on the protest movement in late 2020 and early 2021, see *Return Fire* 6(2), 2021, https://returnfire.noblogs.org/post/2021/03/15/return-fire-vol-6-chap-2-out-as-pdf-chap-1-toner-friendly-version-new-website-features-fixes/ (accessed 21 May 2021).

7. CONCLUSION

1. Chew, Sing C., *World Ecological Degradation: Accumulation, Urbanization, and Deforestation, 3000 BC–AD 2000* (New York: AltaMira Press, 2001).
2. Schwab, Klaus, *The Fourth Industrial Revolution* (Harmondsworth: Penguin, 2017).
3. Anon., 'Introduction to the Apocalypse', *The Anarchist Library*, 2009, https://theanarchistlibrary.org/library/anonymous-introduction-to-the-apocalypse (accessed 20 May 2021).
4. Paying anarchists for their activities is not necessarily contrary to anarchism (depending on the specific doctrine) and workers' cooperatives and 'ethical businesses' are relatively common ways anarchists seek an income, but in disaster anarchism these are marginal. The impossibility of incentivising activities arises because most funding is from 'political principle' sources.
5. crow, *Black Flags and Windmills*, p. 209 highlights it is particularly problematic when well-intentioned 'White Middle Class' or 'folx with privilege' align themselves with community work only to co-opt the work or 'abandon the issues when it wasn't a "hot" anymore'.
6. Sitrin, *Horizontalism*; Zibechi, *Dispersing Power*; Desai, Ashwin, *We Are the Poors: Community Struggles in Post-Apartheid South Africa* (New York: Monthly Review Press, 2002).

7. Firth, *Utopian Politics*.

8. Robinson, 'The oppressive discourse of global exclusion', p. 261.

9. An ASBO is an anti-social behaviour order.

10. Preston, John, *Competence Based Education and Training (CBET) and the End of Human Learning: the Existential Threat of Competency* (Hampshire: Palgrave, 2017).

11. Sassen, Saskia, *The Global City: London, New York, Tokyo* (Princeton, NJ: Princeton University Press, 1991).

12. '#Coronavirus, #Poznan, #Poland: The state will dissapoint you. The #COVID19 epidemic requires mutual aid', *Enough14*, 15 March 2020, https:// enoughisenough14.org/2020/03/15/coronavirus-poznan-poland-the-state-will-dissapoint-you-the-covid19-epidemic-requires-mutual-aid/ (accessed 22 May 2020).

13. Martinez, Miguel A., 'Mutating mobilisations during the pandemic crisis in Spain', *Interface: A journal for and about social movements* 12(1), May 2020, pp. 15–21, www.interfacejournal.net/wp-content/uploads/2020/05/ Martinez.pdf (accessed 16 May 2020).

14. Holanda, Neto and Lima, Valesca, 'Movimentos e ações político-culturais do Brasil em tempos de pandemia do COVID-19', *Interface: A journal for and about social movements*, 12(1), 2020, www.interfacejournal.net/wp-content/ uploads/2020/05/Holanda-e-Lima.pdf (accessed 17 May 2020).

15. Mohanty, Sobhi, 'From communal violence to lockdown hunger: Emergency responses by civil society networks in Delhi India', *Interface: A journal for and about social movements*, 12(1), 23 April 2020, pp. 47–52, www. interfacejournal.net/wp-content/uploads/2020/04/Mohanty.pdf (accessed 17 May 2020).

16. Bau, Hongwei, '"Anti-domestic violence little vaccine": A Wuhan-based feminist activist campaign during COVID-19', *Interface: A journal for and about social movements* 12(1), pp. 53–63, www.interfacejournal.net/ wp-content/uploads/2020/05/Bao.pdf (accessed 17 May 2020).

17. Ng, Lynn Ling Yu, 'What does the COVID-19 pandemic mean for PinkDot Singapore?', *Interface: A journal for and about social movements* 12(1), 2020, pp. 72–81, www.interfacejournal.net/wp-content/uploads/2020/04/Ng.pdf (accessed 17 May 2020).

18. Damier, Vadim and Limanov, Kirill, 'Anarchism in Indonesia', *libcom.org*, 14 November 2017, https://libcom.org/library/short-essay-about-history-anarchism-indonesia (accessed 21 May 2021).

19. Itim, Bandilang, 'Anarchism in the Philippines', *libcom.org*, 14 May 2020, https://libcom.org/blog/anarchism-philippines-14052020 (accessed 21 May 2020).

20. Sims, Holly and Vogelmann, Kevin, 'Popular mobilization and disaster management', *Cuba Public Admininstration Development* 22, 2002, pp. 389–400.

21. Fernandes, Sujatha, *Who Can Stop the Drums? Urban Social Movements in Chávez's Venezuela* (Durham, NC: Duke University Press, 2010).

22. *Freedom News*, 'Organise or starve: Life under lockdown in South Africa's shackdweller movements', 26 May 2020, https://freedomnews.org.uk/2020/05/26/organise-or-starve-life-under-lockdown-in-south-africas-shackdweller-movements/ (accessed 21 May 2021).

23. ACT-UP, https://actupny.org/ (accessed 21 May 2021).

24. Rebón, Julián, 'The politics of protest in Argentina', *Open Democracy*, 12 December 2018, www.opendemocracy.net/en/democraciaabierta/politics-of-protest-in-argentina/ (accessed 21 May 2021).

25. Donaghey, '"It's going to be anarchy" (fingers crossed)'.

26. Jasanoff, 'Learning from disaster'.

27. Foti, 'Mayday Mayday: Euro flex workers time to get a move on'.

28. Ritzer, G., *The McDonaldization of Society* (Thousand Oaks, CA: Pine Forge Press, 2013).

29. Hayes, Dennis and Wynyard, Robin, *The McDonaldization of Higher Education* (Westport, CT: Bergin & Garvey, 2002).

30. Lupton, Deborah, *The Quantified Self* (Malden, MA: Polity, 2016); Moore, Phoebe and Robinson, Andrew, 'The quantified self: What counts in the neoliberal workplace', *New Media & Society* 18(11), 2016, pp. 2774–2792.

31. Preston, *Competence Based Education and Training (CBET) and the End of Human Learning*.

32. Noon, Mike; Blyton, Paul and Morrell, Kevin, *The Realities of Work: Experiencing Work and Employment in Contemporary Society* (Basingstoke: Palgrave Macmillan, 2013), p. 140.

33. Adam, Barbara, *Timescapes of Modernity* (London: Routledge, 1991).

34. Tarì, Marcello and Vanni, Ilaria, 'The life and deeds of San Precario, patron saint of precarious workers and lives', *Fibreculture Journal* 23(5), 2005, https://five.fibreculturejournal.org/fcj-023-on-the-life-and-deeds-of-san-precario-patron-saint-of-precarious-workers-and-lives/ (accessed 21 May 2021).

35. Neocleous, Mark, 'Resisting resilience', *Radical Philosophy* 178(6), 2013, www.radicalphilosophy.com/commentary/resisting-resilience (accessed 21 May 2021).

36. Friedli, L. and Stearn, R., 'Positive affect as coercive strategy: conditionality, activation and the role of psychology in UK government workfare programmes', *Medical Humanities* 41(1), 2015, pp. 40–47.

37. Institute for Precarious Consciousness, 'Anxiety, affective struggle, and precarity consciousness-raising', *Interface* 6(2), 2014, pp. 271–300.

38. Monbiot, George, 'Climate change is not anarchy's football', *Guardian*, 22 August 2008.

39. Harvey, D., *Spaces of Hope* (Berkeley: University of California Press, 2000).

40. Bernes, Jasper, 'Between the devil and the Green New Deal', *Commune Mag* 2, spring 2019, https://communemag.com/between-the-devil-and-the-green-new-deal/

41. Langstone, Delia, '"No shit Sherlock!" Canine DNA and policing public space', *International Journal of Sociology and Social Policy* 41(3/4), 2020, pp. 455–474.

42. Kallis, Giorgos, *Degrowth* (Newcastle upon Tyne: Agenda Publishing, 2017), p. 15.

43. Bernes, 'Between the devil and the Green New Deal'.

44. Kallis, Giorgos, *In Defense of Degrowth: Opinions and Manifestos*, edited by Aaron Vansintjan (Open Commons), https://indefenseofdegrowth.com/ (accessed 21 May 2021).

45. Kallis, *Degrowth*, p. 51.

46. Ibid., p. 51.

47. Morton, Adam David, 'Waiting for Gramsci: State formation, passive revolution and the international', *Millennium – Journal of International Studies* 35(3), 2007, pp. 597–621.

48. Illich, *Tools for Conviviality*.

49. 'Marx's description of the process of capital (economic) exchanges is expressed in the M–C–M' cycle. The M–C–M' cycle is the transformation of money (M) into commodities (C), and the change of commodities back again into money (M') of altered value.' Hean, Sarah; Cowley Sarah; Forbes, Angus; Griffiths, Peter and Maben, Jill, 'The M–C–M' cycle and social capital', *Social Science & Medicine* 56(5), 2003, pp. 1061–1072.

Index

233

Thanks to our Patreon subscribers:

Andrew Perry
Ciaran Kane

Who have shown generosity and comradeship in support of our publishing.

Check out the other perks you get by subscribing to our Patreon – visit patreon.com/plutopress.

Subscriptions start from £3 a month.

www.ingramcontent.com/pod-product-compliance
Lightning Source LLC
Chambersburg PA
CBHW032128020426
42334CB00016B/1081